Julie

cheers

Tony Dmbr

Employment Relations in Non-Union Firms

The form of employment relations and the shape of organisations have changed significantly over the last two decades. Many companies now employ workers who have no access to collective forms of employee representation. The precise relationship between an employee and employer is often ambiguous with complex organisational structures. This book re-evaluates the way employment relations are conceptualised and examines employment conditions in non-union organisations.

The authors present a detailed analysis of the conditions and patterns of employment relations in both small and large non-union firms. They assess the impact of regulation, managerial ideology and market influences on employer strategies to avoid unionisation. Using social and psychological exchange, the book concludes with an assessment of the capacity of workers to act as an agent of change in these non-union relationships. The implications for worker mobilisation, trade union expansion and employer strategies are also considered in the light of detailed case study analysis.

Employment Relations in Non-Union Firms will be of essential interest to advanced students and academics in the fields of Industrial Relations, Human Resource Management and Organisational Analysis.

Tony Dundon is Lecturer in Industrial Relations and Human Resource Management, and research director for High Performance Work Systems, Centre for Innovation and Structural Change (CISC), National University of Ireland, Galway. **Derek Rollinson** is Principal Lecturer in Employee Relations, Organisational Behaviour and Organisational Analysis at Huddersfield University Business School. His main research interests are in the internal dynamics of discipline and grievance handling and control in organisations.

Routledge Research in Employment Relations

Series editors: Rick Delbridge and Edmund Heery
Cardiff Business School

Aspects of the employment relationship are central to numerous courses at both undergraduate and postgraduate level.

Drawing from insights from industrial relations, human resource management and industrial sociology, this series provides an alternative source of research-based materials and texts, reviewing key developments in employment research.

Books published in this series are works of high academic merit, drawn from a wide range of academic studies in the social sciences.

Also available from Routledge:

Rethinking Industrial Relations
Mobilisation, collectivism and long waves
John Kelly

Employee Relations in the Public Services
Themes and issues
Edited by Susan Corby and Geoff White

The Insecure Workforce
Edited by Edmund Heery and John Salmon

Public Service Employment Relations in Europe
Transformation, modernisation or inertia?
Edited by Stephen Bach, Lorenzo Bordogna, Giuseppe Della Rocca and David Winchester

Reward Management
A critical text
Edited by Geoff White and Janet Druker

Working for McDonald's in Europe
The unequal struggle?
Tony Royle

Job Insecurity and Work Intensification
Edited by Brendan Burchell, David Ladipo and Frank Wilkinson

Union Organizing
Campaigning for trade union recognition
Edited by Gregor Gall

Employment Relations in the Hospitality and Tourism Industries
Rosemary Lucas

Employment Relations in Non-Union Firms

Tony Dundon and Derek Rollinson

Routledge
Taylor & Francis Group

LONDON AND NEW YORK

First published 2004
by Routledge
11 New Fetter Lane, London EC4P 4EE

Simultaneously published in the USA and Canada
by Routledge
29 West 35th Street, New York, NY 10001

Routledge is an imprint of the Taylor & Francis Group

Typeset in Garamond by Wearset Ltd, Boldon, Tyne and Wear
Printed and bound in Great Britain by MPG Books Ltd, Bodmin,
Cornwall

British Library Cataloguing in Publication Data
A catalogue record for this book is available from the British Library

Library of Congress Cataloging in Publication Data
A catalog record for this book has been requested

ISBN 0-415-31246-9

Contents

Illustrations

Figures

Tables

Preface and Acknowledgements

The research reported in this book deals with employment relations in non-union firms and the ideas underpinning the research took place in the mid 1990s; initially as a series of discussions between the two authors about what life would be like in the non-union organisation. While both of us had a practical background in dealing with industrial relations in organisations that recognised trade unions, neither of us had ever worked in a non-union firm. For this reason, the rather loose question of what it is like to work in a firm with no trade union presence was one that surfaced in our discussions with alarming regularity.

Although there have always been firms in which trade unions are not recognised by management, until the early 1980s the majority of employees in Great Britain were union members, and their working lives were strongly influenced by these bodies. Since then however, the non-union organisation has become far more commonplace. There has also been a dramatic shift in public policy, including employment legislation that deals with statutory trade union recognition, together with increasing regulation originating in the European Union with regard to both individual and collective rights. Against this background trade unions have sought to rebuild themselves; to some extent by paying increased attention to unorganised sectors of the economy. With these and other issues in mind, our initial query was eventually transformed into a more extensive set of research questions. These addressed the things that we wanted to know about the nature of employment relations in non-union organisations (see Chapter 1) and from this point onwards, the research project rapidly took shape.

The book is intended to appeal to students on final year undergraduate and postgraduate degree programmes, and to academics and practitioners in the areas of industrial relations, human resource management and organisational analysis. In writing the book one of our main concerns has been to enable readers to get a *feel* for the nature of employment in these non-union firms. A second concern is that we should make connections between academic debates and the reality of life in these organisations at the start of the new millennium.

Like many projects of this type, the topic is approached in an interdisciplinary way. In this respect, and in addition to their own knowledge of industrial relations, the authors have been able to bring a blend of social psychological and sociological perspectives to the project, which give a richer and more eclectic view than in many research initiatives. The research was hosted by the University of Huddersfield and here we would like to acknowledge the help of the university's computer department in assisting with questionnaire coding and data input. We would especially like to thank the managers and employees in the four case study organisations, without whose help the research could not have been completed. Any errors or omissions are the responsibility of the authors. Our thanks are also due to our long-suffering wives and children, who at times across the gestation of the project must have seriously questioned the wisdom of being wedded to academics.

Tony Dundon and Derek Rollinson

1   The non-union phenomenon

Introduction

This book deals with the nature of employment relations in non-union firms. In particular, it assesses the ways in which the employment relationship is made, modified and sustained in the absence of a trade union. The aim of this chapter is to set the scene for the remainder of the book. It starts by defining the term 'non-union' and this is followed by an examination of the increased significance of non-union firms in British employment relations. This matter is addressed in three stages: first, by considering the decline of trade unions; second, by examining recent trends in non-unionisation and finally, but more speculatively, by briefly examining future prospects.

Having established the current significance of the non-union firm, the next part of the chapter gives a brief review of the different approaches that have been used to study non-union employment relations. The aims of this investigation are then set-out, and the chapter closes with a brief synopsis of what is covered in subsequent chapters.

An opening definition

Since this book deals with employment relations within non-union organisations, it is fitting that it should open by defining what non-union means. It does not mean, as is sometimes implied, that there are no trade union members within these organisations. Rather, the expression is concerned with an absence of trade union recognition, and this has a legally defined meaning. A recognised trade union can be defined as:

> a trade union recognised by management to any extent, for the purposes of collective bargaining.
> Trade Union and Labour Relations (Consolidation) Act (TULR(C)A) 1992, S178(3)

Essentially collective bargaining is concerned with determining the conditions under which employees exchange their effort for rewards, which, if taken literally, could embrace any aspect of the pay–effort exchange. However, paragraph 3.3 of the recent Employment Relations Act (ERA) (1999) more restrictively defines it as concerning negotiations relating to pay, hours and holidays. In some situations non-union may not mean the complete absence of a trade union. Managers may choose to consult with a union in respect to certain sections of the workforce, while avoiding union recognition for other employees. To put matters simply therefore, non-union refers to an organisation in which management does not deal with a trade union that collectively represents the interests of employees, either for all or part of the workforce.

Of course not all non-union firms are the same. Some organisations may be non-unionised because management uses one or more strategies to avoid the incursion of trade union influence. In others it can occur more by accident than design, simply because trade union organisation has never been an issue. One attempt to map out the diversity of non-union types is provided by Guest and Hoque (1994), who suggest there are good, bad, ugly and lucky forms of non-unionism. The good non-union employer is derived from images of International Business Machines (IBM) and Marks and Spencer (M&S). It provides an attractive employment package and makes use of sophisticated Human Resource Management (HRM) practices, for example, devolved managerial systems, above average remuneration, training and development and recruitment strategies. The bad and ugly non-union firms are often dependent upon larger organisations for their work and operate in highly competitive markets. What can distinguish the bad from the ugly, is that in the latter, management seek to exploit workers, whereas in the bad, management offer poor wages and conditions without intended malice. If there is such a thing as a lucky non-union firm, then remuneration tends to be below the market average with few employee benefits. It is considered lucky because the issue of union recognition has probably never emerged with any significance.

However, there are problems with these conceptual non-union distinctions. One problem is that either/or categories of non-union firm tend to oversimplify and polarise practices that are, in fact, remarkably diverse and complex. It is also possible that so-called good non-union firms can be ugly at the same time; much depends on who you ask, what you ask them and when. As Edwards (1995) points out, while the absence of industrial discontent or union membership may indicate some level of commitment or trust between an employer and employee, it might also be a sign that there is a fear of management, because in the absence of independent facilities for employee voice, there are no remedies for discontent. Confusingly, some of the non-union literature is also replete with language that conveys an impression that unions are somehow less attractive to employees in so-called good companies. Here it is argued that because workers earn above average wages, then harmonious industrial relations are the norm, with little incentive to unionise. In part some of these problems are methodological. For instance, Guest and Hoque (1994) largely base their typology of non-union firms on the results of a survey of managers in these organisations, without asking employees whether they perceived their employers to be good, bad or ugly (Blyton and Turnbull 1998). Thus when non-union is used as a blanket term, it can disguise a wide degree of diversity between organisations and among organisational actors.

The increased significance of the non-union organisation

The decline of trade unions

There have always been a large number of non-union organisations in Great Britain and for that matter, a correspondingly large number of employees who are not members of a trade union. In the last two decades however, the non-union firm has become much more commonplace and at the present time it could well be the most prevalent type encountered in Great Britain. This has not always been the case and to appreciate the current significance of the non-union organisation, it is necessary to examine historic patterns in British trade unionism. Figure 1.1 gives a simplified graphical representation of total union membership and union density (total membership as a percentage of those who could be members) as a time series across the twentieth century.

A number of observations can be made from Figure 1.1. First, trade unions have experienced varying fortunes since the turn of the century. Following a slow early period of growth, union membership fell sharply in

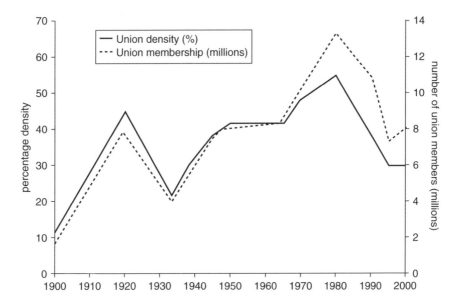

Figure 1.1 Trade union density and total membership 1900–2000.

the early 1930s, recovered after the Second World War, and reached a plateau throughout the 1960s. The peak year for union membership was 1979, thereafter falling back to levels comparable with those in the late 1930s. A second observation is that historically, periods of union decline have been followed by periods of growth, which more than compensated for the preceding losses. For example, higher levels of membership and density in the mid 1940s followed decline in the 1930s, and a similar, but much smaller trend is evident between the early 1960s and early 1970s. More significantly, although there has been a rise in trade union membership since the late 1990s, this has been very modest and nowhere near large enough to reverse the significant losses since 1979. In absolute terms this represents a loss of over 6 million members (from 13.5 million to 8 million), with a decline in density from 55 per cent to 32 per cent over the same period. Moreover, the decline has been virtually continual since 1979 and the level of unionism in Britain is now closer to its previous lowest point, which was encountered during the inter-war period (Cully and Woodland 1996).

A factor related to this decline in membership is the extent to which collective bargaining has an impact on the terms and conditions of employees. This is important because collectively negotiated agreements about terms and conditions not only have an impact in unionised organisations, they also have knock-on effects in firms that do not recognise trade unions. In some of these firms, for example, management uses conditions established by collective bargaining elsewhere as a benchmark against which their own pay and conditions policies are established (Blyton and Turnbull 1998; McIlroy 1995). Between 1984 and 1998 however, the estimated proportion of employees in Britain for whom collective bargaining has the major influence in determining their pay and conditions fell from 70 per cent to 41 per cent (Millward *et al.* 2000). In short, not only are unionised employees a minority in Great Britain, but fewer workers have their terms and conditions influenced by the process of collective bargaining.

In broad terms there is considerable agreement that the decline in trade unions is attributable to four major groups of factors: structural/economic changes; political/legal influences; managerial attitudes and behaviour; and employee attitudes and behaviour. Reference to some of these arguments will appear in later chapters, where we discuss the nature of employment relationships and factors that can affect them. Suffice it to say here, that while there is agreement that all of these factors have been influential in some degree, the reader should be aware that there is far less agreement about the relative influence of any factor on its own. Explaining this decline in trade union influence is a fascinating issue in its own right. However, a detailed explanation is well beyond the scope of this book, the main purpose of which is to explain the nature of employment relations in the non-union firm. Nevertheless, to understand the increased significance of the non-union firm it is necessary to appreciate that along with the decline of trade unions, there have been other influences at work.

The changing contours of the non-union phenomenon

There has been a strong acceleration in the number of non-union firms, and data from the Workplace Industrial Relations Surveys (WIRS) show that the proportion of establishments with union members fell much more sharply after 1984. For instance, between 1980–84 the number of establishments reported in WIRS that had no union members remained constant at 27 per cent (Daniel and Millward 1984; Millward and Stevens 1986), suggesting that there were some gains to offset the decline in traditional unionised sectors. By the time of the third WIRS survey in 1990 however, the proportion of establishments with no union members had increased to 36 per cent, and by 1998 this figure had risen to 47 per cent (Cully *et al.* 1998). As a number of authors note, the net result was that losses during the mid 1980s effectively wiped-out the membership gains of the 1970s (Kessler and Bayliss 1992; Waddington 1992; Bird *et al.* 1993).

There is also important information about the concentration of non-union organisations, both geographically and by industrial sector. Table 1.1 shows that geographically, establishments that did not recognise a trade union were most prevalent in certain parts of the country, notably in London and the South of England. There is also evidence that new towns have emerged as non-union centres, especially where there have been positive attempts to attract inward foreign investment by Japanese and American firms (Oliver and Wilkinson 1992; Smith and Elger 1994). Similarly, certain industrial sectors seem to have a proportionately larger share of non-union firms, and examples include hotels, catering, retailing, hi-technology and professional

Table 1.1 Distribution of non-union organisations by geographical location and type of employee

| | Percentage of employees in workplaces not recognising unions | | | | | |
| | 1980 | | 1984 | | 1990 | |
	Manual	Non-manual	Manual	Non-manual	Manual	Non-manual
London	24	45	32	60	59	71
Outer South East	30	56	41	57	57	64
East Anglia	18	32	50	61	59	53
South West	21	33	36	49	44	64
East Midlands	7	26	37	35	40	48
West Midlands	8	32	14	41	38	50
Yorkshire and Humberside	13	43	14	44	38	57
North West	11	31	15	33	36	45
North	8	28	15	35	35	46
Wales	14	27	27	28	31	58
Scotland	15	37	33	53	38	48

Source: adapted from Martin *et al.* (1996).

service organisations. Younger establishments are also less likely to have a union presence than older firms (Beaumont and Cairns 1987; Beaumont and Harris 1988; McLoughlin and Gourlay 1994).

Perhaps one of the more significant indicators of non-unionism is size of organisation. Table 1.2 shows that workplaces of under 100 employees have both a higher and longer tradition of non-recognition (Millward *et al.* 1992; Cully *et al.* 1998). It has also been reported that union membership (as opposed to union recognition) is at its lowest in smaller firms, with less than 1 per cent of those employed in small private sector establishments being members of a trade union (IRS 1998). Clearly, therefore, smaller establishments are of particular significance when considering non-union relations. Indeed, this would seem all the more important when the sheer volume of Small to Medium Sized Enterprises (SMEs) is taken into account (Dundon *et al.* 2001). In Britain, establishments with fewer than 50 employees account for 99 per cent of all companies, and organisations employing fewer than 500 workers provide 44 per cent of total employment (Storey 1994; DTI 2001).

Therefore, it seems likely that the sheer diversity of organisations could be an important key that helps unlock the mysteries of employment relations in the typical non-union firm.

Future prospects

Given a strong current prevalence for the non-union firm, what then are the future prospects? Is trade union membership likely to increase in a dramatic way once again, or will it remain at its current modest levels for the foreseeable future? To try to give a definitive answer to this question is to risk setting oneself up as a latter-day oracle. However, a classic econometric study of historic patterns of growth and decline undertaken by Bain and Price in the 1980s provides some clues about the broad influences at work. Bain and Price (1983) identify three major groups of variables that are associated with trade union growth and these are shown in Figure 1.2.

The first group, **Contextual Variables**, consists of factors such as workforce structures, management ideologies and social values. Where there is a prevailing *management ideology* that considers trade unions to be an unwarranted intrusion, this will obviously result in opposition to them gaining

Table 1.2 Density of union membership in relation to workplace size

Year	Workplace size (number of employees)				
	25–49	50–99	100–199	200–499	500 or more
Density 1984[a]	26	30	39	47	66
Density 1990[b]	19	25	33	49	53
Density 1998[b]	23	27	32	38	48

Sources: a Calculated from Millward *et al.* (1992: 64); b Calculated from Cully *et al.* (1998: 15).

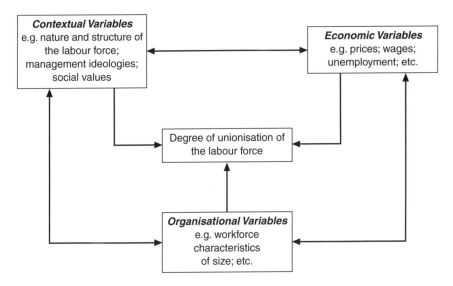

Figure 1.2 Influences on the level of trade union membership.
Source: adapted from Bain and Price (1983).

entry into firms. Because manual workers in most industries have always shown a higher tendency to unionise, and white-collar workers have been somewhat less willing to join, *workforce structures* can also be an important variable. Finally *social values* are important in that the more that unions are accepted as a normal part of society, the more that joining becomes a naturally accepted act.

The second group of factors consists of *Economic Variables*. For example, as the real *prices* of goods rises, employees tend to unionise to protect their standards of living and when real wages rise, people tend to give the credit to trade unions, which reinforces the predisposition of people to join. Another economic factor is *unemployment*. If people are in work and perceive unemployment as a threat, they join trade unions for defensive reasons. However, if they work for an anti-union employer, and fear that their membership might be penalised, there can be a tendency in the reverse direction.

The final group of factors are *Organisational Variables*, such as increasing *concentration of ownership* into large organisations, the use of *atypical or agency labour* and the *social-demographics* of workforce populations. Unionisation is much more common in larger organisations, and with the possible exception of the public sector, unionisation is usually much lower in a workforce that is predominantly female, or has large numbers of atypical and peripheral employees.

From their analysis, Bain and Price draw the conclusion that since the Second World War, these variables have had different effects in different sectors of the economy, and this has a tremendous impact on the capability of trade unions to increase in size after a period of membership loss. In the public service and manufacturing, where, in the past, trade union growth has been the greatest, economic factors, favourable public attitudes to trade unions, and favourable employer policies all combined to give a major expansion. However, in sectors such as private services and the newer, high technology industries, although the first two factors were as positive as else-where, they were not strong enough to overcome the hostility of employers. Indeed, in the hotel and catering sector McCaulay and Wood (1992) found that the likely benefits for workers from union membership were often counter-balanced by fears of management reprisals. While this analysis largely explains matters in the past, its most important implications are perhaps for the future. In the recessionary periods since 1980 the greatest job losses have been in those areas where union growth took place in earlier years. Any compensatory increase in employment has been in white collar work, among females, and in the private services, all of which are the very areas where trade unions found it difficult to mobilise workers, even in earlier years when conditions favoured growth. Significantly, it is in these areas, where the use of agency labour, part-time and casualised work is rife, that future employment growth is most likely. Given the loss of union members and the persistence of non-union organisation, the prognosis for trade unions is not good. Thus non-union relations are likely to remain worthy of further study for the foreseeable future, or as McLoughlin and Gourlay (1994) conclude:

> how employees are managed without unions and the nature of relations with employees where trade unions are absent is an area ripe for further study.
>
> (McLoughlin and Gourlay 1994: 163)

Approaches to the study of non-union relations

In Britain, the traditional approach among industrial relations scholars has tended to focus on the propensity for non-union employees to unionise. There was less about *how* and *why* non-union workers were managed and more interest in the factors surrounding *when* non-union employees would organise. Bain and Price (1983) comment:

> The largest untapped potential for union growth in Britain is among the more than six million workers in private services.
>
> (Bain and Price 1983: 32)

In the US the approach was very different. Foulkes (1980) provided a detailed exploration of the decline in unionisation across the Atlantic and by tracing events back to the 1950s, offered valuable insights into the development of non-union personnel policies. By 1986, Kochan, Katz and McKersie offered a systematic two models analysis of American industrial relations: the unionised and non-unionised. Beardwell (1994) suggests that the neglect of the non-union situation in Britain is due to an entirely different set of political and economic assumptions that informed industrial relations research. To quote:

> non-unionism came late to the party and did not even have the fancy dress of capital letters to ease its entrance. Instead of gatecrashing in a blatant manner, it could be observed as one of the guests quietly holding a drink while HRM and New IR partied noisily in the middle of the throng. So quiet was the entrance of this new neighbour that many only noticed when it was clear that this guest was quite persistent and would be difficult to dislodge.
>
> (Beardwell 1994: 2)

Nevertheless, while it is true to say that there is a dearth of literature about non-union relations in comparison to unionised settings, it should not be assumed that there is a complete lack of information, and several discrete analytical approaches have been identified (Kelly 1998).

The survey approach

This approach draws on a growing strand of survey work, such as the Workplace Employee Relations Survey (WERS) series, or separate surveys tapping employee attitudes (Hartley 1992; McLoughlin and Gourlay 1992; Flood *et al.* 1994; ISR 1995; Jowell *et al.* 1996; Cully *et al.* 1999). Work of this type is useful in identifying the prevalence of non-union firms in key sectors of economic activity, as well as providing important clues about the range of managerial policies and practices. In terms of the concerns of this study, the employee attitude survey approach probably contains more useful insights. For instance, both McLoughlin and Gourlay (1992) and Hartley (1992) suggest that factors of age, gender and skill have little influence on union joining, and that attitudes towards work itself, management and wider social values are far more significant. This suggests a link with the concept of the psychological contract and notions of justice, trust and identity, which will be explained in greater detail in the next chapter.

Managerial accounts of non-unionism

This approach, which largely consists of the accounts of non-union managers (Peach 1983; Tse 1985; Sieff 1990; Billot 1996) also yields some insights. However, given the potential bias in these studies, they must clearly be interpreted with some caution. Nonetheless, provided they are not taken as empirically grounded, they are interesting and contain clear messages that are worthy of recognition. For instance at IBM, Peach (1983) identified a number of factors which seemed to be related to employees' acceptance of the company approach, and these led the Advisory, Conciliation and Arbitration Service (ACAS) not to recommend union recognition. These arguments are redolent of the unitary perspective, often typified as the (M&S) way (Tse 1985; Sieff 1990), the antecedents of which have been an important undercurrent in managerial thinking for some time. In submitting evidence to the Donovan Commission (1968), the (then) Managing Director of the Rugby Portland Cement Company remarked:

> we deplore the terms industrial and labour relations. We prefer human relations, and these relations depend on the tone of one man, the executive; his philosophies, his outlook, his leadership.
>
> (Reddish 1968, in Barrett *et al.* 1975: 299)

One of the problems with these accounts is that they are usually uncritical and lack any analysis of potential conflict in situations where unions are absent. Thus while they offer clues about non-union policies and managerial *intent*, they provide little detailed assessment of how employment relationships are made and modified. Indeed, IBM no longer espouses the full employment obligation and has made workers redundant, while the M&S model has been criticised as ruthless and too demanding on the day-to-day working lives of employees (Turnbull and Wass 1998). In addition, Cressey (1985), Blyton and Turnbull (1998) and Turnbull and Wass (1998) show that much of what has been written about the sophisticated non-union model is more rhetoric than reality, and that it is a phenomenon that invites a high dependency on, rather than a high commitment to the organisation.

Non-union case studies

This is a much wider and deeper approach in terms of analysis and it includes a range of academic-based case studies. These include the work of Foulkes (1980), Cressey (1985), Dickson *et al.* (1988), Bassett (1988), McLoughlin and Gourlay (1992, 1994), Blyton and Turnbull (1998), Beaumont (1995), Bacon (1999), Turnbull and Wass (1996), McLoughlin (1996) and Dundon *et al.* (1999). A common feature which links these is that their prime raison d'être for research is the phenomenon of non-unionism, and so the work tends to be far richer in content than purely managerialist accounts. For example, Foulkes provides a detailed assessment of particular personnel policies in large (US) companies that are linked to managerial union avoidance strategies. A similar theme is evident in Bacon's (1999) Sheerness steel study, suggesting that despite superficial signs of a sophisticated HRM approach, the reality is quite different. That is, management are extremely anti-union, use coercive tactics and abuse the notions of authority and power to secure a preferred way of managing.

Another strand in this literature includes studies that evaluate non-union firms as a by-product of assessing other features of employment relations. That is, the main reason for the empirical enquiry was not non-unionism per se, but some other aspect of the employment relationship. These include studies by Bolton (1971), Roy (1980), White and Trevor (1983), Trevor (1988), Rainnie (1985, 1989), Scase and Goffee (1987), Ram (1991, 1994), Goss (1988), Scott *et al.* (1989), Cressey *et al.* (1985), Claydon (1989, 1996), Roberts *et al.* (1992), Edwards and Whitston (1993), Broad (1994), Scott (1994), McKinlay and Taylor (1996) and Bacon *et al.* (1996). The information that can be derived from this work is highly relevant. While they all differ in their aims and perspectives, these studies offer valuable insights into non-union practices. For example, some of the earlier work by Bolton (1971), a government commission that examined employment in small companies has been highly criticised for its simplistic view, and Rainnie (1985, 1989), Goss (1991) and Scase and Goffee (1987) all found that the small is beautiful notion is misleading. Conflict can be expressed in more subtle ways than in industrial action, for example, through absenteeism and a greater propensity for employees to exit the relationship. While Storey (1994) suggests there is a need for caution because figures about SMEs only represent a statistician's best available judgement, the small business sector is of clear, numerical importance for non-union relations; a point to which we return later.

The labour process approach

Yet another approach is the information derived from the critical literature on labour process theory. Recently this literature has revisited the forms of Tayloristic managerial control in new and emerging sectors of economic activity, many of which are unorganised, for instance, call centres, professional service firms and knowledge-based information technology industries (Thompson and Warhurst 1998; Sturdy 2001). Using Foucault's concepts of power-knowledge within a non-union environment, McKinlay and Taylor (1996) explain how the informality of work processes can establish a distinctive collective identity among non-union workers which protects the group from managerial interference.

More traditional labour process literature, such as Roy's (1980) seminal study on how employers offer sweeteners or combine fear and evil tactics to avoid unionisation has been revisited by Gall (2001) and these classifications are outlined in Table 1.3. Gall's (2001) argument is that in light of the recent Employment Relations Act (1999), non-union employer strategies are developing in more subtle ways than those first used by Roy. For instance, Gall (2001: 3) adds three additional categories to Roy's schema. Some of the approaches, such as evil stuff, resonate in a way that is more applicable to the US than the UK, and so the labels awkward, tame and harm stuff are used to map more recent developments among British non-union employers.

Table 1.3 Non-union management control practices

Non-union approach	Type of employer behaviour and practice
Fear Stuff[a]	Union suppression: Employer behaviour includes blatant intimidation of workers, with the objective of instilling 'fear' (real or otherwise) of managerial reprisals for possible unionisation
Sweet Stuff[a]	Union substitution: Management argue that unions are unnecessary, with better terms and conditions and sophisticated employee voice channels to resolve any grievances
Evil Stuff[a]	Ideological opposition to unions: Management articulates the view that unions are 'reds under the beds', and will be destructive to the company performance
Fatal Stuff[a]	Blatant refusal: Employer behaviour here includes refusal to recognise a union, or at best refusal to 'bargain in good faith'
Awkward Stuff[b]	Stonewalling: Managers create what appear to be legitimate obstacles to union recognition, effectively employing 'delaying' tactics
Tame Stuff[b]	Damage limitation: Employer behaviour can take the form of 'sweetheart' deals, partially recognising 'moderate' unions or creating internal (managerial controlled) staff associations
Harm Stuff[b]	By-passing: Employer behaviour seeks to effectively marginalise collective employee voice, often through specific non-union communication channels

Sources: adapted from Roy (1980) and Gall (2001).

Notes
a = Roy's (1980) original classification; b = Gall's (2001) additional typologies.

HRM and non-unionism

The final approach that is worthy of a mention is that which has been used to test the link between non-unionism and so-called new managerial systems, such as HRM (Beaumont 1995; Guest and Hoque 1994; McLoughlin and Gourlay 1994). Much of this work is underpinned by the idea that since HRM is based on individual and unitarist principles (see Chapter 2), the non-union sector is fertile ground for the use of these new managerial strategies. Problematically, the evidence suggests that this is a sweeping overgeneralisation. For example, the larger and more sophisticated non-union firms in which HRM might be expected to exist, are the exception rather than the rule and the majority of non-union companies are SMEs, rather than large-scale multinationals (Beaumont and Harris 1989). In addition, the desire by management to remain non-union seems to be more associated with competitive market conditions than any clear HRM-type model (Rubery 1987; Kochan *et al.* 1986; Beaumont and Rennie 1986). Even more conclusive is the finding that HRM-related practices are actually more common in unionised establishments (Fernie *et al.* 1994; Cully *et al.* 1998). Among non-union organisations, the workplace industrial relations survey series shows labour turnover and dismissals are higher, and that workers are more likely to experience health and safety problems and face redundancies than in their unionised counterparts (Millward *et al*. 1992, 2000). Furthermore, evidence suggests that High Commitment Management (HCM) practices, which might have links with sustained organisational performance, are just as relevant in unionised as non-union establishments (Cully *et al*. 1998). In short, the literature that depicts the non-union organisation as a model of HRM, which is something distinct from either traditional industrial relations or personnel management, could be conceptually and empirically flawed.

Research aims and questions

Although the brief review of the literature given above reveals that something is known of the non-union situation, compared to the vast amount of information that exists about organisations in which trade unions are recognised, the body of knowledge is patchy to say the least. As we have suggested earlier, the non-union sector is such a significant area of employment, it may well embrace the majority of working people in Britain. As such, it is important to know how relationships in these organisations are made, sustained and modified in the absence of a collective intermediary. It was this that informed the aims of this investigation.

At a general level, one overall aim was to uncover the conditions of employment relations that prevail in non-union firms. Of course, the organisation itself is a context to its system of employee relations and since these contexts differ substantially, a second general objective was to explain the key factors that shape and modify these different relationships. To this end the book seeks to address the following questions and issues:

1   What are the key characteristics that explain the employment relationship in non-union settings?
2   What factors (external and internal) influence how these relationships are made and modified?
3   Given the absence of a trade union, what provisions exist for employees to articulate their concerns (employee voice)?
4   Do non-union firms have a coherent set of employment policies and practices?
5   Are these policies and practices likely to resist the collective mobilisation of workers in non-union firms?
6   Are there any particular patterns or styles of management among different non-union firms?

Outline of the book

The chapters that follow take the reader through the stages that were concerned with addressing the aims of the investigation. Because we felt that it was necessary to approach the matter of classifying relationships in non-union organisations in a way that was relatively unencumbered by prior conceptions, the first step was to review the concept of an employment relationship from first principles. This is described in Chapter 2, which outlines five central characteristics that were used to evaluate employment relationships in the organisations studied. In Chapter 3 some of the internal and external factors identified as those that could potentially play a part in shaping employment relationships are described. Because (even in unionised firms) there have been significant changes in the nature of employee representation and collective bargaining, here we pay particular attention to the matter of provisions that could exist for employee voice. Chapter 4 gives a brief description of the research strategy and methodology used to investigate the case study organisations.

Chapters 5 to 8 present the results from four case studies. Each one contains a description of the organisation itself, a justification for classifying the relationship as a particular, identifiable type, and an analysis of some of the internal and external factors that were influential in shaping and modifying these relationships. In Chapter 9 the data from the four case study firms is integrated to draw more generalised conclusions about non-union employment relations, and the relative influence of factors that affect these relationships. Some of the implications of these findings are also considered in the final chapter.

2   The employment relationship re-visited

Introduction

In this chapter we examine a number of different ways that can be used to portray the employment relationship. These are: the legal view of the employment contract; the traditional industrial relations perspective; and social exchange theory. While each one has its own conception of the most important features of the relationship, none of them embraces all of its aspects and so all of them have their own inherent advantages and limitations. This discussion is used to offer a re-conceptualisation of the employment relationship, from which is derived a typology of relationships that was used to categorise the organisations investigated in this study.

Conceptualising employment relations

There is considerable debate about what constitutes an employment relationship, and what can be taken to be its most important characteristics. For instance, one school of thought draws attention to the idea that the *form*, *shape* and *nature* of work within the modern capitalist enterprise has undergone such a significant transformational change that traditional conceptions of employment have been made obsolete (Cappelli *et al.* 1997; Gallie and White 1998; Felstead and Jewson 1999). According to this viewpoint employers increasingly demand more flexible and accommodative modes of production and service delivery from employees. To achieve this, non-standard patterns of work such as part-time, temporary and casual employment have become commonplace, and employees often have very little (or no) access to collective representation, all of which has resulted in a major reconfiguration of the labour market in most industrialised economies. An allied argument points to the reshaping of organisational structures, where Rubery *et al.* (2001) point out that the traditional and easily understood boundaries between workers and their employing organisation have become increasingly blurred. As such, the *permeable nature* of organisations results in complex multi-employer networking, public-private partnerships, commercial alliances and franchising systems that have serious implications for the legal and socially constructed image of the employment relationship. In other words:

> the notion of a clearly defined employer-employee relationship becomes difficult to uphold under conditions where the employee is working in project teams, or on a site alongside employees from other organisations, where responsibilities for performance and for health and safety are not clearly defined, or involve organisations other than the employer.
>
> (Rubery *et al.* 2001: 1)

In many respects these issues and tensions serve to highlight the indeterminate nature of the employment relationship (Turner and D'Art 2002). It is also important to recognise that while workers and managers have some objectives in common, there are others where their interests can be diametrically opposed. Thus the employment relationship is one in which *antagonism and co-operation* can exist side-by-side (Edwards 1995). To give a simple and somewhat obvious example, employers desire profit maximisation, but at the same time employees want an equitable share in the profits from their labours. Nevertheless, even where interests are in potential conflict like this, it can be argued that there is some scope for them to be reconciled. For instance, one route to profitability is to engage the commitment and cooperation of labour, which can also satisfy employee desires for employment security, social status and identity. A lasting reconciliation of this type usually requires some form of compliance, if not cooperation, although one of the things that stands in the way of this is that the balance of power in the workplace is normally tilted heavily in favour of management (Blyton and Turnbull 1998). Thus the very existence of a trade union reflects a perceived need on the part of employees to erect and maintain enduring checks and balances on management power.

Given the re-shaping of organisational forms, the pattern of work and the changing demographic profile of the labour force, there are a number of perspectives on the nature of the employment relationship. None of these is inherently right or wrong. Rather, they are different paradigms that can be used to view the same phenomenon, and each one tends to be accepted by a particular community of interest. Within each of these paradigms there are different schools of thought that emphasise particular facets of the relationship, and to try to cover all of them would be well beyond the scope of this book. For this reason, the mainstream approaches will be described, together with a note of their particular strengths and weaknesses so far as this study is concerned.

The legal conception of the employment relationship

In theory, this is by far the most straightforward view of what constitutes an employment relationship. On its own, however, it is also the weakest of all theoretical perspectives. Legally, the employment relationship is expressed by the concept of a contract of service,[1] which can be defined as an obligation to work or be available for work, for which payment is promised. This is both an economic and a legal construct (Davies and Freedland 1983; Whincup 1991). In economic terms it forms the basis of wages, holidays and other fringe benefits that are not necessarily delineated by law in an explicit way. However, because it also covers matters that go beyond the simple economic exchange of rewards for service, the contract also influences factors such as how employees are managed in order to meet market demands and the performance of the firm (Clark 1994).

The contract of employment is generally taken to be the cornerstone of British labour law (Kahn-Freund 1967) and three important assumptions underpin the notion of a contract. The first is that the relationship is an individual one. Second, that the parties have different but reciprocal rights and obligations and finally, that the two parties have entered the relationship freely, and with equal bargaining strength. However, there are a number of problems with these assumptions. To start with there is the matter of an imbalance of power in the relationship, about which the employment contract is notoriously silent. The problem is that while the contract assumes that the parties enter the relationship freely and equally, it is completely silent about equality and freedom in an ongoing sense. In addition to the expressly agreed terms such as hours of work and rates of payment, there are other terms of the contract, which are implied in common law. For example, an employee's obligation to give faithful service and abide by works or organisational rules, which are seldom if ever seen before a person actually becomes a member of an organisation. Thus in entering into the relationship the reality is that the employee becomes subordinate to the employer's power, authority and status, which is a far cry from the notion of equal bargaining strength in an ongoing sense (Hyman 1975; Fox 1985). This, of course, is one of the main reasons why employees might see it as advantageous to band together by joining a trade union and to quote from the doyen of British labour lawyers:

> trade unions are more likely to be a more effective force in redressing the imbalance of power inherent in the contract than the law is, or ever could be.
>
> (Kahn-Freund 1977: 10)

Ultimately, the assumption of freedom to enter into the relationship hinges on the idea that either party can refuse to do so, but in a practical sense even this can be questioned. Cohen (1988) alludes to the dilemma between free in theory and forced in practice, by citing the example of an unemployed, unskilled worker faced with the choice between taking a hazardous job, or no job at all:

To infer from the fact that John was free to do other things, that he was therefore not forced to take a hazardous job, is to employ a fake account of what it is to be forced to do something. When a person is forced to do something he has no *reasonable* or *acceptable* alternative course. He need not have an alternative at all.

(Cohen 1988: 245)

Kahn-Freund (in Davies and Freedland 1983: 10) further takes issue with the idea of employee freedom in the contract of employment by noting:

In its operation it is a condition of subordination, however much the submission and the subordination may be concealed by that indispensable figment of the legal mind known as the contract of employment.

(Kahn-Freund in Davies and Freedland 1983)

There are additional problems associated with some of the things that tend to be swept-up into a contract. As noted above, it contains both expressly agreed and implied obligations, yet in practice the parties agree to only some of these beforehand. Although case law and statutory legislation have progressively clarified a number of contractual matters; for example, health and safety, union membership or equal opportunities, some of these rights are more ambiguous in the non-union firm. Employees have to be aware of their rights in order to exercise them, and where there is no trade union to advise people, the law can be so complex that they frequently lack detailed knowledge of their common law rights. In contrast, employers tend to have the services of personnel specialists or other legal advisers at their disposal. A recent example of this is the passage of the Employment Relations Act (1999) which, among other things, contains a provision for statutory union recognition. So anxious are some employers to avoid recognising trade unions that they have sought the advice of US anti-union consultants and law firms who specialise in circumventing or defeating union certification campaigns (Barnett 1999; Logan 2001).

Finally, there are the difficulties that exist because of the changing nature of organisational structures and rules (Rubery *et al.* 2001). Over time, and especially with the increasing use by employers of non-standard forms of work, the distinctions between protected and unprotected employees have been increasingly difficult for the courts to resolve.[2] Such issues are even more complex when it is unclear who the actual employer is, as in the case of agency workers or employees based elsewhere than on the main site or employing location. Even in the case of a single-site employer, a problematic area is the matter of works or organisational rules. The sole author of these rules is invariably the employer and because a prospective employee – or in multi-employer or networked organisations, an employee on loan – is unlikely to have had the opportunity to assent or dissent to these rules, they are effectively imposed in silence. Thus it has been argued that the contract is not even an agreement about terms and conditions, but simply an agreement to enter into a relationship, the terms and conditions of which have yet to emerge (Honeyball 1989).

For all these criticisms, contracting between employer and employee undeniably takes place, and so the legal perspective has a role in conceptualising the employment relationship, whether it is in a unionised or non-union organisation. For this reason, we will return to this matter later, when considering an alternative perspective. The fact remains however, that the legal perspective on its own is incapable of expressing the complexity, subtlety and potential unevenness of the relationship. As noted earlier, one way in which employees can resolve this is by collectivising and using the agency of a trade union to formulate and administer rules and agreements that remove some of the ambiguities and inherent inequalities in the relationship. For this reason it is relevant to consider the Industrial Relations conception of the employment relationship, which is covered next.

The industrial relations perspective

As a subject of study, industrial relations is not a single approach but one that draws on a number of different academic disciplines[3] (Ackers and Wilkinson 2003). It is also a subject that contains a number of distinctly different schools of thought, each of which has its own particular concerns. However, the mainstream view is that industrial relations is concerned with:

> the making and administering of rules which regulate employment relationships; regardless of whether these are seen as formal or informal, structured or unstructured.
>
> (Bain and Clegg 1974: 95)

Since rules cannot sensibly be understood in isolation from the parties to rule making, of necessity this has traditionally embraced the study of trade unions, management, employer associations and government and its agencies (Clegg 1979). Although this takes greater cognizance of the aspects of human agency and capital power, it nonetheless contains a number of difficulties when applied to non-union organisations.

The antecedents of industrial relations are firmly rooted in the institutions of job regulation. Ever since the seminal and pioneering work of Webb and Webb (1897), this has come down to an almost exclusive focus on collective bargaining; a process that has been described as the institutionalisation of conflict (Flanders 1965; Fox 1966). This expression hinges on the idea that the collectivisation of labour is a means of counterbalancing the unequal power in the employment relationship, in which employees, through their representatives, can speak with one voice. Thus the prominence of the industrial relations perspective in academic and industrial circles owes much to a widespread acceptance that collective bargaining is the most practical method of regulating the terms and conditions of employment, thereby reducing the tensions between the parties (Donovan Commission 1968; Flanders 1970; Fox 1985). Problematically, this facility is denied to employees in non-union firms, and while in theoretical terms collective representation can occur in other ways than through a trade union, there is very little evidence of any sustainable alternative system (McLoughlin and Gourlay 1994; Towers 1997).

An important problem with this view is that while IR recognises that antagonism and cooperation exist side-by-side in virtually all organisations, it is the first of these that receives prominent place. This runs the risk of focusing primarily on the institutions of job regulation and conflict resolution, thus regarding other matters in the employment relationship as being of secondary importance. For this reason, industrial relations has devoted scant attention to the non-union situation. Indeed, it is remarkably silent about how rules could be made and modified where employees are not collectivised. So pronounced is this silence that it is all too easy to assume that a non-union organisation is an aberration, or a temporary phenomenon, or even that organisations of this type are all so similar that it is not worth the effort of studying them (Wilkinson 1999). Thus if an exclusive industrial relations framework were to be used to study the non-union situation, there is a great danger that some of the subtleties of the relationship between organisation and employees could be overlooked. It is perhaps for this reason that the term industrial relations now tends to have been eclipsed by the expression employment relations, which accepts that a very wide variety of relationships are possible, some of which are inherently more conflictual than others. In this vein, Edwards (1995) comments that it is only recently that industrial relations texts have acknowledged that there is considerably more to the subject than analysis has hitherto revealed, redefining the relationship between employer and employee as:

> The ways in which employees are rewarded, motivated, trained and disciplined, together with the influence on these processes of the major institutions involved, namely, management, trade unions and the state.
>
> (Edwards 1995: 3)

It should not be overlooked, however, that a traditional industrial relations perspective contains a number of important features that can help in understanding the complexities of managing a non-unionised relationship. It goes well beyond the legal definition of the employment contract and has a higher level of specification and analysis, which overcomes the narrowness of the legal paradigm. It also alerts us to the idea expressed by Dunlop (1958) that industrial relations is a sub-system which mirrors conditions in wider society, in which a set of rules based on societal norms, power and authority and political and legal structures shapes the behaviour of the

actors involved. Additionally, it reminds us that the employment relationship is not a static system of consequences and actions, but something that is
dynamic and always in motion (Hyman 1975). To this end features such as
freedom, conflict, power, authority and legitimacy are not permanent states
but dynamic frontiers of control (Goodrich 1975) that transcend both time
and space. In order to capture some of this dynamic complexity, the discussion will shortly consider a third perspective (social exchange), which can
help to build an analytical framework that is more theoretically robust.
Before doing so however, it is important to consider another development
within industrial relations research, which in some circles has effectively
become a sub-paradigm within the industrial relations perspective.

Across the last two decades the term human resource management
(HRM) has become widely used as a shorthand expression to describe a different (to traditional industrial relations) approach to managing the employment relationship. The term originated in the USA in the early 1980s,
where a number of influential analysts drew the conclusion that in the
highly volatile business environment of the late twentieth century, successful organisations would be those that could compete on the basis of rapid
innovation and quality, together with an ability to cope with change, all of
which would require a particular type of employment relationship. While
there is no universally accepted definition of HRM, most accounts argue
that that its core principles are radically different from traditional industrial
relations, and perhaps the most significant idea is that HRM policies and
practices should primarily be driven by the needs of the business. In the eyes
of commentators such as Hendry and Pettigrew (1990) and Miller (1991)
this results in four key characteristics of HRM:

- a strong emphasis on planning the use of human resources;
- coherent employment policies that are underpinned by a distinct philosophy;
- the machinery of human resource activities is matched with a clearly
  stated business strategy;
- a view of people (employees) as a strategic resource for gaining
  competitive advantage.

These however, are very general principles and in practice it is now
widely accepted that there are a number of variants, the extremes of which
are: soft HRM and hard HRM (Guest 1987; Storey 1987). The **soft** version
is said to stress the word human, and is underpinned by ideas associated
with the human relations movement. That is, employees are viewed as
valued assets, the appropriate use of which leads to a distinct competitive
advantage for the organisation. According to this view, an organisation has
(or should have) policies and practices that are geared to producing innovative, resourceful human beings. Thus there is a high emphasis on eliciting
a degree of commitment to organisational goals, perhaps by devoting

attention to communication and employee involvement (Storey and Sisson 1993; Walton 1985a, 1985b).

In **hard** HRM the emphasis is on employees as a resource. Human resource policies and practices are primarily driven by bottom line considerations and are geared to achieving the strategic objectives of the organisation (Formbrun *et al.* 1984). This can mean that humans are regarded in much the same way as any other resource, for example, land or machinery, which in turn implies a less humanistic approach, and a close watch on effort and headcount. Clearly therefore, HRM can reflect two diametrically opposed sets of policies and practices and while the evidence suggests that most organisations express an underlying philosophy of soft HRM, in practice the hard version is more frequently encountered (Keenoy 1997; Truss *et al.* 1997).

For the purposes of this investigation, the theoretical importance of HRM is that it could be used as a substitute for a traditional industrial relations approach. Indeed, from early on in its development a number of writers such as Basset (1986) and Wickens (1987) argued that HRM is effectively a new model for industrial relations. Moreover, industrial relations scholars such as Edwards (1995), who is quoted above, point out that since HRM is a way of managing the employment relationship, it needs to be included in the study of industrial relations. To this end Guest (1995) outlines four alternative approaches to managing the employment relationship:

Traditional Collectivism:	the use of an industrial relations approach, with no emphasis on HRM
New Realism:	the use of both industrial relations and HRM approaches in tandem, with high priority given to both
Individualised HRM:	the HRM approach substitutes for the traditional industrial relations approach
The Black Hole:	which uses neither HRM nor industrial relations.

In more recent work by Guest and Conway (1999) a large sample of organisations was surveyed, approximately 40 per cent of which were unionised. Of these, approximately half had a high usage of HRM practices, which leads to the conclusion that IR and HRM are not mutually exclusive, but can exist side-by-side. This is consistent with other evidence, which suggests that the take-up of HRM has mostly been in organisations that had previously relied on a traditional industrial relations approach. Interestingly, in non-union organisations a slightly lower percentage of firms made extensive use of HRM practices. However, in the last two decades there has been a very favourable climate for organisations that wish to work without trade unions, and it has been very difficult for unions to halt the spread of non-unionism. As such, there is more than a possibility that some unionised firms have used HRM practices as a tactic to marginalise collectivised employment relations, by substituting individual reward packages, and using so-called joint employee voice mechanisms such as works councils (Dundon 2002; Lloyd 2001). Thus in non-union companies these practices could well be used to give an appearance of providing some of the collective features of IR in a situation where there is no intention of recognising trade unions. For this reason, where reference is made to industrial relations in the book, this should be taken to embrace the use of certain elements of the HRM approach.

The social exchange perspective

Social exchange theory (Homans 1961; Blau 1964; Roloff 1981) has a long pedigree of use in the employment relations literature (Walton and McKersie 1965; Fox 1974; Silverman 1970; Rollinson 1993; Clark 1994). Because it makes use of concepts that reflect broader aspects of social and psychological interaction, it results in an eclectic and arguably much richer view of the employment relationship, which is equally applicable to either unionised or non-union situations and can be particularly useful when considering the latter.

A key advantage in viewing the employment relationship as a matter of social as well an economic exchange is that it results in a recognition that the surrounding social context contains inherent ambiguities, which gives the employment relationship a strong element of indeterminacy (Blau 1964). While it acknowledges that there is an economic dimension to the relationship, it also goes much further by recognising that unlike a pure economic transaction (for example, buying a car or house) in social exchange the parties incur a number of unspecified rights and obligations. An important difference here is that while a pure economic exchange takes place at a moment in time and what is exchanged can be precisely specified, in a social relationship the parties normally expect that the exchange will continue well into the future. Thus the employment relationship is not something static, but has a strong social dynamic (Hammer 2000).

In recognising that the employment relationship is more than a legal contract or centred solely around the institutions of job regulation, social exchange theory alerts us to the complexity of the social as well as economic exchange that takes place. There are five shared properties of this broader, more eclectic theoretical perspective that can be used to characterise the employment relationship, particularly in a situation where unions are absent.

Costs and benefits

When two parties enter into a relationship, they do so with the anticipation of some reward for effort. However, an exchange relationship only brings benefits to the parties if they are also prepared to incur costs. For example, an employee may forgo self-determination in return for salary and other benefits, and while the employer incurs the cost of wages in order to gain the benefits of employee effort, he/she might also seek some degree of commitment (or at least compliance) in the behaviour of workers. Even though they do not have specific or agreed terms about the nature of these less tangible costs and benefits, both parties are (subconsciously) aware of them when the relationship commences.

Fairness

Even if the terms of the exchange are only formulated subconsciously, each party to the relationship is aware of his/her ratio of costs to benefits. There-fore, if either of them perceives that the cost–benefit ratio is heavily weighted in favour of the other party, he/she is likely to feel that the exchange is unfair, and it is doubtful if that party would willingly enter into the relationship. Since there are no absolute standards of fairness people tend to feel that a fair exchange is one in which their costs are matched by the benefits received. Indeed, this idea illustrates why there is an undercurrent of both *conflict* and *cooperation* within the employment relationship. That is, the objectives of employers and workers will quite often differ in both sub-stance and content.

Unvoiced expectations and obligations

Although people obviously weigh up the costs and benefits when a relation-ship commences, they also tend to have expectations that the exchange will continue to be fair, even if what is expected of them changes considerably. Usually this is that the perceived ratio of costs to benefits should never be less favourable than it was at the outset. For this reason, if their costs rise, workers tend to have expectations that benefits will increase accordingly. Similarly, if conditions in the environment force a change in the organisa-tion, the employer can feel that employees are obliged to accommodate themselves to this. Both parties tend to perceive that the other one is under an obligation to comply with these expectations, but seldom, if ever, are these perceived obligations, which Guest *et al.* (1996) articulate as the deliv-ery of the deal, spelt-out by either party at the start of the relationship. Importantly, unsatisfied expectations of this type can help explain why rela-tions between employer and employee fluctuate between cooperative and conflictual situations.

Trust

No one can know for certain whether the other party will honour the terms of the employment relationship, and each party has to take it on trust that the other party will do so. This also applies to the future, and since trust begets trust and mistrust begets mistrust, the degree of trust, or level of work discretion in the employment relationship is one of its key defining characteristics (Fox 1974). For instance, trust or mistrust can help explain the nature of structured antagonisms inherent within the employment relationship and a high level of trust can be a very powerful glue that holds a relationship together.

Unequal power

Social exchange assumes there is always an imbalance of power in a relationship, and the party that is least able to withstand the severing of the relationship is the one who is potentially at a disadvantage in terms of power. This, of course, is the most obvious reason for collectivisation of employees. Whereas an employer is likely to find it comparatively easy to withstand the loss of a single employee, this is not the case if all employees withdraw their labour. Needless to say, the concept of power also has implications in terms of the capabilities of the parties to vary the terms of exchange to their own advantage. Significantly, power can be utilised in both overt and covert ways. For example, evidence clearly demonstrates that trade unions have been an enduring check on the use of unfettered employer power. However, a formal power balance of this type is absent in the non-union situation, and it is unclear how the imbalance is mediated and modified, if at all. In the light of this it could therefore be asked why employees in non-union organisations do not flock to join trade unions? Some insights into this are provided by Kelly's (1998) revision of social mobilisation, which draws on a number of social exchange principles to help understand the process of collectivisation.

Drawing on American social theorists such as Tilly (1978) and McAdam (1988), Kelly (1998) argues that collective mobilisation can flow from employee perceptions of *injustice, attribution* and *identity*, central to which is the existence of *them and us* attitudes. That is, when employees attribute blame to groups such as management, it is likely that they belong to and identify with a social category *the us* (workers) which is opposed to *the them* (management). The propensity to unionise however, can be mediated by other factors. For example, there are important differences between the 'attitudinal' and 'behavioural' experiences of workers (Mowday *et al.* 1982; Cohen 1992; D'Art and Turner 1997). Therefore, in the non-union context, it is possible that a reduction, or even elimination of them and us attitudes can significantly influence the very nature of the employment relationship. A key factor here can be *leadership*. For instance, the actions of leaders (workers, union activists or managers) can influence processes that shape a sense of identity and attribution. In a recent paper on the nature of local union leadership, Darlington (2000) presents a case for political activism as a central lever in the processes of labour organisation. That is, local leaders with a pre-disposition for class-consciousness often defend action and promote a sense of attributing blame to managers. Of course, such activity does not exist in a vacuum and there can be counter forces at work. In the non-union firm managerial hostility, ideology and action can counterbalance a worker's sense of social identity and attribution, and the very nature of such an employment relationship can promote a climate that alters expectations, attitudes and behaviours (Foulkes 1980; Dickson *et al*. 1988; Bacon 1999). Unions might not be outlawed but can be discouraged, either by inaugurating managerial techniques that substitute a worker's sense of attribution, or through more coercive managerial tactics that suppress the triggers to collective behaviour (Gall and McKay 2001).

The psychological contract: an expression of social exchange

A concept that reflects the social exchange view of the employment relationship is that of the psychological contract. The origins of the concept can be traced to ideas put forward by Argyris (1960), who describes it as something that is embedded in the perceptions of both parties (organisation and individual) to the relationship. The potential importance of the psychological contract was first spelled-out in a clear way by Schein (1980), and more recently, there has been a significant reawakening of interest in its application to the employment relationship (Guest *et al*. 1996; Guest and Conway 1997; McFarlane and Tetrick 1994; Mumford 1995; Rousseau and Parks 1993).

Schein draws attention to the idea that in the employment relationship there are really three types of contract. The *formal contract*, which largely deals with the economic aspects of the exchange, and is reflected in the legal conception of a contract of employment. In addition, there is an *informal contract*, some of the components of which are derived from wider social norms about how people should treat each other, while others are more specific to a particular organisation; for example, how much give and take there will be about timekeeping and working late (Brown 1972).

The third type of contract, the *psychological contract*, has contents that are seldom, if ever, explicitly stated. These largely consist of the unvoiced expectations and obligations of the parties, neither of whom could be consciously aware of their expectations until they are not met. Therefore the psychological contract reflects intangible needs, wants and expectations that can vary widely and its details can be very difficult to specify. Nevertheless, some idea of what it might embrace can be seen in Table 2.1.

All three of these contracts have an impact on the nature and shape of the relationship between employer and employee. For the relationship to come into existence the formal contract has to be seen by both parties as acceptable. By putting in place convenient variations through which the parties accommodate to, or oppose each other, the informal contract acts as a lubricant to the formal one. Finally, the psychological contract goes to the very heart of the exchange, by expressing emotional aspects of the relationship.

Table 2.1 The psychological contract – possible expectations of employees and employers

Employee expectations	Employer expectations
• Working conditions will be safe and as pleasant as possible • Jobs will be interesting and satisfying • Reasonable efforts to provide job security • Involvement or consultation in decisions that affect them • Equality of opportunity and fairness in selection and promotion • Opportunities for personal development and progression • To be treated with consideration and respect • Fair and equitable remuneration	• Acceptance of main values of the organisation • Diligence and conscientiousness in pursuit of objectives important to the organisation • To avoid abusing the trust and goodwill of superiors • To have concern for the reputation of the organisation • Loyalty and willingness to tolerate a degree of inconvenience for the good of the organisation • Trustworthiness and honesty • To conform to accepted norms of behaviour in the organisation • Consideration for others

Source: adapted from Rollinson *et al*. (1998).

Re-conceptualising the employment relationship

From the arguments above, it can be expected that all three types of contract will exist in employment, whether unionised or non-unionised. In conjunction, these three elements can be used to describe approaches to making and modifying the employment relationship in a way that transcends the unionised v. non-unionised dichotomy. Formal contracts will be present in both types of organisation, because for all the limitations of the legal view of the relationship, wherever there is paid employment, there are contracts of employment (even unwritten). However, it can be expected that the importance of the other two types of contract will vary considerably. At the risk of oversimplifying matters, in the unionised situation the relationship may be more focused on the combined use of formal and informal arrangements. That is, trade unions will attempt to establish frontiers of control that reflect (or better) the floor of rights established by employment legislation. They will also try to institutionalise custom and practice (the give and take inherent in the informal contract) into a fairly permanent set of mutual rights and obligations (Brown 1972).

In the absence of a collective organisation however, there is no independent mechanism outside managerial-inspired techniques for employees to become involved. Therefore, the informal and psychological elements probably play a greater role in shaping the features of the exchange. In this respect Rousseau (1995) draws an important distinction between two types of psychological contract. **The Relational Contract** describes the situation in a unitary (single source of authority) organisation. This is said to reflect the relationship between an employer and employee in which each party attempts to accommodate to the needs and expectations of the other. In contrast, a **Transactional Contract** may exist in more pluralistic organisations, and describes a relationship between the parties that is characterised by regulatory interests. Here mutual responsibilities tend to be more formally and precisely defined through structures and institutions which mediate the terms of the exchange. Interestingly, there is recent evidence that where the terms of the psychological contract are made more explicit, perceptions of fairness and trust are stronger (Guest and Conway 2002).

Using Hyman's (2001: 1–5) recent geometry of trade union identity and purpose, a triangular approach can be applied to help simplify the story. This is shown in Figure 2.1.

Each point on the triangle corresponds to one of the employment relationship models reviewed thus far. In some organisations the relationship may be tilted more towards one point than another. The *legal construct* of the employment relationship may be more relevant in a single or more stable employer enterprise; perhaps those less exposed to the environmental influences that intrude across permeable organisational boundaries. One tilted towards *joint regulation* may be dominated by collective bargaining institutions or European Works Councils, thereby relying to a greater extent on formalised systems of joint regulation to mediate terms and conditions. The *social (psychological) exchange* paradigm could have a great deal of value in understanding the complexity of the employment relationship in non-union, informal and smaller social settings. However, a relationship in an organisation resting at any single point of the triangle is likely to be unstable. For instance, other than in an illegal situation, it is unlikely that an employment relationship devoid of any legal considerations would be encountered. Even in a non-union setting, where the emphasis could rest on informal and psychological aspects, it is possible that there will be employee and employer interactions that are used to moderate the terms of that relationship, for example, forms of non-union consultation and employee involvement. Thus in practice, the employment relationship is likely to incorporate features of

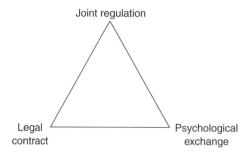

Figure 2.1 A stylised view of different employment relations perspectives.

all three points, with differences in degree depending on the context and market conditions faced by the organisation.

With this in mind a scheme was developed to categorise employment relationships. Our aims in doing this were twofold. First, to develop a scheme that could be used in either unionised or non-union situations. Second, to derive a scheme of categorisation that reflected the central characteristics of the relationship between an organisation and its employees and in particular, a scheme that revealed differences between organisations in terms of their approaches to deriving and modifying the details of the relationship. To avoid a reliance on any one of the three perspectives out-lined above, this involved a degree of re-conceptualising the employment relationship. For instance, because of the absence of trade unions, who inject a strong element of formality into the regulation of the exchange that occurs in the employment relationship, it was necessary to place a greater emphasis on informal and psychological aspects of the exchange. Drawing on evidence culled from a wide variety of literature in the subjects of industrial relations, employment studies and organisational behaviour, five central characteristics of the employment relationship were selected. Although there are other characteristics that could have been incorporated, those used were chosen because of their potential to reveal differences that could be important in terms of meeting the aims of this investigation. It was acknowledged from the outset that in practice, these characteristics are likely to be inter-connected, a point to which we return at the end of the chapter. For the present however, and in the interests of identifying them in a clear and unambiguous way, they are described separately. In what follows each characteristic is described, and its importance in reflecting the nature of the employment relationship in a non-union situation is explained. The following chapter gives an indication of some of the factors that we antici-pated would have an impact on the nature of these characteristics of an organisation.

Regulatory approach

In the absence of a trade union there is bound to be an element of ambiguity about how rules are made and modified. Theoretically, it is possible for this to be the prerogative of just one party – the employer. As such, this charac-teristic reflects the extent to which the exchange of rewards for effort is subject to unilateral regulation by the management of a particular organ-isation.

Marsh and McCarthy (1968) argue that regulatory procedures should be both *acceptable* and *appropriate* to both parties, which tends to reflect a post-Donovan pluralist ideology. Nevertheless, it would not be putting matters too strongly to suggest that the traditional industrial relations approach contains an unvoiced assumption that unilateral management regulation is near universal in the non-union situation, which in some firms extends into undermining the basic floor of employment rights established by legislation. Indeed, it is possible that this assumption accounts for the lack of interest in the non-union organisation that is characteristic of traditional industrial relations. However, the presence of a trade union is no guarantee that unilateral regulation by managers is absent. For example, it has been argued that even in unionised organisations management has de-incorporated itself throughout the 1980s and 1990s (Dunn 1993; Poole and Mansfield 1993), which suggests that *appropriateness* or *acceptability* has come to mean what is acceptable or appropriate to managers. Indeed, Parry *et al.* (1997) show that in what remains of the privatised coal mining industry in Great Britain, although trade unions are still recognised and the structures of collective bargaining have remained intact, management has abandoned any semblance of joint regulation. Beyond this, Brown and Rea (1995) comment that managers seem to have searched for ways of regulating practices without sacrificing their power and authority, by what Marchington and Parker (1990) suggest is pushing negotiation down to consultation, and consultation down to communication.

Just as the presence of a trade union is no guarantee of acceptability and appropriateness, the absence of a trade union does not mean that these matters are neglected (Terry 1999). Indeed, Lloyd (2001) gives a case study example of an aerospace company that had de-recognised trade unions and reintroduced collective representation in a form designed to make it acceptable to the workforce. Moreover, in the last two decades many unionised and non-union organisations have trimmed their workforces down to the bare minimum. Most of them have also sought a high degree of employee flexibility and commitment, in order to be able to respond to the increasingly volatile and turbulent nature of product markets. In doing so there is a sense in which they have probably become far more dependent on employee goodwill (see comments on the HRM approach earlier). Since people are always much more committed to implementing decisions that they have helped to make, one way to foster goodwill is to give them a say in matters that affect them. While this does not necessarily mean that employees are admitted to the management decision-making process, an important tool for achieving goodwill has been to try and harness employee voice. As Brown and Rea note:

> Voice may be mobilised through joint consultative processes without necessarily committing management to explicit negotiation. Consultation does not offer outcomes in the form of agreements, nor is its conduct so obviously dependent on the two sides' power relationship.
>
> (Brown and Rea 1995: 366)

There is some evidence that the methods which allow employees to have a say have become more embedded in organisations (Marchington *et al.* 2001). These include two-way communication flows, regular and informal exchanges of information and cross-functional team working. Similarly, Cressey *et al.* (1985) and Ram (1991) discuss the implication of a socially negotiated order, in which regulation may be seen as unilateral, but nonetheless involves important informal and socially constructed forms of interaction between employee and employer.

For these reasons an organisation's regulatory approach is a characteristic that reflects the essential nature of its relationship with employees, and there are two main reasons why this feature should be included in an evaluation of the non-union situation. First, since non-union organisations are increasingly commonplace, it is important to test the unvoiced assumption of traditional industrial relations that this is synonymous with unilateral regulation by management.

Second, the extent to which an employer embraces methods that allow employees to have a say in matters that affect them is not only an important feature of the employment relationship in its own right, it is also indicative of a measure of exchange at the emotional/psychological level. As such, it is likely to have a bearing on other characteristics of the relationship, for example notions of fairness, equity and justice.

Human resource strategy

This characteristic reflects the role that managers intend employees to play in achieving business objectives, together with the ways in which they are expected to play this role. In broad terms it could be expressed as a bipolar continuum with two extremes. At one extreme employees are viewed simply as a factor of production, the costs of which should be minimised. Here the emphasis is on obtaining compliance in employee behaviour and, because they are seen as a disposable asset that can be dispensed with when it has served its useful purpose, developing employees to reach their full potential would be considered unimportant. Non-union organisations with this strategy would probably be keen to suppress any tendencies for the workforce to unionise. At the other extreme employees are seen as valued assets, which can be developed to give the firm its competitive edge. A corollary of this is that there would be a degree of investment in employees to develop their skills, together with some emphasis on engaging with them to elicit their commitment. Non-union organisations with this strategy would probably be more likely to use a union substitution approach, in the hope that this would convince employees that collectivisation is irrelevant. To some extent there is a correspondence between these two extremes and what are referred to earlier as the hard and soft versions of HRM. Importantly, Storey and Beardwell (1995) recognise that both of these extremes exist in non-unionised organisations and describe the former as a reactive, *minimalist* strategy, while the latter is referred to as a more proactive *maximalist* strategy.

Irrespective of whether an organisation is unionised, this characteristic can have a huge impact on its relationship with its employees (Kaufman and

Taras 2000). For instance, a minimalist approach implies little in the way of security for employees and in all probability there would also be a high degree of direct control over their activities. This could result in employees having a low degree of attachment to the organisation, or at best one that rests purely on a calculative involvement. In the unionised situation, where a vehicle exists to mobilise the collective power of employees, it could be expected that employees would mandate their union to press for a large number of rules to constrain management's freedom of action. In the non-union context however, they do not have this facility and so the nature of an organisation's human resource strategy can be a particularly important way of characterising the relationship. Where the strategy is minimalist for example, it could be expected that the relationship could be somewhat exploitative, with very definite efforts by management to remain non-unionised (Blyton and Turnbull 1998; Foulkes 1980; Sisson 1993). Since employees are seldom blind to attempted exploitation, this could result in a very poor psychological contract, or at least one in which employees feel that they need to find ways to make it transactional, rather than relational.

For all this there is an ongoing debate about whether organisations have clear strategies with respect to human resources. Where the expression human resource strategy is used in the literature, any element of strategy is usually considered to be downstream of product market and business strategies, and so it might attract a minimum of conscious thought (Kochan and Katz 1988; Purcell 1987; Sparrow and Pettigrew 1988; Storey 1995). For this reason any strategy could be emergent, rather than carefully thought through in advance (Mintzberg 1973). Be this as it may, there is a powerful alternative argument which holds that even if they do not recognise it themselves, managers inevitably have strategies, simply because they have goals and develop recipes (strategies) for achieving them (Thurley and Wood 1983).

Trust

In this investigation trust is loosely defined as the extent to which either party perceives that the other one will honour the obligations of exchange inherent in the relationship, without recourse to policing activities to ensure that this takes place. Importantly, this means that each party not only perceives that the other one behaves honorably, but that the party is predictably honorable, which makes predictability the very essence of trust (Grey and Garsten 2001). Clearly this goes to the very heart of any relationship, be it personal or occupational, and so it is an important characteristic of the employment relationship, whether or not an organisation has a trade union presence. However, in the unionised situation, although trust is highly desirable, it might not be so essential. Here, the parties normally construct explicit, mutually agreed rules of conduct that specify their reciprocal rights and obligations, together with limits to their discretionary powers. These go hand-in-hand with procedures that can be brought into play to deal with situations in which either party seems to have failed to honour the agreement.

Although it is currently fashionable to deprecate bureaucratic rules, they bring a strong element of predictability to both parties in the employment relationship. Because the making and modification of rules is less prominent in the non-union situation, trust can become the vital cement that holds the parties together in relationship. Being able to trust the other party to play fair means that people can get on with whatever it is that they have to do without having to look over their shoulders to ensure that the other party is not stealing an unfair advantage. Moreover, because either party is able to be less apprehensive about whether the other one is being truthful, this also means that it can be much easier to modify the terms of the relationship.

Despite the apparently straighforward nature of the above definition, trust can be a somewhat imprecise and slippery concept because:

> To trust is to observe a diffuse pattern of mutual obligations. The nature of what each owes the other is not precisely defined and each trusts the other to maintain reciprocity over the long term. Of course either side may betray this trust.
>
> (Fox 1985: 69)

This tells us that trust is not a tangible attribute, but more a matter of perception, in which what is perceived to exist is often inferred from indirect evidence. For instance, if workers are subject to tightly specified work procedures and their behaviour is policed by supervisors to ensure conformity, they are likely to perceive that management does not trust them to honour their side of the exchange – a low trust situation. Conversely, the greater the degree of discretion extended to workers, the more they are likely to feel that work rules and policies embody high trust (Fox 1985: 109). This does not necessarily mean that work must always have a high discretional content to engender trust. Indeed, workers might actually be satisfied with low discretion roles, and even unpleasant and repetitive work can have a certain amount of intrinsic value (Noon and Blyton 1997). This is particularly important in the light of recent developments, which are not primarily aimed at generating trust, but make use of the related concept of empowerment, which tends to be seen by many mangers as a way of engendering a greater degree of discretion and commitment within the workplace (Ashness and Lashley 1995; Cunningham *et al.* 1996; Wilkinson 1998).

In general terms empowerment is concerned with engaging employees at an emotional and physical level (Ashness and Lashley 1995), the implication being that initiatives such as this reflect greater trust, and a belief that workers will fulfil their obligations more willingly because they are granted increased task autonomy. Claydon and Doyle (1996) point out that there are two assumed features of empowerment, which make it particularly appealing to managers. First, it seems to offer a way of obtaining higher levels of performance from employees, without the imposition of regimes of strict supervision and control. Second, it has a humanistic rhetoric, which allows managers to feel that they are doing the right thing by giving employees autonomy and the opportunity for self-development and personal growth. When taken together, these give rise to a management assumption that empowerment benefits everybody. Employees are more satisfied with their work, because they have more interesting and responsible jobs in which they are trusted to behave responsibly, which in turn raises their keenness and commitment. In return managers get a more efficient, effective and flexible workforce. This however, is empowerment in theory and in practice matters are not quite so clear cut. First, the rhetoric of empowerment can also be a way to avoid dealing with employees on a collective basis. The whole idea promotes a sense of individualised autonomy and can become a more sophisticated (if not sinister) way of inducing employees to internalise management's values and ideologies, in what appears to be a decision made of their own free will (Willmott 1993).

Second, empowerment initiatives are commonly introduced where downsizing/delayering has, or is, taking place and it is convenient, or even necessary to devolve day-to-day decision making, because staffing levels have been reduced to a bare minimum. Since there is a widespread tendency for managers to assume that more interesting work is a sufficient reward in itself, employees often find themselves working much harder for the same level of pay (Cunningham *et al.* 1996), which can have serious implications for the perceived fairness of the situation.

Finally, there seems to be a great deal of ambiguity and imprecision about what managers mean when they speak of having an empowered workforce (Collins 1999; Cunningham *et al.* 1996). In some instances employees simply find themselves working much harder, with jobs that are no more interesting than before. It is hardly surprising therefore, that empirical studies often reveal that empowerment initiatives fail to deliver their expected advantages and that employees wind-up less committed (Cunningham and Hyman 1999). In this respect it is interesting to note that there is a stream of evidence using a combination of indicators, which reveals declining perceptions of trust and empowerment among employees. A summary of some of this work culled from the results of annual Social Attitudes surveys in the 1980s and 1990s is shown in Table 2.2.

Note that for all four indicators in Table 2.2, the general picture is one of less trust and empowerment. Between the early 1980s and the mid 1990s, fewer employees believed they had a say in work-related decisions, and even fewer saw relations between workers and managers as very good. Moreover, between 1986 and 1995 those who believed managers/big business will try to get the better of workers if given the chance (e.g. a shift in the cost–benefit advantage) increased from 54 per cent to 62 per cent.

Table 2.2 Survey indicators of employee trust and empowerment

	1984	1985	1986	1987	1989	1990	1991	1993	1994	1995
Employees' say in decisions affecting their work (%)										
Should have more say	36		46	44			45	52		
Satisfied with the way things are	63		53	54			54	47		
Management will always try to get the better of employees if it gets the chance (%)										
Agree			51.5	51.6	60.9	61.3	57.9	62.7	63.4	64.0
Disagree			24.6	27.3	19.8	19.0	19.2	15.4	15.0	14.2
Big business benefits owners at the expense of workers (%)										
Agree				53.9	51.1	52.8	52.4	49.5	54.8	60.1	61.7
Disagree				19.0	22.1	21.5	22.6	18.5	17.0	13.6	15.3
In general how would you describe relations between management and other employees at your workplace? (%)										
Very good	36	38	34	34	32	38	34	31	29	30
Quite good	47	45	47	48	49	44	45	47	47	45
Not very good at all	16	16	19	18	18	17	21	20	24	24

Sources: adapted from British Social Attitude Surveys: Hedges (1994/95) and Kelly (1998).

Informality–formality in regulation

This characteristic can be defined as the extent to which formalised interactions, rules and procedures are used as the main way of setting and modifying the terms of the employment relationship. Although this has some connection with the characteristic described earlier as regulatory approach, it is not the same thing. Whereas the regulatory approach focuses on the degree of management prerogative, and is largely applicable to visible forms of regulation, this one deals with a less visible, but highly important characteristic: whether informal methods are also used.

Some element of informality pervades all employment relationships. This is recognised in the concept of an informal contract, which expresses the give and take, or pattern of indulgency between the parties, for example, in terms of temporarily suspending the formal exchange requirements in order to cope with day-to-day exigencies. It is also recognised in the idea of a psychological contract, which deals with the matter of social exchange. The importance of formality is that in large organisations, a great deal of employee behaviour is regulated by the application of bureaucratic control methods (Durkhiem 1933; Ray 1986). In smaller firms however, many of which are not unionised, relations between the parties are often more direct and personal. Indeed, despite the Donovan prescription for greater formality in unionised organisations, managers often have to rely on informality or custom and practice to modify working arrangements on a day-to-day basis. Thus the very existence of informal relations becomes an enduring feature of some employment situations (Brown 1972; Delbridge 1998), which in many ways reflects the quality of the relationship, as well as the social dynamics of the workplace. For this reason it tells us a great deal about *how* the relationship is modified, as well as the *methods* used to regulate it. Importantly, Purcell (1979) points out that there is a strong connection between trust and formality. That is, a degree of formality indicates that both parties are willing to commit themselves to certain patterns of action in the future, which may promote trust. However, if one (or both) parties has too great an insistence on formality about everything, this is often taken by the other party to indicate that there is a lack of trust.

This characteristic of informality–formality can be particularly important in examining the non-union situation. The absence of a collective organisation of employees removes the necessity for the existence of a forum in which formal agreements can be made, e.g. a joint trade union–management committee of some sort. In these circumstances the extent to which management is prepared to formally commit itself reveals a great deal about the relationship. In addition, the inclusion of informal relations adds a stronger focus on social exchange, which gives a much richer picture than an exclusive reliance on structural and institutional indicators of job regulation. Moreover, there is a great deal of evidence to show that line managers find it necessary to engage in informal relations with workers to ensure an efficient level of production and, potentially, to sustain the relationship (Delbridge 1998; Gratton *et al.* 1999). Thus by taking note of informal practices, it is sometimes possible to reveal more subtle features of the relationship. For example, McKinley and Taylor (1996) show how workgroup values help generate identity, attribution and a capacity for resistance between non-union employees and management. Equally important is the empirical evidence from smaller firms, where Scott *et al.* (1989) note that informal routinisation can serve to obscure the employment relationship with family and personal ties. This suggests that informality may be indicative of a more individualised approach, which could avoid collectivism, and thus maintain or legitimise non-unionism as being in the interests of employees and owner-managers.

Them and us

A state of them and us is an extremely potent way of characterising the nature of the relationship between an organisation and its employees. In the simplest possible terms it can be described as the extent to which employees conceive of the employment relationship as one in which there are two parties with potentially opposing interests. This idea has its origins in work on intergroup conflict and in particular, the in group and out group phenomenon (Alderfer and Smith 1982; Allport 1954; Ashtorth and Mael 1989; Huse and Bowditch 1973; Kolb *et al.* 1974). In employee relations terms, them and us attitudes play a central part in Kelly's (1998) case for social mobilisation in terms of *attribution*, *injustice* and the transition from an individual to collective *identity*. Strictly speaking however, attitudes are not directly indicative of patterns of behaviour, but of behavioural intentions (Ajzen 1988). For this reason, it is necessary to distinguish between *attitudinal* them and us and *behavioural* them and us. In the former, employees tend not to endorse managerial objectives or subscribe to the idea that management and workers are part of a unitary whole. In behavioural them and us however, they might well go one stage further, by expressing support for trade unions as bodies that pursue employee interests against management.

Clearly this characteristic could be illuminating in any situation where there are employees and managers. However, it is particularly important in a non-union organisation because in practical terms, behavioural them and us is made more difficult for employees. Here it is important to note that a number of authors have shown empirically that even where employees appear to display positive attitudes towards the opponent group (managers), the underlying basis of social identification expressed as them and us attitudes is still present. As such, behavioural intentions and collective identities are strongly correlated (D'Art and Turner 1997; Kelly 1997a, 1997b; Kelly and Kelly 1991), but because avenues for formal protest are blocked off, employees might attempt to locate other, less organised ways to express their feelings, for example, absenteeism or quitting. In addition, this characteristic is important in the non-union situation because it is indicative of employee reactions to what they could perceive to be key features of the psychological contract, with all that this implies in terms of feelings about fairness, justice, trust and unequal power.

Potential connections between characteristics

As was pointed out earlier, it can be misleading to view any of the five characteristics in isolation. Some of them, for example, the regulatory approach used, its degree of formality and the nature of the psychological contract are likely to go hand-in-hand. Similarly, trust and the existence of them and us attitudes, or employee commitment, could also be connected as defining features of an employment relationship. For this reason it is important to re-emphasise that the main purpose in developing this list of characteristics was to be able to characterise the essential nature of employment relationships in a broad way, which avoids some theoretical and methodological limitations inherent in the traditional approaches outlined earlier. To close the chapter it is therefore fitting that the five characteristics should all be presented in order to conceptualise the range of different employment relationships used to categorise the organisations investigated. This is shown in Figure 2.2.

At the left-hand extreme is an *exploitative* relationship, in which the main features include managerial-imposed regulation; a low emphasis on engaging with employees; and adverse psychological aspects of the relationship

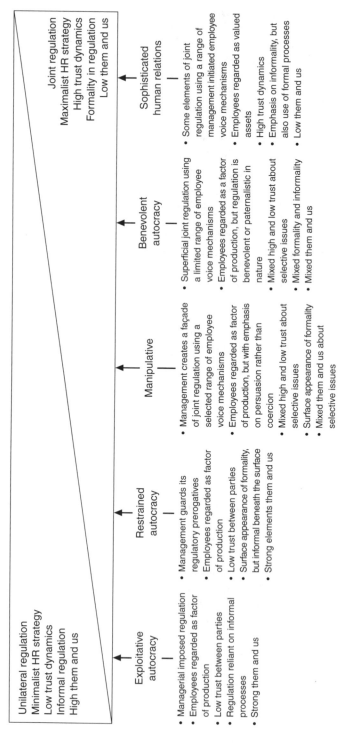

Unilateral regulation
Minimalist HR strategy
Low trust dynamics
Informal regulation
High them and us

Joint regulation
Maximalist HR strategy
High trust dynamics
Formality in regulation
Low them and us

Exploitative autocracy

- Managerial imposed regulation
- Employees regarded as factor of production
- Low trust between parties
- Regulation reliant on informal processes
- Strong them and us

Restrained autocracy

- Management guards its regulatory prerogatives
- Employees regarded as factor of production
- Low trust between parties
- Surface appearance of formality, but informal beneath the surface
- Strong elements them and us

Manipulative

- Management creates a façade of joint regulation using a selected range of employee voice mechanisms
- Employees regarded as factor of production, but with emphasis on persuasion rather than coercion
- Mixed high and low trust about selective issues
- Surface appearance of formality
- Mixed them and us about selective issues

Benevolent autocracy

- Superficial joint regulation using a limited range of employee voice mechanisms
- Employees regarded as a factor of production, but regulation is benevolent or paternalistic in nature
- Mixed high and low trust about selective issues
- Mixed formality and informality
- Mixed them and us

Sophisticated human relations

- Some elements of joint regulation using a range of management initiated employee voice mechanisms
- Employees regarded as valued assets
- High trust dynamics
- Emphasis on informality, but also use of formal processes
- Low them and us

Figure 2.2 Conceptual characteristics of different types of employment relationship.

such as low trust and high them and us attitudes. Small establishments have typically been associated with this state of affairs (Rainnie 1985; Scott *et al.* 1989; Scase 1995), but in the absence of a trade union, larger organisations have also been shown to display similar characteristics and practices (Foulkes 1980; Cressey 1985; Blyton and Turnbull 1998). At the other extreme is a more trusting relationship, which is characteristic of a human relations approach. Larger and more sophisticated non-union organisations have been associated with this type of relationship (Foulkes 1980; Dickson *et al.* 1988; Turnbull and Wass 1996).

The other types of relationship, extending from restrained autocracy through manipulative to benevolent autocracy lie between these extremes and are inserted to account for the complexity and variation in types. All of the organisations are ideal types. That is, each one represents a set of characteristics that prior literature indicates could theoretically exist in combination, but whether or not these exist in practice remains an open question, which can only be answered by conducting investigations in actual organisations. Indeed, it was acknowledged from the outset that while an organisation could be very close to one of these ideal types, it might not fit exactly because it differed in terms of one or more of the key characteristics. As will be seen later when results are presented, an attempt will be made to locate organisations along this continuum and where there is a lack of exact fit with one of the types, an explanation for this state of affairs is given. In the meantime it is important to explain something of the factors that were anticipated to be influential in shaping relationship characteristics, together with the research philosophies and methods used to collect data. These matters are covered in the following two chapters.

3 Factors affecting the employment relationship

Introduction

In this chapter we describe the factors that can influence the nature of employment relations in a firm and explain some of their effects. While these forces are at work in nearly all firms, their influence can vary over both time and space and so an employment relationship is essentially a dynamic state of affairs. Indeed, some of the forces described in this chapter might not have an influence in a particular firm, and so the chapter deals with what are really *potential* forces. For this reason, the first section of the chapter gives a conceptual map of these factors and this has two main purposes: first, it structures the discussion for the remainder of the chapter and second, it provides a framework for analysis in chapters 5 to 8.

Factors influencing employment relations: a conceptual map

Whether or not a firm recognises trade unions, there are many things that could influence the nature of its employment relationship. However, to simplify the discussion these have been reduced to the four main groups of factors shown in the oval shapes in Figure 3.1: Management Attitudes to Trade Union Recognition, Management Style, Employee Relations Climate and Employee Voice.

Two of these major influences, Management Style and Management Attitudes to Trade Union Recognition, have arrows feeding into them from boxes on the left-hand side of the diagram. This indicates that they tend to be influenced by other matters, some of which emanate from outside and some from within the firm.

Given that employment relationships are highly dynamic, uneven and at times contradictory, these factors represent a somewhat simplified picture. Nevertheless, they help convey the idea that there is a set of potential influences that shape the nature of relationships. For our purposes, of course, we are interested in non-unionised employment relations. In the remainder of the chapter the four major influences will be discussed in turn, to explain

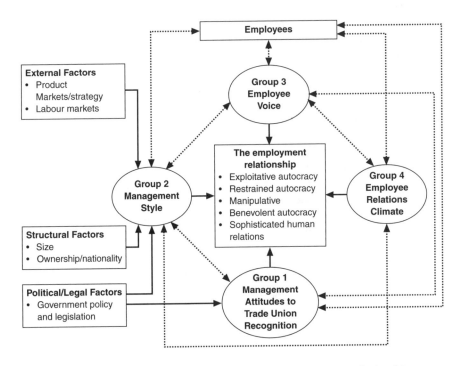

Figure 3.1 A conceptual map of factors affecting the employment relationship.

how each one has an impact on the nature of the relationship, and also how matters upstream of a particular factor shape its nature. Finally, to explain how they could affect each other, some of the other connecting influences (shown in the diagram by dotted lines) are explored.

Group 1: Management Attitudes to Trade Union Recognition

A common characteristic of all the firms in this study is that they are non-union. Thus it might seem strange to include this as a factor that could be responsible for differences in the nature of employment in these firms. However, a firm that recognises trade unions is not necessarily pro-union; for example, recognition can be grudgingly granted, and managers take steps to marginalise trade unions, so that they have little or no influence. Neither is a non-union firm automatically one that is rampantly anti-union.

One way for a firm to become non-union is for management to formally de-recognise trade unions, in which case they are excluded from a formal role in collective bargaining and/or consultation. De-recognition is essentially a union exclusion strategy and by definition, a firm that is already non-union does not need to go to these lengths to remain union-free. Where managers wish to remain in this state however, there would seem to be two basic options. First, any attempt to unionise can be resisted (still union exclusion), which in the light of recent legislative changes could become increasingly difficult, but not impossible. Second, substitution tactics can be brought into play, in which case managers could seek to persuade employees that a trade union presence is not in their best interests.

Wood *et al.* (2002) show that since the introduction of union recognition legislation, about half of the employers reported in their survey adopted non-supportive measures in relation to union recognition requests. Further, even among those employers who were supportive of a union claim for recognition, this did not guarantee union success. Significantly, in all nineteen cases where the employer was non-supportive, recognition claims failed; and in a further seven cases where the level of employee support for a union was tested by a ballot, only three resulted in recognition being achieved. As Wood *et al.* (2002) comment:

> Reliance by unions on an employer initiating discussions is not likely to yield large numbers of recognitions. Moreover, there are sufficient numbers of employers who responded to union approaches for recognition in a non-supportive way to suggest that building up substantial membership is *not* an inevitability for unions.
>
> (Wood *et al.* 2002: 221)

Managerial attitudes to recognition may or may not be influenced by statutory recognition, but what is equally significant is how employers respond to the idea of union recognition. On one hand, attempts to unionise have been resisted (union exclusion) by employers in both overt and covert ways (Dundon 2002; Logan 2001). On the other hand, managerial attitudes to union recognition may promote substitution and/or collective marginalisation tactics, which seek to persuade employees that a trade union presence is not in the employees' best interests (Gall and McKay 1994; Claydon 1996). These take a variety of forms, of which the most frequently cited reasons (by managers) include:

- the need to re-align industrial relations practices with new company structures, following organisational re-structuring, merger or acquisition;
- bargaining and negotiation having become artificial, because of a decline in union membership and activity within an organisation;
- management decide that unionisation is no longer an appropriate part of organisational culture, and instead embraces a widespread use of HRM techniques, to promote a more individualistic (rather than collectivist) approach to labour relations;
- opportunism: management sees de-recognition as a cost-reducing strategy, which can be embraced because of declining union power and influence.

(Dundon 2002)

Thus whether or not a firm is unionised, management attitudes to a trade union presence in the firm can be an important influence on the employment relationship. As will be seen from Figure 3.1, these attitudes can be affected by many factors and these will be covered later in the chapter when discussing the interactions between factors. For the present, because it also has an important influence on Management Style, it is more convenient to focus attention on an external factor that has a huge impact on management attitudes to recognition: the *Political/Legal Context*.

Government policy and legislation

The role of the state has long been recognised as an important influence on employment relations in Britain (Phelps-Brown 1959; Donovan 1968; Clegg 1979; Wedderburn 1986). Moreover, there is an abundance of evidence to show that government policy has influenced regulation, especially through reforms to collective bargaining (Clegg 1979; Wedderburn 1986; Pendleton and Winterton 1993) and here it is important to emphasise the strong link between government policy and legislation.

Although the legal and economic view of the employment relationship (i.e. the contract of employment) has a number of limitations, the impact of labour law cannot be ignored. Indeed, juridification, that is, the extent to which the legal system influences employee relations, has an important social and economic dimension which has the capacity to influence behaviour (Von Prondzynski 1985). The government is the only institution that has the capability to make new laws, or abolish old ones, and in doing this it effectively establishes the rules of the game. Since 1979 employment law has been a central plank in the restructuring of industrial relations, with an average of one major piece of statutory legislation every two years (Ackers *et al.* 1996). In this period state support for non-collective mechanisms has been used to promote an ideological, political and legal assault on collective representation (Kessler and Bayliss 1992; Edwards 1995; Ackers *et al.* 1996). This assault was underpinned by an ideology and rhetoric which treated trade unions as a supply-side constraint to the free operation of the labour market and for some authors trade unions were even treated as the cause of unemployment (Hayek 1980; Minford 1982). In effect the state vigorously encouraged non-union relations, with the argument that greater managerial freedom, informality and control over human resources would yield economic advantages to employers (Department of Employment 1981, 1991). One of the most significant ways in which the state can promote widespread changes of this type is to set an example with its own employees (Armstrong 1969) and to cite an example given in what is perhaps the most extensive British study of non-union employee relations to date:

At midday on 2 March 1989 Gareth Morris walked out of the gates at the Government Communications Headquarters (GCHQ) for the last time. Mr Morris had been sacked, ending 40 years of trade union membership at GCHQ. He was the last union member left at the centre, a ban on the membership of independent trade unions having been instituted some five years earlier by Mrs Thatcher's Conservative government. This attitude was one which held that trade unions were a barrier to the efficient operation of the labour market and that employers should look to non-union firms for examples of how to manage their industrial relations. The banning of trade unions at GCHQ showed that the government was prepared to practise what it preached.

(McLoughlin and Gourlay 1994: 1–2)

Clearly, this dramatic example of de-unionisation sent a clear signal to British industry from the government of the day that henceforth, non-union was to be considered the preferred form of employment relations.

While the election of a new Labour government in 1997 brought with it a greater emphasis on individual employment rights and statutory trade union recognition, there also appears to have been a general unease about extending collective representation rights. Speaking to the Trades Union Congress (TUC) shortly before the election, Tony Blair explained that unions should not expect favours, but fairness. What is significant about Blair's comment is that it appears to mark a break with what Callinicos (1996) describes as a well-established principle of Labour Party policy: the political expression of trade union bureaucracy. As such, even under a new Labour government, state policy appears to be tilted towards a political-business, rather than political-union stance, which suggests that management is likely to remain the dominant actor.

State policy has a tremendous effect on the attitudes and expectations of managers (Poole and Mansfield 1993). It is not so much that it has a direct effect on the employment relationship, but rather it shapes the perceptions of the parties about the nature of the exchange relationship (Kochan *et al.* 1986; Kochan and Katz 1988). Indeed, because there are a number of contradictions or ambiguities about the direct influence of the law, the perceptual effect could be by far the most influential one. For example, with the exception of a few well-publicised cases (notably print and newspapers), British employers seem to have been unwilling to use the law to seek injunctions against unions (Evans 1987) or actively promote a non-union relationship by legal measures. Moreover, because of other mediating factors, such as the economy, product or labour markets can sometimes be a more significant influence. Thus the direct link between labour law reform and an impact on the employment relationship is often uncertain (Kessler and Bayliss 1992; Dunn and Metcalf 1996). Nevertheless, the impact of the law is potentially important for a number of reasons.

Measures such as the abolition of the closed shop, secondary picketing and restrictions on industrial action have arguably restricted the ability of unions to represent and recruit members. Thus the law could have prompted a more individualised and unilateral managerial approach (Bacon and Storey 1993; Brown and Rea 1995), which has been translated into less formal regulatory methods as a central characteristic of the relationship. Indeed, the Employment Relations Act (1999) excludes employees in organisations that employ less than 20 workers from important individual and collective rights, which could mean that some relationships will become more formally regulated, while those in smaller firms are more informally determined. As a result, previous developments such as de-recognition practices and current legal provisions such as recognition rights could impact on HR strategies (Smith and Morton 1993; Gall and McKay 1994; Claydon 1989, 1996).

These matters raise the issue of whether legislation has an indirect or direct influence on the terms of the relationship. Perhaps the greatest potential impact of the law is on the perceptions and behaviours of the parties. That is, they perceive that the socio-legal environment is beneficial (or not) to non-unionism, which could affect matters in less direct ways. For example, by specifying employer and employee rights, it can be argued that the law has sought to substitute individual for collective work relations (Wedderburn 1986; Whincup 1991; Bacon and Storey 1993; Legge 1995). This could well have an impact via other influences, such as managerial style and employee voice (Boxall and Purcell 2002; Purcell 1987). For the future, conforming to legal developments arising from the European Employee Information and Consultation Directive will require management to establish employee consultative systems (Hall *et al.* 2002). This could establish an important chain of events that influences the industrial relations climate in a firm, which in turn shapes the choices made by employers about collective and/or individual employment relations systems.

One of the main concerns of this investigation was to evaluate whether management have (or perceive they could use) the backdrop of the law to modify the employment relationship in the absence of trade unions. Therefore, the broad operational definition of Management Attitudes to Trade Union Recognition adopted for this investigation, was the extent to which management in each organisation perceives that state policy gives an advantage or hindrance in maintaining a non-union relationship.

Group 2: Management Style

The expression management style is widely used in subjects such as Organisational Behaviour, usually to distinguish between different leadership styles; for example, democratic/participative versus autocratic. In employment relations however, it is used in a more global way, to refer to management's overall approach to handling relations with employees and in particular, to reflect the way that management exercises authority over subordinates. Managers have a variety of ways of influencing the actions of subordinates, and are also likely to have preferred ways of managing human resources, which in part, arise from their beliefs about the legitimate role of management in the enterprise. However, there are all sorts of internal constraints that can exercise a mediating influence on style and so a particular style should not be taken as an infallible indication of the way that a manager will behave in all circumstances, but rather, his/her preferred way of doing things.

The original scheme for describing styles was devised by Alan Fox (1966, 1974) who drew a fundamental distinction between two contrasting management frames of reference: unitarist and pluralist. Unitarism and pluralism are ideological frames of reference, which reflect beliefs about whether or not an organisation is (or should be) made up of members who have unity of goals and purpose, or at least one common goal and purpose that transcends all others and makes them all pull in the same direction. In Fox's view, style is driven by a manager's ideological preferences, whereas later writers, such as Purcell (1987) place less emphasis on ideology as the prime determinant of style. Nevertheless, there is widespread agreement that style is closely associated with management behaviour, and so it is likely to have a strong impact on the employment relationship, and could have a particularly strong effect on HR strategy (Purcell 1987; Purcell and Ahlstrand 1993; McLoughlin and Gourlay 1994). Indeed, it has been suggested the personnel policies of an organisation are a strong indicator of style (Purcell 1987; Marchington and Parker 1990; McLoughlin and Gourlay 1994). Note however, the word used here is policy. Policies are rules that guide decision making, as and when certain contingencies arise (Ansoff 1965), whereas a strategy is a plan or design to achieve aims, goals or objectives (Johnson and Scholes 1999). Thus, style is very different from strategy (Tyson 1995) and policies can restrict both strategies and styles.

The matter of differences between style and strategy was addressed by Storey (1983, 1986), who suggested that the very existence of strategy is questionable. Instead, he argues that British managers merely justify their actions by calling them strategies, and that these actions are often short-term, self-interested and inchoate (Storey 1986). Conversely, Marchington and Parker (1990) suggest that management is often aware of its inaction, and that the absence of action does not necessarily mean a lack of strategy. Thus although style and strategy are concepts that are theoretically separate, in practice, and depending upon the particular circumstances and ideological values, they can be heavily entwined (Tyson 1997; Torrington and Hall 1998).

Management style could have a strong impact on other characteristics of the employment relationship. For example, from a labour process perspective, managerial styles of controlling labour have been linked to different phases of capitalist development (Braverman 1974; Edwards 1979; Burawoy 1979, 1985). This suggests that external factors are likely to influence style, a point to which we return presently. For the moment it is sufficient to note that Friedman (1984) suggests that in terms of style, management can choose between allowing freedom and responsibility to employees, or exercising direct control over their activities. The former style implies that employees are seen as a valued resource, which possibly indicates high-trust relations and a proactive HR strategy as characteristics of the relationship. In contrast, direct control symbolises a coercive approach, redolent of Goss' (1991) style of sweating in small firms. In this, employees are seen as an untrustworthy, disposable factor of production, which in turn implies unilateral methods of regulation.

As noted above, style is essentially a preferred way of doing things, which in part reflects beliefs about what management sees as its legitimate role in the enterprise. As such, it is likely to have an impact on whether management attempts to regulate the relationship unilaterally, or jointly in conjunction with employees (Brown and Rea 1995). Therefore, it is hardly surprising to find that the concept of *individualism* v. *collectivism* has been used as a general proxy to indicate particular managerial preferences (Purcell 1987; Bacon and Storey 1993; McLoughlin and Gourlay 1994; Purcell and Ahlstrand 1994). Purcell (1987) defines *individualism* as the extent to which management gives credence to the individual's feelings and encourages development of employees' work capacities. *Collectivism* however, is not so much concerned with recognition of trade unions, but whether management recognises the right of employees to have a say in decisions that affect them. Therefore, style might also impact on another influential factor that has yet to be discussed: namely, employee voice. Indeed, voice and collective styles have both been shown to influence regulation as one of the characteristics of the employment relationship (Brown and Rea 1995). However, some caution is needed in using the concept of individualism v. collectivism. A number of authors, notably Bacon and Storey (1993) and McLoughlin and Gourlay (1994) argue that individualism and collectivism are not mutually exclusive. Rather, both can exist simultaneously within an organisation and the important feature that distinguishes a particular style is where the balance or blend between them is struck. For instance, individualism as defined by Purcell (1987) implies a more proactive HR strategy, high-trust relations and a more relational psychological contract, whereas collectivism could result in psychological contracts that are more transactional in nature.

In the context of non-union relations, McLoughlin and Gourlay (1994) make important links between style and the characteristics of the relationship used in this study (see Chapter 2). They use a scheme for classifying styles, which is based on two independent dimensions of collectivism–individualism and the degree of strategic integration of HR policies. This gives four distinct style types and since this, with slight modifications, is adopted for this investigation, it is shown in Figure 3.2.

Strategic integration

	High	Low
Individualism	**Traditional HRM** Employees viewed as central to achieving the goals and objectives of the firm. A proactive HR strategy is used, together with individualisation of the relationship. Managers point to the irrelevance of trade unions, which is redolent of a 'union avoidance' approach and results in some tendency for a low demand for trade unions on the part of employees. Mostly a unilateral approach by management to making and modification of the terms of the relationship, with some tendency towards 'them and us' in the relationship.	**Benevolent autocracy** Close, friendly and informal contact between employees and managers. High employee skills tend to give a degree of labour-market independence from the employer, which can influence the degree of unilateral regulation by management and the degree of informality in regulation. Managerial preferences tend to be for high degrees of individualisation to foster close links with and between employees, together with high trust relations.
Collectivism	**Strategic HRM** Trade union recognition for some, or all parts of the workforce. This gives some element of joint regulation, but probably limits are placed on trade union demands, by carefully framing agreements to distinguish between negotiable and non-negotiable areas. Fairly high degree of formality in regulating the relationship.	**Opportunist** Fragmentation of policies and practices and a lack of formalisation. Minimalist HR strategy, with little development of employees, who are essentially seen as a 'cost that must be contained'. Some degree of collective regulation, perhaps as a hangover from earlier times when unions were recognised. Strong element of 'them and us' in the relationship.

Figure 3.2 Management styles in non-union organisations.

Source: adapted from McLoughlin and Gourlay (1994).

Factors influencing Management Style

External factors: product and labour market strategies

As noted earlier, Fox (1966, 1974) who first commented on the importance of management style took the view that it is ideologically driven, whereas later writers such as Purcell (1987, 1999) regard style as something that can be a way of implementing a particular set of policies and strategies. The academic debate on this issue is far too complex to be repeated here, but whichever of these ideas is most correct, both theories put business objectives upstream of style, which in essence means that they have an effect on management styles. Business objectives are broadly what the firm seeks to achieve vis-à-vis its market environment and in the strategy literature, management's perceptions of the market result in a business strategy (Weik 1979, 2001), from which are derived sub-strategies for technology, capital and human resources etc. Human resource strategies can broadly be conceived of as the intended role for people management to achieve business objectives and in this, there is very strong evidence that product market considerations can have a huge impact on management choices (Godard 1997).

Strategy can also dictate the technology chosen to deliver a product/service and this has a direct impact on work processes, which can be a key influence on employment relations (Fox 1985; Pollert 1988; McLoughlin and Clark 1994; Garrahan and Stewart 1992). For example, the drive for flexibility and efficiency from technical restructuring can translate into exploitation through low wages, casualisation or insecure (e.g. temporary) work (Pollert 1988). Nevertheless, Blauner (1964) Child (1972) and Thompson (1983) all suggest a paradox in the influence of technology and its impact on management style. On one hand, increased technical control of work processes can mean less demand for labour and result in employees being viewed as a disposable factor of production that can be replaced by capital. Conversely, employees with a high degree of technical expertise obtain a greater degree of influence over the labour process, which gives them a degree of bargaining power and an enhanced capacity to modify the relationship. Finally, as Fox (1985) notes, because it governs what work is done, how it is done and the relationships that prevail between those doing it, technology has a social impact. Thus social relations can alter because of technology (McLoughlin and Clark 1994).

Labour market conditions are an important determinant that affects the management of employment relations (Kochan *et al.* 1986; Marchington and Parker 1990). For example, Bacon (1999) notes that although the company had experienced a period of growth and product market stability, employee relations at a non-union steel plant on the Isle of Sheppy contained a strong element of them and us between the parties. This, in part, could be traced to the effects of local social and economic factors. That is, social deprivation and unemployment in the area helped consolidate management's anti-union approach. In a different way, McLoughlin and Gourlay (1994) comment on the high cost of living in the South East of England as a source of influence on the union substitution practices adopted in their non-union case study firms. Other studies have also shown that local market circumstances have an important influence on managerial strategies to avoid unions (Foulkes 1980; Broad 1994; Gunnigle 1995; Flood and Toner 1997). For example, Gunnigle (1995) comments that management in some non-union firms consciously articulate the possibility of job insecurity (legitimized by local market circumstances) to suppress unionisation and that:

> many of the non-union companies studied are adopting more of a stick than a carrot approach to sustaining non-union status. Such an approach is heavily reliant on a slack labour market.
>
> (Gunnigle 1995: 37)

Structural factors: ownership, nationality and size

Ownership and nationality issues can affect management style in a number of ways; in particular, by importing managerial ideologies into subsidiary plants (Cressey 1985; McLoughlin and Gourlay 1994; Gunnigle 1995). Others have considered the impact of the 'Japanisation' of British workers, where attempts have been made to import Japanese management practices into subsidiaries (Reitsperger 1986; White and Trevor 1983; Wilkinson and Ackers 1995; Stephenson 1996; Broad 1994). For example, practices such as *Kaizen* can be seen as a form of union avoidance that replaces functions hitherto performed by a union (Stephenson 1996).

The influence of the founding owners of a firm may also influence key aspects of the employment relationship. For instance, Legge (1995) comments on the Harvey-Jones style of open, joint consultative management at ICI, suggesting that regulatory mechanisms are less unilateral because of the more consensual approach among senior managers. In the past, Quaker-type employers often valued employees as an organisational asset, rather than adopting a commodity market approach (Whitaker 1986). In addition, evidence from the SME literature (Goss 1988; Scott *et al.* 1989; Wilkinson 1999) would suggest that founding owners can instil a distinctive managerial legacy on employment relations. In many small, family-owned firms for example, the approach to employment relations is often typified as what the owner believes is good for the business is assumed to be good for employees (Roberts *et al.* 1992).

Many studies of employment relations treat size of organisation as a variable factor, and there are a number of ways in which size can influence employment relations. Although size can be assessed in several different ways (Curran 1990; Storey 1994; Holliday 1995), for this investigation, it is taken to be the number of employees, which is important for two reasons.

First, in sociological and psychological terms, the number of employees within an organisation is likely to influence the degree of interaction between the parties, which can be tremendously important in the absence of trade unions. Larger organisations have been linked to more militant workforce attachment (Dubin 1973), bureaucratic regulation (Durkhiem 1933; Ingham 1970; Silverman 1970) sophisticated HR strategies (Peach 1983; Tse 1985; Turnbull and Wass 1996). In modifying the employment relationship, management can have the added concern that in larger organisations it is more difficult to satisfy employee expectations as size increases.

Second, while non-union companies are likely to vary in size, previous literature has an unfortunate tendency to adopt an either/or approach. That is, non-union firms are either regarded as large, atypical employers (such as M&S and IBM) that use sophisticated human relations approaches to avoid unionisation, or they are located within the SME sector, symbolic of the bleak-house/sweatshop organisation, which suppresses unionism. This conceptual distinction was discussed in Chapter 1 and viewed as too simplistic, which gives rise to a need to account for differences in organisational size and type.

Political/legal factors

Government policy and legislation were covered earlier when discussing management attitudes. Thus little need be added here except to point out that the more antagonistic stance of the state in the 1980s was often articulated in an uncompromising manner which not only shaped the opinions of management but also had a strong potential to affect their behaviour. To quote:

> Those who opposed the new policies increasingly ran the risk of being seen not as critics with whom to debate and compromise (the supreme pluralist virtue), but as a domestic enemy within, which must be defeated ... (quoting government spokesman). The mining dispute cannot be *settled*. It can only be *won*.
>
> (Wedderburn 1986: 85)

As a result, management attitudes became increasingly self-confident (Poole and Mansfield 1993) and while this does not necessarily mean that managers have become more aggressive or macho, the environment in which they operate has created an added degree of self-confidence in modifying the employment relationship. Thus managerial preferences in the non-union setting imply a greater focus on unilateral regulation, and as has been noted elsewhere:

> Britain is approaching the position where few employees have any mechanisms through which they can contribute to the operation of their workplace in a broader context than that of their own job.
>
> (Millward 1994: 133)

Moreover, it can be noted that government policy towards such issues as union recognition has been linked with particular (exploitative) managerial styles, such as those at the Grunwick processing plant in 1976 (Purcell and Sisson 1983). This is likely to be an important source of influence on employment relations, for example, on the dimensions of regulation and trust, and also on managerial attitudes towards union recognition.

Group 3: Employee Voice

Employee voice is an important area of some significance in employment relations. Boxall and Purcell (2002) argue that it is less concerned with whether there are restrictions on managerial power, than with how much reliance can be placed on management in modern democracies. In simple terms employee voice can be described as methods that provide for employees to have a say in matters that affect them. Freeman and Medoff (1979) suggest that it makes good sense for both company and workforce to have a voice system, which on one hand can lead to improved organisational performance, and on the other can deflect conflictual issues between employer and employee. In this sense Freeman and Medoff (1979) view trade unions as the best agent for providing voice, and voice itself as something that could minimise employee exit from the organisation. For this reason, voice is often justified against the criterion of organisational performance. Nevertheless, there are additional arguments about why voice opportunities should be provided, notably in terms of the issues of legitimacy and human rights (Adam 1995; Towers 1997; Boxall and Purcell 2002). Therefore, given that the topic has attracted interest from a variety of perspectives, it is worth noting that the expression employee voice can have different meanings and interpretations. These are summarised in Table 3.1.

First, voice can be taken to mean the facility to articulate an individual dissatisfaction, for instance, where the employee seeks to resolve an issue

Table 3.1 The meanings of employee voice

Voice as:	Objectives of voice	Voice mechanisms	Potential range of outcomes
Articulation of an individual dissatisfaction	To rectify a problem with management and/or promote better relations with an individual employee	Complaint to a line manager Use of grievance procedure Individual speak-up programme	Exit of employee – enhanced employee loyalty
Expression of collective organisation	To provide for a countervailing source to management	Trade union recognition Collective bargaining Industrial action	Partnership – derecognition
To tap into employee creativity/ideas Contribution to management decision making	To dilute the demand for collective representation To obtain improvements in efficiency	Upward problem-solving groups Quality circles Suggestion schemes Attitude surveys Self-managed teams	Individualised commitment – disillusionment and apathy
Mutuality Human Rights Belief that 'workers ought to have a say'	To achieve long-term viability for organisation and its employees	Collective agreements Works councils Non-union forms of employee representation	Influence over management decisions – tokenism

Source: adapted from Marchington *et al.* (2001).

through the grievance procedure, and he/she is dealt with on an individual basis. A second meaning given to the expression is the existence of collective representation as a counterbalance to management power, for example, through unionisation and collective bargaining. Third, voice is sometimes described as the capability to harness employee ideas and creativity. Although an allied objective here might be to dilute the demand for collective representation by targeting employees directly, the aim could more simply be that of seeking improvements in efficiency (e.g. through quality circles or teamworking). Thus the range of possible outcomes might be to internalise organisational commitment among employees, or to avoid generating disillusionment. Finally, voice may be based on notions of human rights and mutuality, either through joint consultation, collective bargaining and/or non-union systems of employee representation. Possible outcomes under this heading may range from having a significant influence over managerial decisions, to little more than a token or symbolic employee contribution.

In unionised firms, formal recognition of a trade union makes the provision of voice mechanisms a virtually automatic feature: usually through collective bargaining and/or joint consultation. Similarly, in non-union firms collective forums for employee voice are not unknown (Terry 1999; Lloyd 2001; Gollan 2002). However, in neither case does this ensure that mechanisms are used to their best advantage, or that they have a high utility in employees' eyes. In Gollan's (2002) study of News International for example, it was found that according to employees and non-union representatives, the Employee Consultative Council (ECC) lacked effectiveness. Marchington *et al.* (2001) report that in both union and non-union firms, employee voice mechanisms are often defined according to management's own interpretations of what the expression voice is taken to mean. This can sometimes be little more than communication and/or upward-problem solving techniques, such as project teams, staff briefings, attitude surveys or suggestion schemes. Needless to say, systems such as these are likely to shape the prevailing climate in an organisation and influence the extent to which employees feel that they have a say on matters that affect them.

In the non-union setting, the use of employee voice may serve to consolidate managerial control. Foulkes (1980) for example, notes that mechanisms such as in-house company counselling, staff committees and feedback meetings emphasise the importance of employee voice in remaining union-free. Paradoxically, for union avoidance to be sustainable, there is a need to expend time, effort and resources on voice channels; or what Flood and Toner (1997) suggest is the catch-22 face of non-unionism. This dilemma for management was evident in Broad's (1994) analysis of a Japanese organisation, where management used the company council to remain union-free. However, when workers perceived this mechanism to be a tool that was used exclusively for managerial, rather than employee concerns, workers eventually identified more with the union than with the company committee. Thus to employees, the perceived utility of voice mechanisms has the potential to be shaped by other factors that can modify the relationship; not least management style.

For the above reasons in this investigation it was considered important to not only evaluate the existence of voice mechanisms, but also their perceived utility among employees.

Group 4: Employee Relations Climate

A simple definition of organisational climate is:

> a characteristic ethos or atmosphere within an organisation at a given point in time, which is reflected in the way its members perceive, experience and react to the organisational context.
>
> (Rollinson 2002: 597)

Note that climate is an experienced state of affairs, which can be thought of as the way that people describe the organisation to themselves and interpret what they find (James and Jones 1974; Jones and James 1979). In addition, climatic conditions can sometimes be quite transient. Moreover, because it is how people experience things, it affects their attitudes, which in turn has behavioural implications (Schneider *et al.* 1980).

Although it has some similarities with the allied concept of culture, as applied to organisations it has been in use for much longer and its origins can be traced to the pioneering work of Lewin (1951). The explanatory importance of climate lies in its use as an intervening variable; that is, while other factors that influence the nature of the employment relationship, they act *through* climate, which can modify their effects in some way. For instance, an autocratic management style, or an absence of employee voice opportunities, which are unhealthy in their own right, could result in a climate that makes severe them and us attitudes virtually inevitable. It is also important to note that culture, which currently tends to be the more fashionable topic, is not the same thing as climate, although at least one authority in the area argues that climate and culture tap similar phenomena, but from different methodological perspectives (Denison 1996).

One thing that links the concepts of culture and climate, is the importance accorded to values. Values are a fundamental part of any culture and, to some extent, a culture is what gives people their values. Climate however, is much more a reflection of whether current organisational conditions are in accordance with the values that people hold, and this is one thing that makes the concept more useful for this study (Nicholson 1979). It is an atmosphere or set of feelings experienced by those who are party to the relationship (Rollinson 2002) and in the words of Koys and DeCotiis (1991) climate is an experience-based, multi-dimensional and perceptual phenomenon that has the capacity to influence behaviour. However, while climate could influence the characteristics of the employment relationship in a number of ways, it does not arise of its own accord, but because of the effects of other factors discussed earlier; for example, management style, employee voice and management attitudes to union recognition.

After Rim and Mannheim (1979) employee relations climate is taken to be a reflection of the way that employees and managers see each other, which takes account of the idea that once formed, climates can be extremely resistant to modification. That is, when one party perceives that the other behaves towards them in a certain way, the recipient tends to respond accordingly, which in turn evokes perceptions and behaviour in return. Thus climate can quickly become a self-fulfilling prophecy (Biasatti and Martin 1979). If, for example, the climate is harmonious, issues tend to be approached by both sides in a joint problem-solving way (Harbison and Coleman 1951), and where it is hostile, it can result in an extremely frosty atmosphere, where each side tries to undermine the other.

While evaluation of climate can be very difficult because of its highly perceptual and unquantifiable nature, a number of attempts to do this exist in the employee relations literature. For example, Purcell (1979) uses orthogonal indicators of trust and formalisation. In addition, Kelly and Nicholson (1980), in discussing climate in relation to strike processes, suggest that managerial ideologies, actor perceptions of conflict and the economic environment will be mutually reinforcing indicators of climate. More useful for this investigation however, is the twin-dimensional approach offered by Nicholson (1979), using two indicators. The first is termed issue-centred climate, which expresses the type of problems and degree of satisfaction with problem-handling in the organisation. The second is termed inter-personal climate, which reflects patterns of interaction and the satisfaction of the parties with their opposite number. In this view, key actors (more specifically, their interactions) can influence climate.

The interrelationship of factors

While the four major influences on the employment relationship have been discussed separately, this does not mean that they are unconnected. Indeed, this is shown in Figure 3.1 and for completeness, this final section of the chapter traces some of these links. However, it is beyond the scope of this book to give an exhaustive list of all these cross-linkages and so those that are discussed are given purely for illustrative purposes. This will be done by returning to each of the four major factors in turn and in addition, reference will be made to an influential factor that appears in Figure 3.1, but which has received scant attention so far: that is, employees themselves.

Management attitudes to trade union recognition

As noted in the earlier discussion, there are strong grounds for suggesting that government policy and legislation have influenced these attitudes. Note however, that management style is also affected by the same factor and for this reason it is logical to suggest that there is a reciprocal link between attitudes and style. For example, a government message about the economic advantages of being union free could be expected to give rise to a negative orientation to trade unions on the part of management, together with styles that relegate employees to a strictly subordinate role in an organisation. The same is probably true of ownership, or the national origins of the firm, which also produce effects through management style. Attitudes are also likely to be influenced by employee pressures, or rather, management's perceptions of pressures that emanate from employees. One of the strongest influences on attitudes to an object is prior experience (Tversky and Kahneman 1973; Fazio and Zanna 1978; Regan and Fazio 1977). Thus to the extent that managers have had significant (good or bad) experiences of dealing with trade unions, present attitudes can be affected. The same is almost certainly true of the types of employee voice mechanisms used. It is management that decides whether or not workers should have voice opportunities and managers, rather than workers, decide what voice mechanisms will be used (Marchington and Wilkinson 2000). Thus past experiences with certain types of voice mechanism, and in particular, non-union systems of employee voice can shape management preferences for what is currently used (Kaufman and Taras 2000).

Employee relations climate

Climate is almost completely determined by factors associated with people. If employees perceive that managers are not to be trusted and tend to behave in this way towards managers, they will probably look for evidence to confirm their assumptions; perhaps by seeking what is described in Chapter 2 as a transactional, rather than relational psychological contract. Provision of employee voice opportunities could play an influential part here. A lack of voice opportunity, or a perception that voice mechanisms have little utility could easily be interpreted as a sign that management is not only untrustworthy, but also has a style that includes dictating the terms of the relationship.

Climate has been shown to influence, and be affected by managerial styles and strategies (Foulkes 1980; Purcell 1979). Indeed there are implications that climate is, in part, a manifestation of managerial ideologies. Thus it could influence the HR strategy that management adopts, i.e. either proactive or reactive. In addition, a particular managerial style can promote a climate of subordination, compliance or even fear within the relationship (Roy 1980). A non-union example of this was the style of management noted by Billot (1993, 1996) to exist at Co-Steel, Sheerness. Here workers were *coerced* to *comply* by language that was often couched in the rhetoric of commitment (Leahy 1996), which had an impact on trust as well as both attitudinal and behavioural them and us as key characteristics of the relationship (Bacon 1999).

Employee voice

From the above, it is clear management attitudes to recognition can have a huge impact on the provision of voice mechanisms. These attitudes will affect how managers attempt to make use of any voice mechanisms that are established. This is also likely to be true of management style. If managers have preferences for behaving in certain ways towards employees, there is likely to be an impact on whether they consider it legitimate for employees to have a say in matters that affect them.

Management style

Mention has already been made of reciprocal influences between style and attitudes to recognition. However, it is also important to note that similar reciprocal influences can exist between climate and style. As noted, climate can become a self-fulfilling prophecy and where employees demonstrate their lack of trust in management, it can sometimes result in managers behaving in a less than trustworthy way. In relationships, trust tends to beget trust in return, while mistrust begets mistrust (Blau 1964).

Summary and conclusions

In this chapter we have given a brief overview of a number of factors that can have a strong impact on employment relations in the non-union firm, four of which are portrayed in the conceptual model given at the start of the chapter. Some of these factors, for example management style and management attitudes to trade union recognition can be mutually reinforcing and although others, such as employee relations climate and employee voice can also act in this way, they can also exert a counter-influence that holds the relationship together. As a prelude to describing employment relations in the four case study organisations, the next chapter gives a brief outline of the research methods and methodologies used in this investigation.

4 Research methods and methodologies

Introduction

This chapter gives a brief overview of the research methods used for the investigation. It commences with a description of general research strategy and the data collection methods used. As a prelude to the more detailed results contained in Chapters 5 to 8, the chapter then describes exploratory research that took place before case study work commenced. This was an important precursor to later investigations and, among other things, was used to identify and select four non-union organisations for more detailed investigation.

General approach

As can be seen from the research questions given at the end of Chapter 1, the central concern of the investigation was to explain the nature of the employment relationship in non-union firms. Employment relationships are made and modified through social processes, for example in the union situation, collective bargaining and consultation are typically used (Clegg 1979). Where bargaining is absent however, the processes used can sometimes be near invisible, and some of them are more in the nature of pressures and influences that the actors experience, rather than visible events and happenings. With this in mind, answering the research questions requires an appreciation of both objective and subjective factors.

In general terms, the approaches that could be used to answer the research questions fall between two extremes, each of which has its own advantages and limitations (Cook and Selltiz 1964; Chalmers 1982; Hakim 1994). At one extreme is the *classical approach*, which has its roots in natural science. It uses a detailed review of all possible variables and factors prior to empirical investigation, together with a rigorous use of deductive reasoning to develop theory and hypotheses for testing. While this encourages rigour and thoroughness, the approach also has its limitations. There is a risk of ignoring emergent data, which only becomes evident once fieldwork has commenced (Gouldner 1955). Moreover, it can be difficult to capture the complexity of social interaction (Silverman 1970), particularly where deeper analysis is required to explain the subtlety of the processes involved (Glaser and Strauss 1967; Buroway 1979; Brown and Wright 1994).

At the other extreme is the *grounded theory* approach, the antecedents of which lie in anthropology. Here the researcher enters fieldwork with no prior hypotheses and the aim is to gather sufficient high quality information to allow theory to emerge from an interpretation of what is encountered. The main advantage here is that the potential richness of data avoids the limitations of the classical approach. Nevertheless, the approach also has its inherent limitations. Because it relies on development of theory after field-work, the importance of prior empirical work in the area is sometimes over-looked.

This investigation does not easily lend itself to either of these pure approaches, and instead uses elements of both to give what is usually described as a middle range approach (Broadbent and Laughlin 1997; Laughlin 1995). For instance, in Chapters 1, 2 and 3 prior literature is used to illustrate the need for further empirical inquiry into non-union employ-ment relations and establish a conceptual understanding of the features likely to explain key processes and issues. Note however, that although a conceptual model is given in Chapter 3, no explicit hypotheses are developed for testing. Thus the role of the model is as a device to alert the researcher to keep his/her eyes open for certain factors and influences that could be at work, but without being blind or insensitive to other infor-mation.

A fundamental feature of the research design was to use a strategy of pro-gressive narrowing of information sources. Fieldwork commenced with a very broad, exploratory study from which four organisations were selected for further investigation. Detailed evidence was then collected from this nar-rower range of organisations, using data collection instruments that were designed to allow the flexibility of rich, deep and complex factors to emerge from what are essentially dynamic processes. The aim here was to allow the importance of organisational-specific contexts to be understood and this utilised a case study methodology, which has its own advantages and limita-tions.

With its emphasis on the collection of rich and detailed information, the case study can be particularly useful in explaining dynamic social processes, and the essence of this type of work is that it uses a wide range of methods for collecting data. For instance, interviews, which range from closed to semi-structured or completely unstructured methods are widely used (Edwards and Scullion 1982; Darlington 1994; Scott 1994). The use of questionnaires is also commonplace, because these can bridge the gaps between qualitative and quantitative methods and facilitate the manage-ment of a mass of information (Yin 1993; Hartley 1994). In addition, but perhaps less frequently, direct observation is used and this can range from detailed participant observation, such as Buroway's (1979) involvement on an assembly line, to less intrusive and opportunistic forms of observation as the occasions arise during periods of fieldwork (Hartley 1994). Nevertheless, there is an important limitation of the case study approach. Because it focuses on events within a particular context, it can be very difficult to generalise from the results. For this reason, Scott (1994) suggests that case study results mean something rather different than, for example, social surveys:

> Case studies are not about indicating how common a particular phenomenon is, but rather about helping to understand situations ... this means using the evidence of behaviour in particular enterprises to shed light upon issues which are common to a wide range of business organisations.
>
> (Scott 1994: 30)

As such, the main purpose of case study analysis is in building and testing theory (Eisenhardt 1989; Yin 1993) and the theory itself can be grounded as well as emergent (Glaser and Strauss 1967). Indeed, certain insights may not even become evident until the research is in progress. As Hartley (1994) comments:

> Case study researchers, in their pursuit of delicate and intricate interactions and processes occurring within organizations, will use a combination of methods, partly because complex phenomena may be best approached through several methods, and partly to triangulate and thereby improve validity. A case study ... emphasis [is] on understanding processes alongside organizational contexts.
>
> (Hartley 1994: 209–10)

Data specification and collection methods

Data specification

The information we felt it necessary to collect for organisational case studies was strongly guided by the way that we conceptualised and defined the various factors that could be at work. These matters are discussed in the previous two chapters and information was collected to enable an assessment to be made of these matters in each case study organisation. For example, Chapter 2 gives five characteristics that were used to categorise the employment relationship in a particular organisation. Namely:

- its dominant regulatory approach
- its human resource strategy
- levels of trust in the employment relationship
- the degrees of informality–formality in regulation
- them and us attitudes in the organisation.

Similarly, Chapter 3 describes a number of factors, which prior literature in the area indicates could have a strong impact on the nature of the employment relationship in a particular organisation. Since we wanted to be able to explain relationships as well as categorise them, information was collected on:

- employee relations climate
- management styles
- employee voice mechanisms
- management attitudes to trade union recognition
- certain external factors such as markets, together with structural factors such as ownership/nationality.

Data collection methods

All methods of data collection have their own strengths and weaknesses and in work of this type the nature of the information required (tempered of course, by practical considerations) is often allowed to dictate the collection method used. For this reason a fairly wide range of collection techniques was utilised. However, a guiding principle was that in order to add validity to any conclusions drawn, the technique of triangulation would be applied in analysing results (Denzin 1970; Jick 1979). That is, we wanted to have more than one indicator of a particular factor or phenomenon, and wherever possible, the data for each of these different indicators should desirably be collected by a different method: a multiple indicator approach. The methods used and the type of information gathered in this way are given in what follows.

Self-completed questionnaires

In general, these were used wherever it was necessary to obtain information from a large number of people. For example, this method was used for the exploratory survey of companies reported later in this chapter. This survey sought background information about non-union employee relations in a range of different organisations and because the aim was to elicit factual information about policies and procedures, rather than explanations for why these policies and procedures had been adopted, the questions asked were not overly sensitive. In the subsequent case studies, questionnaires were also used to obtain information from a large sample of employees in each organisation, and here the reasons for using this method were rather different. On some matters it was necessary to have information about employee perceptions and attitudes, for example, about management's behaviour, and the utility of voice mechanisms. For these issues, attitude measures based on well established and tested scales were developed (modified for the non-union context), and these provided an opportunity to collect factual and biographic data about employees as well. Finally, a questionnaire, which elicited factual information about the organisation was completed by the senior manager of each company.

Interviews

While self-completed questionnaires have the advantage that questions are asked in the same way of everybody, they have a pronounced weakness when it comes to collecting information of certain types. For instance, sensitive information can be difficult to obtain in this way, even where the respondent is guaranteed anonymity. Similarly, questions about complex topics might need to be explained to the respondent, or the respondent probed for his/her exact meaning in an answer. In these cases, interviews are likely to yield more useful information than questionnaires and much of the data in the case study organisations was collected in this way. This was particularly the case where there was an indirect reason for requiring the information. For example, one of the things we wanted to know was whether management behaviour, and management attitudes towards trade unions were influenced by government policies and legislation. Note that the aim here was not that of exploring the direct effect of government policy and legislation, but whether it had an effect on management policies and action. This is much more likely to be revealed by a sequence of carefully designed questions, than boldly asking in a questionnaire: to what extent are your policies and attitudes towards trade unions influenced by the policy of the government? This implies that the respondent might slavishly follow government policy, rather than thinking for him/herself. Similarly, there was sometimes a need to explore meanings and perceptions with employees and once again for information of this type, interviews were used.

Document survey

In certain cases it was possible to elicit the required information by going to the other extreme of relying on company documentation. For instance, this was possible when collecting information on organisational policies and rules. Here the difficulty is not usually in collecting the information, but analysing it and for this, the techniques of content analysis were used.

Observation

During visits to each firm, a rudimentary form of observation was possible. This involved direct, non-participant observation of both work processes and the interaction between parties.

The exploratory survey

Before embarking on detailed case study work in specific organisations, we undertook a small-scale exploratory study of a wider cross-section of firms and this had three main purposes.

First, we wanted to obtain what can best be described as a feeling for the area. That is, to sensitise ourselves to a number of issues and themes that the prior literature suggested could be prominent in the non-union situation. Second, to identify appropriate non-union firms that would potentially be willing to cooperate in later detailed case study investigations and build working relationships with managers in these organisations. Third, because we considered it important that the study should contribute to the body of knowledge in a general way, we wanted to be sure that our case study organisations were typical of a wider population of non-union firms. For this task we elected to conduct an exploratory postal survey of firms using questionnaires.

The sample

Using a standard commercially available index of organisations, 200 were selected for the survey, from which 38 usable and completed questionnaires were returned. Table 4.1 shows the response rate in relation to sector distribution, and it is worth noting that despite a low response rate, the distribution between manufacturing and service sector organisations is maintained at 50 per cent.

Table 4.1 Unionism and non-unionism by sectoral distribution in exploratory sample (N = 38)

	Service sector		Manufacturing sector		Totals	
	%	N	%	N	%	N
Firms recognising trade unions	18.5	7	29	11	47	18
Firms recognising trade unions and staff associations	2.6	1	2.6	1	5	2
Firms recognising only staff associations	7.9	3	0	0	8	3
Firms recognising neither trade unions nor staff associations	21	8	18.4	7	40	15
Totals	50	19	50	19	100	38

As Table 4.1 shows the manufacturing sector dominates in terms of union recognition at 29 per cent, compared to 18.5 per cent for unionised service sector firms. As such, it might be expected that non-unionism is to be found predominantly among service sector respondents. However, while services make-up the majority of completely non-unionised respondents (21 per cent), at 18.4 per cent manufacturing is not that different, and so it is inaccurate to assume that non-unionism is largely associated with the service sector. What is perhaps more significant is that 40 per cent of all organisations had no employee intermediary (i.e. no trade union or staff association). This is comparable with results obtained in the third Workplace Industrial Relations Survey (WIRS3), in which 36 per cent of the sample had no union presence (Millward *et al.* 1992). It is also comparable with the latest Workplace Employee Relations Survey (WERS), in which 47 per cent of workplaces had no union presence (Cully *et al.* 1998). However, while both of these workplace surveys report findings relevant to the private sector, unfortunately there is no evidence in terms of sector distribution. What they do reveal is a distinction between manual and non-manual employees. In 1990 the distribution between manual and non-manual workers in firms with zero union density was reported as 42 per cent and 49 per cent respectively (Millward *et al.* 1992). This is consistent with what we found in our small survey and is shown in Table 4.2.

In this sample of non-unionised companies the manual to non-manual employee ratio was 13.6 per cent to 12.2 per cent, and the unionised ratio was 37.6 per cent to 13.3 per cent respectively. Thus of the 47,600 workers covered in this pilot survey, 26 per cent had no intermediary representation

Table 4.2 Distribution of union and non-union establishments by the number of manual and non-manual employees

	Manual employees		Non-manual employees		All employees	
	%	N (000)	%	N (000)	%	N (000)
Firms recognising trade unions	37.6	17.9	13.3	6.3	51	24.2
Firms recognising trade unions and staff associations	2.6	1.25	0.75	0.35	3	1.6
Firms recognising only staff associations	0.6	0.3	19.3	9.2	20	9.5
Firms recognising neither trade unions nor staff associations	13.6	6.5	12.2	5.8	26	12.3
Totals	54.4	25.9	45.6	21.7	100	47.6

Source: adapted from Millward *et al.* (1992).

with their employer and 20 per cent were covered by an in-house staff association. Although smaller, the sample here is in line with other studies, which gives some reassurance that it is representative. However, some qualifications must be noted. The non-manual figure (45.6 per cent) is disproportionately high, given the inclusion of 8,000 employees from just one respondent – a major high street building society, which recognised an in-house staff association rather than a trade union. Moreover, the average size for union-recognised organisations in the survey is 1,300 employees, while for non-unionised establishments the mean size is 800. If the largest non-union employer (3,400 workers) is excluded, the mean size would be reduced to 560 employees. This is consistent with other evidence which suggests that the typical non-union organisation is likely to be found among small-to-medium sized enterprises (Beaumont and Rennie 1986; Beaumont and Harris 1989; IRS 1998; Winters 1999).

The question of ownership of non-union organisations has been highlighted by a number of authors (Dickson *et al.* 1988; Cressey *et al.* 1985; Millward 1994; McLoughlin and Gourlay 1994; Gunnigle 1995) and respondents were asked about ownership and/or their parent company in relation to the country of origin. Of the fifteen non-union establishments shown in Table 4.1, the majority (11) were British-owned and of the remaining four firms one was a Canadian-owned steel manufacturer, two were American-owned service sector companies and one was a manufacturing firm that is part of a French and Singapore consortium. Thus non-union status was tilted towards British rather than foreign ownership. With the exception of one manufacturing organisation – the Canadian-owned steel manufacturer, Co-Steel Sheerness, which de-recognised both the Iron and Steel Trades Confederation (ISTC) and the Amalgamated Engineering and Electrical Union (AEEU) in 1992 – none of the foreign-owned firms had ever received a request for trade union recognition. However, among British-owned firms those that had been approached by a trade union about recognition in the past had all refused.

In summary, in this sample non-union firms were predominantly British-owned SMEs, relatively evenly split in composition between manual and non-manual employees, and at that time unlikely to experience a recruitment drive or recognition request from a trade union.

Employment relations and the non-union firm

An important issue revealed by the exploratory study was that of management attitudes towards trade unions. This was tapped by questions which sought managers' views on what they considered to be the most important employment relations issues in their company and what they found to be most satisfactory (or unsatisfactory) about the non-union employment relationship. A summary of responses to the latter is given in Table 4.3.

As can be seen, management clearly expressed views that an employment

Table 4.3 Management perceptions of advantages and disadvantages of non-union status (N = 15)

	Manufacturing		Services		All firms	
	%	N	%	N	%	N
Main advantage						
Greater managerial freedom	85	6	75	6	80	12
Easier employee communications	70	5	62	5	66	10
Greater employee commitment/loyalty	57	4	37	3	53	8
Lower labour costs	14	1	37	3	26	4
Main disadvantage						
Less employee loyalty/ commitment	70	5	87	7	80	12
Difficult employee communications	70	5	75	6	73	11
Higher labour costs	28	2	12	1	37	3

relationship without trade unions brought both advantages and disadvantages. In terms of advantages, respondents believed that the workforce was more committed, loyal and dedicated to its job than if a trade union were present, which gives some indication that managers perceived trust to be an important dimension of the relationship. The view that non-union status means that employees are treated as individuals was also mentioned as an important factor in 66 per cent of all non-unionised firms. Significantly, 80 per cent of respondents reported that greater managerial freedom was the main advantage of a non-unionised workforce, implying that unilateral regulation was a potentially important feature. On the other hand, managers also saw some disadvantages; in particular, communicating with employees appeared to be something of a double-edged sword. While two-thirds of managers saw employee communications as an advantage in the absence of a union, over 70 per cent believed that communicating to employees without a trade union could also be a disadvantage. A possible explanation for this is an example of what Flood and Toner (1997) refer to as the catch-22 face of non-unionism. That is, where there is no union, while management perceived it to be easier to get its message across without potential distortions, this goes hand-in-hand with the disadvantage that effective communications along individualistic lines requires a degree of time, effort and money.

Pay and employment conditions

It can also be noted that there is another paradox revealed in Table 4.3. While 26 per cent of respondents believed that lower labour costs are an advantage of non-unionism, another 37 per cent suggested the reverse. This could mean that higher labour costs are associated with paying a premium rate to remain union free. However, an alternative interpretation could be that the 26 per cent of firms who believed that non-union status gives management the opportunity to pay lower wages were pursuing a union suppression strategy. In other words, because of the union absence management took advantage of the situation and some clues about this are revealed in answers to a more specific question about pay and benefits, the responses to which are summarised in Table 4.4.

As can be seen, equal percentages of respondents (47 per cent) said that pay was either better or the same as that for other companies in the same industry/area, which, if taken at face value means that employees were unlikely to feel deprived. However, it is necessary to exercise a degree of caution about this. The question was asked of managers and so there is a potential for bias in answers. Indeed, Table 4.4 also shows that only one respondent admitted that pay was worse than that for other similar organisations.

When considering fringe benefits as part of a firm's labour cost, the idea that firms might be prepared to accept high labour costs to remain non-union is hardly supported. Less than half of the respondents reported that they provided an occupational pension scheme for all employees. None provided paternity leave or childcare at the workplace and only one firm provided local sports and social facilities. Three offered some employees private medical insurance; and four provided company cars to senior managers or

Table 4.4 Pay and non-pay benefits of non-union status (N = 15)

Pay and non-pay benefits	Manufacturing		Services		All firms	
	%	N	%	N	%	N
Compared to other firms in the same industry/ area, is the pay in your firm for the typical employee:						
better	57	4	37	3	46	7
about the same	42	3	50	4	46	7
worse	0	0	12	1	7	1
Occupational pension scheme	28	2	62	5	46	7
Medical assistance (e.g. BUPA)	14	1	25	2	20	3
Free parking	57	4	88	7	73	11
On-site catering (e.g. canteen)	86	6	100	8	93	14
Paid holiday leave	100	7	100	8	100	15
Protective clothing	86	6	25	2	53	8

sales representatives. The most common non-pay benefit was either a free car parking space, or canteen facilities on site. All non-unionised respondents provided paid holiday leave, with the amount of leave varying between three-weeks-three-days to six-weeks-two-days per year for employees, the average being four-weeks-four-days.

Management style and selection of case study organisations

As noted earlier, one of the main purposes of undertaking the exploratory research was to be able to identify suitable organisations for in-depth case studies. The main vehicle for making this selection was what we learned about the management style within the organisations surveyed.

The different ways of conceptualising management style are discussed in Chapter 3 (Fox 1966; Purcell and Sisson 1983; Purcell 1987; Sisson 1989; Marchington and Parker 1990; McLoughlin and Gourlay 1994). From these, the one we used was based on the framework devised for non-union firms by McLoughlin and Gourlay (1994). This uses two dimensions – degree of strategic integration and the extent of individualism v. collectivism – to classify styles into one of four types: *Traditional HRM*, *Strategic HRM*, *Benevolent Autocracy* and *Opportunistic*. This is done by counting the human resource policies and practices that are in place in a firm, which lays the original scheme open to the criticism that it focuses more on scope than the depth of the key indicators. Therefore, the scheme was adapted slightly by collecting information that gave a somewhat more sophisticated interpretation of Purcell's (1987) distinction between collectivism and individualism, and made use of the categories devised by Gunnigle (1995), which included a note of whether management have a propensity or willingness to engage in Employer Associations, which could be another form of corporate (non-union) identity. In a later study, Gunnigle et al. (2001) conclude that participation within the inner circles of influential employer bodies, such as Chambers of Commerce, may actually reinforce and promote non-union status.

A second aim was to examine the extent to which management claimed to treat employees in a collective manner, for example, by adopting harmonised/equalised terms and conditions and non-union employee voice mechanisms. These indicators were used to capture the broad proxies of management style using a multiple-indicator approach. For example, in addition to the existence of a personnel department or senior manager on the company's board, additional questions probed respondents for further information, such as the other responsibilities of the personnel manager, and the size of the personnel department where relevant. Thus the single response of yes or no to a personnel director with a seat on the company's board is complemented by other detailed information and the number of non-union organisations falling into each of McLoughlin and Gourlay's categories is shown in Figure 4.1.

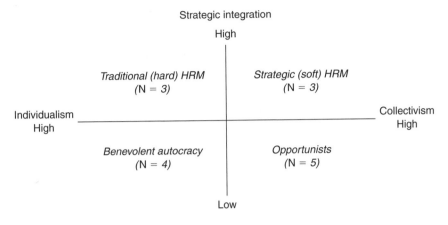

Figure 4.1 Management styles in non-union organisations surveyed (N = 15).

Sources: adapted from McLoughlin and Gourlay (1994); Purcell and Sisson (1983).

Selection of case study organisations

Seven general criteria were used to select organisations for more detailed case study investigation. These were as follows:

1 organisations were selected to reflect a cross-sample of different sized firms;
2 a cross-sectoral distribution of companies was chosen to include both service and manufacturing activities;
3 the firms were chosen to reflect a geographical diversity within Britain;
4 the firms were chosen to reflect more than one category of worker, so that non-unionism would not be confined to an exclusive occupational group. This was considered potentially useful in explaining differences and similarities between non-union companies;
5 since younger organisations have been noted to be a particularly prominent feature of non-unionism during the 1980s (Beaumont and Cairns 1987; Beaumont and Harris 1988; McLoughlin and Gourlay 1994) firms were selected to include those that commenced trading both before and during the 1980s;
6 because foreign-owned firms offer the potential to import managerial systems which can be derived from foreign customs and cultures (Cressey *et al.* 1985; Gunnigle 1995; Wilkinson and Ackers 1995) it was considered desirable to reflect different patterns of ownership;
7 since we wanted to reflect a number of different approaches to people management in a non-union context, firms were selected to reflect the use of different management styles (See Figure 4.1).

Table 4.5 outlines the results obtained in evaluating management style (a tick indicates the presence of an attribute). It also shows the four firms

Table 4.5 Management style in non-unionised organisations (N = 15)

Dimensions	Service sector firms						Manufacturing firms								
	A	B	C	D	E	F	G	H	I	J	K	L	M	N	O
Collective															
Parent company recognise trade union															✓
Parent company recognise staff association														✓	
Company member of employer association						✓	✓	✓	✓		✓	✓	✓	✓	✓
Firm use services of employer association	✓						✓	✓	✓		✓	✓		✓	
Employee committee/works council	✓		✓		✓	✓		✓	✓				✓		
Annual pay review for all employees	✓				✓	✓	✓		✓		✓	✓	✓		✓
Single-status/harmonised terms/conditions	✓	✓		✓	✓	✓				✓		✓			✓
Non-pay benefits all employees (e.g. pension)	✓	✓		✓	✓	✓		✓	✓	✓		✓			✓
Job evaluation scheme for all employees	✓														
	6	2	1	2	4	5	3	4	5	2	3	5	3	3	5
Individual															
Individual pay reviews	✓	✓		✓	✓	✓	✓	✓	✓	✓	✓	✓	✓	✓	✓
Individual performance pay/PBR	✓	✓		✓	✓						✓		✓	✓	✓
Regular individual appraisal methods	✓	✓	✓	✓	✓		✓	✓			✓	✓	✓	✓	✓
Appraisal methods linked to pay award	✓	✓		✓	✓						✓				
Incentive and bonus schemes	✓	✓		✓		✓	✓	✓		✓	✓		✓	✓	✓
Employee suggestion schemes	✓					✓								✓	✓
Multi-skilling/occupational demarcation	✓												✓	✓	✓
Individual communication channels	✓	✓	✓	✓	✓	✓	✓	✓	✓	✓	✓	✓	✓	✓	✓
De-recognised trade union															
	8	6	2	6	5	4	4	4	2	3	6	3	6	7	7

Strategic integration

	A	B	C	D	E	F	G	H	I	J	K	L	M	N	O
Personnel department/specialist on-site	✓					✓							✓		
Personnel director on company board	✓	✓				✓						✓	✓	✓	✓
Devolved line management decision making	✓	✓	✓			✓						✓	✓	✓	✓
Personnel role as specialist advice function	✓		✓		✓			✓							
Formal discipline and grievance policy	✓	✓		✓	✓	✓	✓	✓	✓		✓	✓	✓		✓
Formal employee training programme	✓	✓		✓	✓	✓	✓	✓	✓		✓	✓	✓		✓
Formal recruitment policies	✓	✓		✓	✓	✓	✓	✓	✓		✓	✓	✓		✓
TQM programmes	✓			✓		✓			✓	✓	✓		✓	✓	✓
Company 'mission statements'	✓				✓	✓	✓	✓				✓	✓	✓	
Employee involvement schemes				✓	✓	✓	✓	✓	✓	✓	✓	✓	✓	✓	✓
	9	3	2	6	6	6	5	5	4	2	6	6	8	3	6
Total Score	23	11	5	14	15	15	12	13	11	7	11	14	17	13	18

Notes

Company 'A' is Delivery Co. (case study in Chapter 8).
Company 'C' is Water Co. (case study in Chapter 5).
Company 'F' is Merchant Co. (case study in Chapter 7).
Company 'K' is Chem Co. (case study in Chapter 6).

chosen for detailed case study analysis. Fuller details of these firms are given in Chapters 5 to 8, which respectively report the findings in each one.

In terms of the selection criteria, it is worth noting why each organisation was included in the study. Water Co. was a multi-site SME in the service sector, which, as a relatively young organisation, had experienced a turbulent market. It also had different types of occupations employed across different geographical sites, and was a foreign-owned company, which could be an important source of influence in making and modifying the employment relationship. The prevalent management style in the firm was classified as opportunist and ad hoc.

Chem Co. was different from Water Co. in that it was in the manufacturing sector and thus employed very different groups of workers, for example, skilled technicians, as well as semi-skilled process operatives. In addition, the market for chemical products was considered to be an important difference between the two firms. While Chem Co. was similar to Water Co. in that it was a multi-site SME, it differed in having experience of a long established non-union relationship during the height of union membership in Britain. It was also UK-owned and therefore differed in terms of ownership as a possible influence on the relationship. In addition, the prevalent management style in the company, while basically autocratic, was also somewhat benevolent.

Given its size, occupational structure, market sector and age, Merchant Co. was different from the previous two organisations. In addition Merchant Co. had some (albeit minimal) experience of union de-recognition during company acquisitions and had implemented a redundancy programme in the face of a turbulent product market. Unlike the two previous organisations it had a personnel department, and this could have an impact on important relationship influences. For example, in terms of management style, it was classified as traditional (hard) HRM.

Finally, as part of a large, foreign-owned multi-national organisation that is well established in terms of age, Delivery Co. complemented the data set for this investigation in having important key differences. It had a geographically dispersed range of different types of occupational groups, its own separate personnel department, and was engaged in a competitive service sector market. Finally, initial indicators of the employment relationship at Delivery Co. pointed towards a more sophisticated non-union model and its management style was nearer to strategic (soft) HRM. Taken together, these initial features for Delivery Co. complement the diversity of other non-union firms discussed above. These then were the four organisations chosen for detailed case study investigation, the results of which are explored in the following four chapters.

5 Water Co.

A case of exploitative autocracy

Introduction

This chapter presents results for the first of the four case study organisations. This is Water Co., a small-to-medium sized enterprise (SME) that employs 120 people across five different sites in the UK. It is a relatively young company, having been established in the mid 1980s at the height of the Thatcherite enterprise culture, and therefore provides an interesting context for exploring non-union employment relations. It is also foreign owned. An American–Canadian mineral water company owns Water Co. in the UK, although in practice a distant relationship is maintained between the American–Canadian owners and the UK senior management team. In effect, managerial decision-making powers remain with the Chief Executive for both commercial and employment matters for all UK sites.

The chapter commences by categorising the type of employment relationship at Water Co. This is followed by a detailed explanation of the effects of why Water Co. has a highly exploitative relationship based on managerial action and intent. It also shows how the nature of the relationship impacts on management styles, employee voice, the psychological exchange and employee attitudes towards trade unions.

Employment relationship: key characteristics

In terms of the key characteristics of the employment relationship set out in Chapter 2, Water Co. is categorised as exploitatively autocratic because:

- the regulation of employment is exclusively managerially imposed, and dependent on the particular managerial style of key actors;
- the notion of HR strategy is extremely minimalist, with employees regarded as a highly disposable factor of production;
- there are few mechanisms for employees to express their voice and in general, there is a low level of trust between employees and employer;
- a discernible pattern of them and us exists between employees and management;

- the relationship is highly dependent on informal customs at workplace level.

Notwithstanding the above, the case study also illustrates how labour, as an agent, has the capacity to react and influence the nature of employment relations. In this respect, the non-union relationship at Water Co. is potentially unstable.

Influences on the employment relationship organisational context

Structure and the nature of work

Water Co. is the smallest and newest company in this study. It commenced trading in 1987 as the British subsidiary of a well-known French mineral water company. With increasing competition and a poor share of the UK market, Water Co. was sold in 1992 to a Canadian firm for £4 million. In 1993 Water Co. traded at a £650,000 loss, on an annual turnover of £3 million. This led to a reduction in the numbers employed, with the closure of a distribution centre in High Wycombe. In 1994 the firm obtained its first modest (£50,000) profitable returns and in 1995 the Warrington distribution centre was opened, which increased the workforce from 95 to 120. By 1996 the company had grown substantially in commercial terms, and was independently valued at £38 million. At the time of this research, Water Co. returned a pre-tax profit of just under £3 million with 120 workers.

While Water Co. is a stand-alone, small-to-medium sized enterprise, it is also part of a larger multinational firm. Internationally, the organisation employs just over 800 employees: 300 in the USA, 400 in Canada and 120 in the UK. In practice, the principal owner is its American parent organisation, which has commercial interests in three other mineral water companies. The US office is regarded as the strategic base of the company and profits are remitted to the American parent, which ultimately retains all strategic decision-making powers, although management in Britain has the freedom to make its own commercial and human resource policies.

The British operation, which is the subject of this case study, is a multi-plant establishment. Its head office is located in the Midlands, which incorporates a distribution centre and clerical support section. There is a processing plant for the bottling of water in Derbyshire, and there are two other distribution centres: one in London and one in Warrington. Within this geographical structure there are four main business functions. The largest of these is distribution, with 55 employees, followed by administration and finance (30), production (25), and sales with approximately 10 employees. This is shown in Figure 5.1.

There are several important points about the nature of employment at Water Co. For the 55 employees within distribution, there are three separate

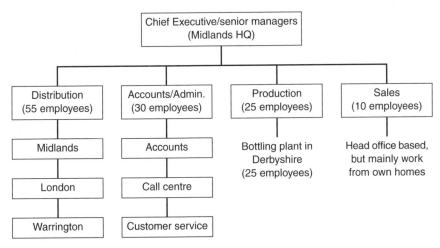

Figure 5.1 Organisational structure of Water Co.

sites. The largest of these is the Midlands head office (35 employees), followed by London and Warrington. Each distribution site also employs different occupational groups and has a site supervisor, a route-manager (who maps out the best delivery route for drivers), sanitation engineers (who maintain and repair water coolant machines at customer sites) and delivery drivers.

All white-collar workers are based at the Midlands head office. This comprises an accounts department (about 4 employees), customer service (about 8 employees) and a call-centre (about 15 employees). In addition, the sales team (10 employees) is also predominantly based at the head office, but in practice, people tend to work independently from any company site (travelling the country as sales reps), or work from their own homes. During several visits to the company's head office, it was evident that the nature of work gave rise to many serious antagonisms with respect to call centre workers, who were subject to a greater degree of managerial control than other employees. To some extent this can be explained by their interface role with customers, but can also be traced to the technology used in the call centre, which exacerbated a physical and social division of labour. The call centre was a small department of approximately 15 staff, each located at an individual workstation that consisted of a computer terminal and a telephone head set. An electronic message board was displayed at the end of the office, which informed all employees how many customer calls had been answered, how many were on-line waiting and the overall percentage rate of calls answered.

Significantly, the nature of work meant that employees worked in almost total isolation. Beyond the computer screen, workers could see one of two things: a partition screen which prevented any contact with co-workers, and the large electronic message board which flashed a team success rate across the room. There was also a high degree of managerial surveillance. Call centre operatives had little space or opportunity to leave their workstations. The supervisor sat in close proximity to employees and seemed to have one main objective: to prohibit employees from speaking to one another. One employee commented:

> they say it's better with the new computer system, but it's not ... we're seen as the ones who can make the real money cos we sell the stuff and speak to the customers all day ... so they always want to screw yeah.
>
> (Call centre employee)

In terms of the characteristics of the employment relationship discussed in Chapter 2, this pointed to managerially imposed regulation. For instance, an average of three minutes was allowed for each telephone call, which included 45 seconds to type one sentence about the customer's query on screen. Once a telephone call had been completed, the computer-operated telephone system gave a 50 second delay between answering the next call and closing the previous caller's account details on screen. Hence the 45 second time lag to type one sentence before the account details disappeared from the screen (an automatic operation when a call has been terminated), and the next customer in line being put through (again, an automatic operation when the previous call had been terminated). In short, within 50 seconds of ending one telephone conversation, the next call was automatically fed to the nearest operator, while the computer screen re-set itself ready for the next input.

In contrast, the nature of work for employees at the production plant was very different, suggesting that informal influences form an important dynamic to the relationship. The production plant employs 25 workers and operates a double shift system (6am to 2pm and 2pm to 10pm) with continuous production operations. Workers are located at different stages in the production process of bottling mineral water and in general, methods of supervisory control were less intrusive than elsewhere in the company. Workers would frequently stop work outside of break times, engage in conversation, play cards or extend their lunch break to play soccer, with no immediate concern from either of the two supervisors on site. When asked about this, one employee commented that:

> well, they just leave us to it really ... if you need a piss, then you need a piss, that's that.
>
> (Production employee)

Thus although the nature of work in the call centre was highly regulated, there tended to exist considerable variation across the company in terms of informality and managerial control practices. Call centre operatives, located at the head office, were in close proximity to senior managers and had to deal with customers on a direct basis. In contrast, production workers were distant from the watchful eye of senior managers and the situation for delivery drivers was altogether different.

Many worked for periods of time on the road, or based at customer sites, delivering and installing water coolers. As such, relations between supervisors and these groups of workers developed in an entirely different, largely informal manner to those of head office or call centre employees. Although these differences in the nature of work and organisational structure are quite subtle, they allow us to understand that even within a small enterprise, the relations that develop over time and among workers and line managers can influence the way the relationship is experienced, regulated and mediated.

Having said this, it would be misleading to assume that work in the production plant or for delivery drivers was somehow easier or generally more favourable than for call centre operatives. Management viewed the workforce as highly disposable. Over 75 per cent of all workers were aged between 21 and 30 years of age, with another 16 per cent aged over 40. Just over 50 per cent of all workers had been employed with the company for one year or less. Indeed, apart from six people (the Chief Executive, two senior managers and three clerical employees), no other worker had been employed at Water Co. for the duration of the company's short history and there was a particular reason for this. It was common practice for employees to be dismissed and later re-employed as a tactic to avoid the employees' having a legal entitlement to protection against unfair dismissal. As workers approached two years' continuous service, supervisors in the bottling plant explained that the employees' temporary contract would not be renewed: 'of course they would be able to come back in a few weeks later' (production supervisor). In several interviews the Chief Executive expressed his concern that workers have too many rights these days, and comments by one employee were equally revealing in this respect:

> if you get sacked that's it ... they say it, you leave ... sometimes someone down there [i.e. Midlands HQ] says something about it, but not really ... lads come and go here all the time.
>
> (Processing plant employee)

The major industrial relations decisions, concerning pay, terms and conditions, or the tenure of people's employment, remained the exclusive prerogative of the Chief Executive. Occasionally there was some involvement with other senior managers, but there was no formal mechanism for joint management decision making or for employees to articulate their concerns. In practice, managerial choice remained the prerogative of the Chief Executive, with employees regarded as no more and no less than a disposable factor of production.

Market factors

It has been noted elsewhere that context-specific factors, such as the availability of other jobs as well as labour and product markets, are important
features that influence managerial strategies (Marchington and Parker
1990). The products sold by Water Co. are of two types. The first is small
bottles of mineral water, typically 75ml and 150ml sized bottles, which are
sold to the general public from retail outlets – shops, pubs and cafés. Water
Co. does not sell these products directly to end customers, but to wholesale
distributors, and the market for these products accounts for less than 20 per
cent of the overall business for the company. The second area is the main
trading activity for Water Co. This involves the sale and distribution of
mineral water to commercial customers, mainly factories and offices who
provide the product to their employees or the general public. The water is
sold in 20 litre bottles, which are located in a water cooler/dispenser leased
to the customer. The market environment is highly competitive, and price
and speed of delivery are regarded as the most significant factors influencing
customer satisfaction. Moreover, market demand for bottled mineral water is
subject to seasonal fluctuations, with customer demand often dependent on
exogenous factors such as hot weather.

The volatility of the market for Water Co. products is extremely relevant
to the nature of employment and managerial approaches. The most influential market factor was identified as price, rather than the quality of water.
That is, although numerous respondents would refer to the natural properties of the water sold by the company, it is price rather than anything else
that persuades customers. One particular tactic used by the Chief Executive
was to head-hunt well-known sales representatives from other firms in the
industry. This was more than a policy of finding key employees with knowledge of the industry. At a time of increasing market competition for
bottled mineral water, the recruitment of well-known sales representatives
also widened Water Co.'s commercial base, because it was understood that
poached employees would bring new customers with them.

The intensity of market pressure suggests that employees were regarded
as an easily disposed factor of production, rather than as a valued asset. As
noted above, many employees were subject to dismissal, as a tactic by management to avoid employment rights, only to be re-employed a few weeks
later. Overtime working was generally high, due to a seasonal (summer)
demand, especially for delivery drivers. Sanitation engineers often had to
double-up and make deliveries while servicing and repairing customer
equipment. The Chief Executive summed-up this impact:

> Sometimes people that we would employ today who are qualified for the
> job doesn't mean they would be in 12 months' time, because the busi-
> ness is fast-moving and that much bigger now, we can't really afford to
> invest in people for the future ... we need to obtain them quickly and

that means looking outside more than inside these days, if we're to achieve market leadership.

(Chief Executive)

As Ram *et al.* (2001) note, the importance of market conditions and the ways in which management respond to these can be more than a contextual footnote. At Water Co. market pressure led to a pattern of flexibility, irregular working hours, job insecurity and the recruitment as well as the displacement of key employees. This in turn shaped the style of management and the specifics of any social and psychological exchange within the relationship.

Management style and the psychological exchange

In Chapter 3 the issue of management style was discussed. Having unpacked the typical dimensions used to assess management style (such as the range of HR policies and the extent of individual and collective integration), it was felt that a deeper analysis was required. That is, management style can also be influenced by the key features of social exchange discussed in Chapter 2, particularly the relationships between trust, fairness and management's ability (or willingness) to deliver on the deal. The objective here is to explore the impact of style through managerial *action*, *intentions* and employee *experiences* encountered at Water Co.

The range of policies and practices that might indicate union avoidance for either anti-collectivist or pro-individualist reasons were found wanting at Water Co. There were no defined procedural arrangements for dealing with discipline or appeals; no equal opportunities policies, few formal health and safety procedures, and recruitment and selection tended to be ad hoc and informal. Indeed, some employees reported that they had never received an employment contract or written statement of their terms and conditions. The dominant style tended to emanate from the personal traits of the Chief Executive, who regarded employment relations matters as irksome and annoying. His style was highly autocratic. For example, while line managers reported that they had authority and responsibility for employee relations, including such matters as recruitment, discipline and dismissal, ultimately decisions had to be ratified by the Chief Executive. One supervisor in the London distribution centre summarised the *action* arising from the Chief Executive's own style in a few simple words:

no one is ever sacked here, but a lot are told to leave!

(Distribution supervisor)

The nature of such autocracy was often intentional and purposeful. A new pay review and appraisal system was introduced, for which decisions were ultimately made by the Chief Executive. There was no scope to involve line managers or consult with workers in determining pay, and the whole philosophy expressed by the Chief Executive was that management are here to manage, and employees to work. The new pay system helps to capture his preferred way of managing, and its impact on the psychological contract.

The smallest single group of employees within the company (the sales reps) were used as a benchmark to develop a new bonus and commission-based pay system. Briefly, every category of employee had his or her regular salary replaced with a lower basic wage, plus an element of commission or a bonus, depending on overall company performance and individual effort. Within this scheme, occupational or specific job tasks were regarded as largely irrelevant and in a personal message to employees, the Chief Executive wrote:

> with our new incentive package for remuneration and performance I'm convinced everyone can meet the new challenges and reap the rewards by striving for customer quality and individual self-betterment ... we should all benefit in our success in the near future.
>
> (Chief Executive)

What emerged was a diverse, arbitrary and often complicated wage structure. At the Midlands head office, sales reps, call centre staff and customer service employees all received the lowest basic pay in the company, the rationale for which was explained by one of the senior managers:

> well you have to understand they [call centre staff] have the easiest chance to earn the readies because they speak to customers all day long ... and they [sales reps] have a better chance to sell the coolers than anyone else.
>
> (Senior manager: head office)

With a lower basic salary, supplemented by commission on the number of successful calls for call centre workers, the level of earnings was clearly a prerogative of management. The pace for answering customer telephone calls was determined by the telephone system mentioned earlier. Moreover, the capacity to boost earnings ultimately depended upon customers external to the employment relationship. One operator remarked:

> if we answer more and more calls our bonus is up, but if we're answering fewer calls the company is probably more productive – not so many mistakes for them [customers] to get you about.
>
> (Operator: call centre)

The paradox is that if call centre operators answered a greater number of telephone queries, this implied a measure of customer complaint, rather than improved organisational performance. Employees were not blind to the fact that their earnings capacity could be improved by poor quality service, nor were workers ignorant about managerial intentions to reduce the wage bill. To quote:

> I'm one of the longest serving [sales] reps, and I do think it's one of the better places I've worked ... you've got to remember these are all young lads [meaning sales reps], not so many stay that long in the offices, maybe the odd dozen or so ... as soon as they realise the bonuses don't come that easy, they're off.
>
> (Sales representative)

The same system existed for other employees. Delivery drivers received a bonus on the number of deliveries made over and above targets set by management, and sanitation engineers earned commission for the number of water coolers serviced at customer sites. Indeed, it was common practice for sanitation engineers to make deliveries of water while out visiting customer sites as a way to boost basic salary.

Issues associated with the appraisal system also revealed deeper, qualitative indications about managerial intent. Every employee in the company was subject to an annual appraisal and supervisors conducted the appraisal interview around pre-set performance targets determined by the Chief Executive. There was no method of consultation and employees we spoke to were first informed of the new targets during the appraisal interview. Most workers expected targets to increase, and a few of them reported that the appraisal was rarely used for anything else other than to inform them of the Chief Executive's new expectations. There was no mention of staff development or talk of training opportunities during the appraisal and for management, the exercise ensured that people understand what is expected of them.

Ultimately, reducing labour costs was the overriding objective in appraisal setting, shaped as much by the external demands from customers as they were by internal managerial preferences. Sales reps explained that while they anticipated an increase in targets, their appraisal focused on maintaining the underlying success rate of the company as determined by management, often regardless of other external market influences. One sales employee explained:

> We all get tough targets and that's alright – I mean it's how we make our crust anyway, but this time round making a profit isn't in it. We've to keep pace with the last two years' growth ... they're talking of something like a 60–80 per cent increase just to keep level. There's no chance ... with the spell of weather we've been having.
>
> (Sales representative)

Targets set for the year were established against a large increase in the volume for water sales over the preceding two years, the most pronounced market growth for the company. Yet the weather which fuelled this growth was not evident. In short, it wasn't hot enough to sell the same amount of water.

In summary, while management style can be based on the scope of policies and the extent to which practices are integrated (or their absences exposed), at a deeper level of analysis managerial *intentions* and worker *experiences* suggest that management style was more complex. At Water Co., a single dominant actor, the Chief Executive, pursued his preferred way of managing and in terms of the key features of the employment relationship, the intentions of management seem to paint a picture of low trust, with little indication that employees are treated as an asset.

Employee voice and the psychological exchange

In social exchange terms the levels of involvement, communication and consultation are important features that can signify delivery of the deal. In essence, employee voice reflects the extent to which workers have a say in matters that affect them, together with the ways in which this can occur.

Other than the annual appraisal mentioned above, which was little more than a top-down way of informing employees of targets, team working was the only other formal mechanism for employee voice reported at Water Co. Formally, there was a cascade system of communicating information via working teams. However, this was often piecemeal, with meetings occurring as infrequently as quarterly or annually. Moreover, the use of systematic voice arrangements tended to be confined to the occasional intervention by senior management. From the perspective of employees, such briefing systems were regarded as a means to communicate something major or important, rather than to involve workers on a day-to-day basis. The Chief Executive summed-up the absence of any systematic voice policy at Water Co. thus:

> we don't consult [*employees*] we impose when we really know it's not so good to do it that way ... several things we have introduced have not gone smooth and some of them have been where we have implemented them.

(Chief Executive)

Given the absence of formal voice mechanisms, it could be expected that employee perceptions of actually having a say would be found wanting. However, the evidence is far from straightforward and Table 5.1 shows that worker perceptions are somewhat contradictory. Over half of those surveyed said that employee views are considered by management when making decisions, and another half said that management often communicated changes. In contrast, however, 63 per cent reported they do not speak to management about their wages, with another two-thirds (59 per cent) suggesting that employees are not involved in management decision making.

Table 5.1 Employee voice at Water Co. (percentage of respondents)

Question/statement	Agree	Not sure	Disagree
In your job do you often inform supervisors that you can do your job well	50	17	33
In your job do you often suggest to supervisors improvements in the way your job could be done	33	35	53
I speak to management often about my wages and conditions	20	17	63
Employees are very much involved with management in making decisions in this company	23	18	59
When decisions are taken which affect my pay or work, employee views are taken into account by management	57	13	30
Management often communicate changes about work	58	10	32

Note
N = 61.

Thus at Water Co. there are key features of the employment relationship that contradict one another. While there is an absence of voice mechanisms, together with an indication of low trust, there also exists an undercurrent of informal social dynamics that seems to satisfy certain elements of a psychological contract. What seems to be important here is the nature of informal exchanges at workplace level as a means for workers to get by, and minimise the degradation of an otherwise harsh managerial style.

Shopfloor relations and employee well-being

It is evident that workers at Water Co. experienced a number of exploitative and contradictory issues in their day-to-day work environment that shaped the nature of employment relations. They were subject to an autocratic management approach, experienced few of the dimensions associated with a favourable psychological contract and had no access to collective representation. Yet employees at Water Co. were by no means passive recipients of these conditions, and on several occasions during the research a number of issues were observed and discussed with workers, which demonstrate how labour remains a cohesive agent against managerial power, despite the absence of a trade union.

One issue serves to illustrate the importance of them and us attitudes and the processes in which workers develop a sense of identity and attribution. At the Warrington distribution centre, the use of company vehicles became a contentious issue during the research. Briefly, most employees were in charge of a company vehicle of some sort; either a small van for sanitation engineers who serviced water coolers, or larger trucks for delivery drivers. A decision was made at the head office that in future, all employees would no longer be able to use company vehicles outside working time. Consequently, employees were required to make their own travel arrangements to and from work.

The reaction of employees was extremely important in shaping relationship dynamics. Workers viewed the use of company vehicles as a legitimate practice. Significantly, the close-knit working bonds strengthened the workers' sense of *identity* along with their perceptions of *attribution* and *blame* towards management for the removal of a long established custom and practice and in response, workers disrupted delivery schedules. For instance, the start times at the Warrington site varied between 6am and 8am, and employees explained they had real and genuine difficulties in getting to work on time. The site was located on a trading estate adjoining a motorway, and such public transport that did exist did not start until other retail outlets in the area opened for business. Crucially, this was much later than the start times at Water Co. While some employees had their own transport, others did not, and reliance on public transport proved to be more disruptive for the company than it did for workers. One employee explained:

> It wasn't that we were deliberate, I mean we didn't sit down and work out what we'd do. We had a good go at Kenny [supervisor] and let him know it was all shite. I suppose we just knew that if we didn't give one another a lift, Kenny would have to sort something out.
>
> (Delivery driver)

Thus while there was no formal dispute or grievance activated by employees (other than complaints in-passing to the site supervisor) workers clearly articulated their sense of *injustice*. More importantly, and in relation to social exchange, employees developed an understanding (possibly with supervisory knowledge) that their own actions of not giving one another a lift to work would be more damaging to the company than to themselves. The supervisor explained that when he had to report that deliveries were late starting, head office managers soon restored the custom of vehicle use outside of company working hours.

A second issue, which further illustrates a lack of trust as well as managerial-imposed regulation, emerged around a new marketing campaign initiated by the Chief Executive. The objective was to market the company and obtain new customers in Scotland. To this end the whole sales team were taken to Edinburgh for a full week to blitz the area, with the support of one sanitation engineer to install water cooling machines in customers' premises. However, the role of a sanitation engineer was not part of the plan until the last minute, mainly because no one had considered the installation of water coolers should the Edinburgh week attract new customers. The Warrington site was asked to send one of its sanitation engineers to support the sales team. The Warrington supervisor commented:

> the chief executive didn't want excuses why we couldn't do it, he just wanted it done. That's how it works here. The problem [is] I had one sani on holiday and the others were booked-in for deliveries and servicing elsewhere the next day.
>
> (Supervisor: Warrington)

The particular issue is illustrative of the relationship between managerial action and workers' sense of *injustice, attribution* and *identity*. Briefly, the employee was recalled from his holiday, not because of some emergency within the company, but because the Chief Executive had issued the instruction to support his latest idea. The employee concerned had returned from a week's family holiday in Wales to find the Warrington supervisor waiting outside his home with a hire van loaded with water, coolers and a mobile phone. His instruction was to drive to Edinburgh that day and support the sales team for a week. Notwithstanding the complaints raised by the employee on his own doorstep (his family suitcases yet unpacked) the issue demonstrates the power of managerial intent in the absence of any independent representation:

> It wasn't whether I went or not. You have to understand it was whether I was history or not ... even though that was never said to me directly ... I knew what it'd mean ... and no, they never sold one bloody cooler all the time I was up there.
>
> (Sanitation engineer)

At the bottling plant in Derby the nature of shop floor relations were equally significant, but in a different way. Unlike other sites, at Derby it was common for employees and supervisors to mix and socialise together. For instance, shift managers and workers would play soccer together during lunch breaks, were all members of a football team which played in a local league, and card schools and betting syndicates existed with line managers and employees as members. Significantly, shop floor relations were often couched in terms of a distinctive language and discourse particular to the site. In many ways there existed a particular site sub-culture, which was much more deeply ingrained than at other Water Co. locations. For example, some employees were observed on several occasions to use personal and insulting names when addressing supervisors, such as 'you're a prick'. In return, supervisors generally gave as good as they got, rather than resorting to their role of superior actor in the relationship. When discussing this with employees, it was explained that it's always been that way and one employee responded:

> well, they're easy-going up to a point ... [supervisor A] tells you
> straight but [supervisor B] is too much of a prick ... we've often said he
> needs one of those jobs worth hats.

(Employee: bottling plant)

The same conversation ended:

> but he's all right, really, for a dick-head.

Thus against an initial image of personal dislikes, there was a hidden sub-text based on shop floor customs and legacies particular to that site. In this instance informality served to ameliorate some of the degrading aspects of work, and fill a void in terms of a psychological exchange for workers (and supervisors).

At the Warrington site there was also a distinctive use of banter and language between employees and supervisor. On several occasions there were full-blown shouting matches concerning allegations of favouritism. It was claimed that certain drivers were given easier deliveries, with some customer sites regarded as the more lucrative jobs because of multiple drops at one location, which also meant that targets could be met quicker with subsequent bonus payments. Other examples included employees ignoring instructions to finish their coffee break and load vehicles. Indeed, despite threats of discipline from the supervisor, employees would hardly acknowledge they had just been told to carry out their work, even though they knew their break time was over. A particular form of company-speak was often used, with one supervisor known by his method of warning people that they will be history, which meant they might be dismissed. In many ways, employees recognised this was an abuse of the managerial prerogative and on at least one occasion, the issue of union membership was discussed among workers, to be vehemently opposed by management through overt threats. One driver remarked:

> I've told Kenny [*supervisor*] before – so it's not that he doesn't know – if
> he gives me any of that you'll be down the road crap, or I'm history,
> he'll take his head home in a bag, and I've told him, he's not talking to
> me the way he treats some of these young lads. Stupid threats, that's all
> he's good for.

(Delivery driver)

This shop floor level research provides a unique opportunity to capture some of the more salient issues related to employee well-being and psychological exchange within the employment relationship, and this was further assessed through a series of indicators. As shown in Table 5.2, about half of the employee respondents (52 per cent) indicated that they share the same values as the company and 50 per cent are willing to stay with Water Co. if offered another job elsewhere.

Table 5.2 Psychological indicators of employee well-being at Water Co. (percentage of respondents)

Question/statement	Agree	No opinion	Disagree
The values of this company are similar to my own personal beliefs	52	28	20
There are good career and promotion prospects in this company	31	13	56
I am willing to stay with this company if offered another job on similar terms and conditions	50	22	28
I am loyal to my employer	67	18	15
There is a great deal of tension at my workplace between management and employees	54	20	26
I am willing to put in a great deal of effort for the success of this company	85	8	7
I am satisfied with my pay and conditions	42	0	52

Note
N = 61.

Yet some of the other indicators paint a more complicated and contradictory picture of the dynamics of the relationship. For example, while 67 per cent agree they are loyal to the company, just over half (54 per cent) suggest there is a great deal of tension at their workplace. Similarly, a significant majority (85 per cent) are prepared to put in extra effort to help the company be successful, though less than half (42 per cent) are satisfied with their pay.

As a source of employment modification, this shop floor data demonstrates that the complexity of interactions among co-workers, supervisors and company management is likely to be an important factor. For many workers at Water Co., helping the company to be successful not only indicated a sense of organisational loyalty, it also served to ameliorate some of the exploitative aspects of work and people management in the organisation.

Worker attitudes to trade unions

Given these contradictory and exploitative experiences of the employment relationship at Water Co., workers nonetheless remained unorganised. The attitudes of these employees towards trade unions were collected and assessed by answers to interview questions and responses to questionnaire items, which are shown in Table 5.3.

Overall, workers were generally supportive of the principal values of trade unions, although it seemed there was less agreement about the ability of a union to improve pay or terms and conditions. However, the influence of

Table 5.3 (Non-union) employee attitudes to unions at Water Co. (percentage of respondents)

Question/statement	Agree	No opinion	Disagree
Trade unions provide necessary protection for employees generally[a]	100	0	0
Trade unions can be beneficial to employees[a]	100	0	0
Trade unions are generally a good thing for workers[a]	100	0	0
There are benefits in having the views of all employees represented to management[a]	100	0	0
Trade unions are, on the whole, sensible[a]	56	25	19
A trade union would make my job more secure in my company[b]	75	12.5	12.5
My pay/conditions would be improved if a trade union represented my interests in this company[b]	37.5	25	37.5

Notes

N = 16.[c]

Factor analysis revealed two factors, a = ideological union factor; b = instrumental union factor, c = data had to be collected by interview after management deleted all union related questions from the employee survey.

management style and action discussed above cannot be isolated from these attitudes. For instance, all respondents agreed that trade unions can protect worker interests and that there seemed to be some value in having all employee views represented to management. Nevertheless, when asked about trade unions in relation to improving pay or their terms and conditions, workers seemed less convinced. Perhaps it is not too surprising that 75 per cent thought their job could be more secure if they enjoyed collective representation, given that management displaced workers at an alarmingly frequent rate at Water Co. In contrast, only about one-third (37.5 per cent) agreed their pay and terms and conditions could be improved with trade union representation.

The rationale behind the formation of such attitudes requires a more qualitative interpretation. No employee expressed any negative sentiments about unions generally, although the role for a union within the context of the immediate work environment was often contrasted with a hostile perception of managerial behaviour towards unions. Of the 16 respondents interviewed, 10 of them suggested management would not allow a union, while 2 believed there was no need for a union and another 4 commented that they had never thought about a union.

Three of these 16 respondents had been former union members (all with a previous employer), and two were currently union members. Both of these were employed at the Warrington distribution centre. Surprisingly, one was the supervisor, who explained he was a union member from a former occupation (joiner), and union subscriptions were paid by direct debit that had never been cancelled. He thought the union was the General, Municipal and Boilermakers' Union (GMB), but was not sure, and had never received any union services. The other employee was a sanitation engineer who joined the Transport and General Workers' Union (TGWU) after starting employment with Water Co. When asked the reasons for joining, he reported it was in response to despicable treatment by management. This is the same sanitation engineer who had to travel to Edinburgh immediately after his family holiday, as described earlier. Significantly, he had no former union experience and the motives for joining appeared to be a sense of injustice and attribution derived from his experience of management action. He explained:

> I've no doubt whatsoever, if [the supervisor] or [the Chief Executive] knew about the union I'd be on my bike … it's more protection for when I need it, than anything else.
>
> (Sanitation engineer)

Other employees, who had a favourable orientation to unions, tended to justify the union absence because of management action and possible reprisals. For example:

> The actual mention of a trade union would get management's back up here.
>
> (Production employee)

> I think if you had a trade union which actually had some pressure, which might be able to change things, I think management would be a little terrified to say the least.
>
> (Bottling plant employee)

> I'm not quite sure how unions work, the bits I've heard, I think they'd be useful here. [But] if you were to welcome a union, then you'd have to ask yourself the question, would I be jeopardising my job if the union didn't get in? The management theory is that the company's done well so far so why have one, and then to put your case to welcome one, means your going to be very, very unpopular, and that's not a good situation to have with the management here.
>
> (Sanitation engineer)

In summary, it can be suggested that while employees seemed to have a broadly positive perception of trade unions (and there was no suggestion that a union would be inappropriate), the most significant factor here was clearly managerial hostility.

It is also worth commenting on some of the difficulties of collecting research data at Water Co. Unlike the other case studies in this book, employee attitudes towards trade unions could only be obtained by interview at Water Co. After the authors had negotiated access to the company, printed and distributed questionnaires to employees, a number of questions were removed that asked about employee views of trade unions. This first became apparent when questionnaires were returned from employees in the post. On inquiring about this change, it was explained that this happened while the owner was visiting the UK as questionnaires were about to go out. The Chief Executive (somewhat apologetically) commented that it was the owner who noticed the bundle of questionnaires and asked what they were for. When the Chief Executive explained, the owner was reported to have said he wanted all questions about unions removed. His argument:

> well, we don't want to give them [*employees*] any ideas?

However, the story does not end here. While the American owners wanted to remove the possibility of giving employees any ideas about trade unions, the Chief Executive was less diplomatic about the matter. Having made our protests about this interference in the design of the research instruments, the Chief Executive allowed us to ask employees the same set of questions during interview and whether this would trigger unionisation or not seemed not to matter to him. That is:

> they weren't having one [a union] anyway.
>
> (Chief Executive)

Summary and conclusions

In the introduction to this chapter we categorised Water Co. as having a highly exploitative and autocratic non-union pattern of employment relations. This was demonstrated through a minimalist HR strategy, together with the centrality of managerial-imposed regulation. There was very little opportunity for employees to articulate their voice, and many workers had never received a contract of employment. Virtually no policies existed in relation to health and safety or equality of opportunity. Furthermore, there was clear evidence of them and us attitudes between employee and employer, coupled with relatively low levels of trust. Taken together, these factors suggest that the behavioural intentions of workers in terms of collective mobilisation were restricted by the influence of management style, action and intent. In short, management's approach was unambiguously one in which employees were viewed as a highly disposable factor of production.

However, the data also suggests there are a number of significant contradictions in the notion of stylised employment relations. The absence of formal employee voice mechanism did not always mean that employees lacked a say. In addressing some of the features of a psychological contract, employees found expression for their feelings through informal social dialogue and some comfort from a sense of group identity (often incorporating supervisory grades) at workplace level. To some extent this was based on the personal ties of friendship between workers and supervisors, but also based on a sense of identification among workers, who recognised themselves as a separate group with very different interests to those of management.

In terms of union exclusion, managerial style and hostility is particularly important. As Cully *et al.* (1999) comment, one of the more difficult hurdles for collective mobilisation seems to be the ability of unions to overcome the anti-union sentiments expressed by employers. Water Co. is unashamedly anti-union, but although workers might well have been sympathetic to the idea of unionisation, they also seemed to question the efficacy of a union in terms of protecting them against potential managerial reprisals. Significantly, this does not negate the capacity of labour to act as an important agent in the processes that mediate employment relations. Despite the absence of collective representation, workers were not passive recipients of the conditions they experienced. Rather, they exerted influence in return and in so doing, partially shaped how management regulated the employment relationship.

6 Chem Co.

A case of benevolent autocracy

Introduction

Like Water Co., Chem Co. is a non-unionised small-to-medium sized enterprise (SME). It employs 130 workers across two sites: one on Merseyside and the other in Leeds. As with Water Co., there is no personnel or HR function, with employment relations being the responsibility of the Operations Director. However this is where the similarities end. Chem Co. is a much older establishment, having commenced trading in 1975. It is also wholly UK-owned, and employs different occupational groups with a very different skill mix: process operators, skilled and semi-skilled workers, technicians and chemical engineers. The organisation manufactures intermediary chemicals, which are then used by a small number of large firm customers, such as ICI and Unilever.

The employment relationship: key characteristics

Chem Co. has a very different employment relationship to Water Co. This can be characterised as highly autocratic, with elements of restrained benevolence. In many ways, the relationship is perhaps more unstable than that identified for Water Co., although for very different reasons. In particular:

- The regulation of employment was for the most part managerially led. However this also included a subtle blend of both individual and pseudo-collective aspects, in order to avoid potential triggers to unionisation.
- HR strategy emphasised a caring benevolence for workers, though the reality of what this meant for workers varied for the different occupational groups.
- A wide range of voice mechanisms existed, although the facility for employees to have a say remained limited and was subject to strong managerial control.
- Work structures were highly formalised. However, formality also tended to polarise relations, given the small social setting of the workplace.
- Management style was by far the strongest influence, with the ideological preferences of one single actor being particularly important.

Influences on the employment relationship organisational context

Structure and the nature of work

Chem Co. came into existence in 1975 and was the result of an amalgamation of a number of small chemical dye manufacturers, which followed hard on the heels of a decline in the textile industries in Lancashire and Yorkshire in the late 1960s. Under the general auspices of the then Bradford Dyers' Association (BDA), a number of experiments were conducted in the early 1970s to switch production from textile chemical dyes to bromide and bleaching agents. In 1975, Chem Co. was established as it is today, with 130 employees across two sites.

Chem Co. is an organisation with a large proportion of manual employees and the company is engaged in manufacturing as well as processing chemical products. In contrast to Water Co., it represents a long-term non-union relationship in a company that expanded during the zenith of unionisation in the 1970s. The company also employs a mix of occupational groups that could more easily be associated with unionisation than non-unionism (e.g. production and process operators, manual workers and skilled engineers).

The main site is in Merseyside, with another site in Leeds. Both are multi-purpose plants and shortly before the study commenced another site in the north west of England was closed because its plant and machinery was outdated. Investment in technology at both Merseyside and Leeds meant that the company was capable of producing the same output with some reorganisation across the two remaining sites.

Chem Co.'s business activities include over 150 products, all concentrated in a niche market for intermediary chemicals. For example, products include chemical compounds for washing powder, fabric conditioner and paints. As such, there are a few important contracts to supply Imperial Chemical Industries (ICI) and Unilever. Unlike other SME-type companies, which may experience customer-chain dependency (Blyton and Turnbull 1998), Chem Co. has a diversity of customers, although ICI and Unilever account for about 45 per cent of all business. In addition, there is a growing business in flame retardant chemicals for the textile industry, bromides for photography (Agfa and Kodak) and products for the pharmaceutical industry.

Recession in the late 1990s hit the bromide side of Chem Co.'s activities, which led to some research and development investments in search of new products. With new laboratory equipment and increased production capacity from investments in capital, Chem Co. patented a range of new products targeted at the pharmaceuticals industry. Currently, these products account for 30 per cent of Chem Co.'s business activity.

The organisational structure of Chem Co. reflects its geographical distribution, which is split along three principal lines: Merseyside, Leeds, and Group Services. While both the Leeds and Merseyside facilities can produce broadly the same products, the latter is by far the largest in terms of volume and number of employees. The Group Services function is also based at the Merseyside plant, and acts as an umbrella title for non-chemical support services, such as Accounts, Marketing and Sales.

In commercial terms, Chem Co. has experienced a shift from being a loss-making organisation (deficit of £112K) in the early 1990s, to a growing share of the domestic market, with some export trade beginning towards the end of the 1990s. By 1998 Chem Co. had a total turnover of £29.5 million, of which £300K was retained as profit, and the company was independently valued at £7.7 million.

There is no personnel manager or personnel department at Chem Co., and all employment matters are dealt with by the Operations Director, below whom are site managers, then supervisors and team leaders, who cover either technical (e.g. laboratory), maintenance or process activities. There is a separate Employee Works Committee for each site, chaired by the Operations Director. For Group Services there are department managers, for example for accounts and clerical support. The organisational structure of Chem Co. is shown in Figure 6.1.

At Chem Co. the greatest impact on the nature and organisation of work came from new technology. The bulk of employees at both plants are process operators engaged in the manufacture of a variety of chemical and pharmaceutical products. Technical and professional employees are based in particular laboratories related to specific chemical manufacturing (for example paints, pharmaceuticals or washing powder). However, they also work on the line from time to time in a quality assurance capacity, ensuring that large batches are produced correctly. The majority (80 per cent) of the workforce is male.

For almost all employees in the company, changes to the organisation of work had been introduced through considerable technological investments.

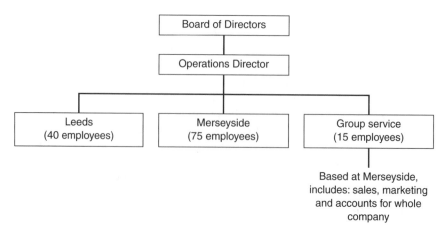

Figure 6.1 Organisational structure of Chem Co.

The Operations Director explained that new technology impacted on everyone and everything in the organisation. The main investments focused on laboratory research and development activities, together with an upgrading of processing technologies at both plants. In terms of work organisation, the new technology introduced new multi-function working cells on process lines.

Briefly, manufacturing and chemical production is structured around small cells (or teams) on a 24-hour, 365-day shift pattern. Process operatives are classified as semi-skilled and work on different job tasks, depending on the type of chemicals being manufactured. Separate cells, consisting of between three and twelve workers who conduct all stages of process manufacturing, with employees rotating between different jobs on a particular line. In the past these were demarcated jobs, depending on the separate stage of manufacture.

For some product lines the sequence of work activity was dictated by the technical processes used. For example, in the processing of paint pigments for ICI, or washing powder ingredients for Unilever, the pace of work was largely determined by technical operations. On the paints line, cell teams of between three and five people would follow a two- or three-hour cycle in which various chemical ingredients would be added at pre-determined stages. These were mixed in large vats, and the flow of processing was determined by valves opening and closing at set times. Once the process had commenced, it required little employee effort and the pace of production was largely fixed, because certain ingredients were mixed and diluted for a period of time before subsequent stages could begin. Each cell team would be responsible for several separate production jobs running at different stages, moving between these while the mixing and diluting of paint pigments was occurring elsewhere on the shift. Consequently, and given the capital-intensive nature of the work, only a few employees were required to manufacture large volumes of such chemicals. In this respect, the technology had an impact on the level of labour supply. Further, there was an overlap between technical demands and managerial decision making. In particular, supervisors on the paints line would suggest that it was the technology used which demanded a system of 24-hour, 365-day processing. However, deeper analysis suggests that the demands of technology were at times secondary to managerial action. For example, while it was reported that it was easier to run certain parts of the plant continuously than to close down a particular line and re-open it at a later date, ultimately such decisions were also couched in a language of economic efficiency as well as a technical rationale. One supervisor commented:

> to close this section down would cause mayhem … we'd need at least a full day to get it working properly again … Safety and maintenance would have to be called in, and probably a few contractors to dismantle and then reassemble half the pipework once it'd stopped … that's not going to be seen as a very proficient way of managing.
>
> (Supervisor: paint line)

Thus on the one hand, the capital-intensive nature of chemical process technology dictated a system of shift working and influenced the pace and nature of work organisation. On the other hand, however, this was often blurred by managerial reasons for economic efficiency, and the precise causal symmetry between technology and the role of management as an influence on the relationship was a complex issue.

The consequences of multi-skilling and de-skilling of labour were of greater significance for employees working on pharmaceutical products. For example, the technology used to manufacture pharmaceutical products lends itself to greater flexible variation in terms of changing the pace and nature of work. The nature of pharmaceutical processing did not require chemical ingredients to be diluted and mixed at set periods of time, as was the case with paint pigments. One immediate difference was the extent to which supervision was considerably more intense and bureaucratic in contrast to work outside pharmaceuticals. For example, team leaders would constantly monitor and check employee performance by walking the line, ensuring there were no bottlenecks and that each stage was running smoothly. Furthermore, once employees entered certain parts of the pharmaceutical line, departure for even the most basic of human needs was frowned upon. This was due to lost production time, given the required safety precautions. That is, employees had to shower both before entering and upon leaving the cell area, and remove protective clothing because of the dangers from chemical dust.

There also appeared a rudimentary form of labour aristocracy across the organisation, especially in the technical and research and development areas. Rather than de-skilling work, as in the case of production mentioned above, professional and technical employees working in laboratories had the scope to broaden and up-skill their work. Here, the nature of work gravitated around a small number of highly specialist workers developing new products. This meant that employees in research and development were afforded a greater degree of task freedom. For example, many had very specific technical or chemical qualifications, and tended to rely on experimentation in their day-to-day work, which allowed them to upgrade and widen their own personal expertise. The Operations Director explained that this led to certain frustrations in managing such employees:

> I can't be an expert at everything and we encourage R&D to be active in what they want to do really, and in the main they are. The odd person here isn't but the vast majority of people follow the sort of professionalisation needed for our business if you like; specialisms in chemistry, things like Phosgene, Flora, Nitrous compounds, that kind of thing. So I have to rely on specialists to know what's happening and what's not happening with certain people, which isn't that satisfactory for me ... I've got a few I can trust and have learnt to live with it that way. And there's really the biggest reason not to have a trade union because I'd

then be thinking, well, who is trying to call the shots – some union steward or a chemist; or even worse, both perspectives to deal with.

(Operations Director)

The overall significance of technology as a tool to affect employee behaviour was at times complicated and uneven. In some areas, the pace of output could not be altered by technology, yet in others it could. Where technical operations meant production schedules were fixed, there was often less demand for labour and the nature of such work was de-skilled on particular lines. Furthermore, those employees with technical and scientific knowledge were afforded a greater degree of freedom in their work, which pointed to a greater degree of trust for some occupational groups.

Market factors

As briefly mentioned above, Chem Co. manufactures and sells intermediary chemical compounds. It makes over 150 different products, with about half of its core business focused on particular markets to supply a few large customer organisations (ICI, Unilever, Kodak and Agfa). Following a recession in the mid 1990s, Chem Co. diversified and patented a number of new chemical compounds that account for another 40 per cent of the company's business, mostly for new pharmaceutical and drug industry products.

In general terms the nature of the product market was explained as highly competitive, although this was not related to similar companies entering the market. Indeed, ease of entry for competitors was constrained by a number of factors, including the capital and financial resources needed to set up a chemical company. Furthermore, among those competitors that did exist, it was explained that it was a practice across the industry for similar small-scale chemical companies to be relatively well-known to one another, and each usually concentrated on a distinct market niche.

A more complicated facet to market competition was the nature of commercial contracts with customers. These contracts were often of a long duration (typically three to five years) and once signed implied a degree of market stability. For example, at the time of this study, Chem Co. had been manufacturing paint pigments for ICI for about eight years, and the contract had only been renewed once. The Operations Director explained the market thus:

It is common for small chemical sites like us to invest in production facilities such that we have, when we have a clear knowledge of future plans ... customers recognise that, and we work within that system quite well I'd say.

(Operations Director)

However, while actual market entry may be difficult for organisations outside the industry, market pressures remained important. This was mainly due to customer relations with powerful large organisations. The Leeds manager explained that customers can also be competitors, and this could be used in subtle ways in negotiating commercial contracts. For example:

> we're a small fish in a big pond, we are a chemical manufacturer and most of our competitors are our customers ... ICI might come along to us and say can you make X Y Z and we would say, yes, OK. Another part of ICI might be saying, hang on we'll make that instead, internally, so competitors can also be customers.
>
> (Site manager: Leeds)

In addition to the complexities of market competition and relations with customers, labour market factors pointed to a number of contradictions. In the main, there was a low labour turnover rate for all employees, although occasionally the turnover for process operators would peak and trough, according to one departmental supervisor. All employees were permanent, mostly full-time, and although agency staff had been used in the past, these had not been employed for some years.

The development of an internal labour market pointed towards a benign form of benevolence within the employment relationship, although this differed across occupational categories in the company. Briefly, a few problems had occurred when trying to recruit less skilled employees for production at short notice, often owing to tight customer deadlines. One response was to encourage existing workers to nominate friends or family members as prospective employees when vacancies arose.

The recruitment of process operatives, often through existing employees, introduced a form of internalised peer pressure for people to conform to expected standards and behaviours, and at times this appeared to be articulated unconsciously. The Operations Director commented:

> I took on one young lad, he's bloody useless really, but we took him on straight from school because his dad's worked here for about 8 years, and we did ask for nominees, so we took him on and put him on a Modern Apprenticeship for one day a week at the college. Now I've got the college ringing me up, and did you know, these days people don't fail Apprenticeships, they just haven't passed them yet! What a load of crap, in my book if they haven't passed then they've failed ... As far I'm concerned his dad can sort him out.
>
> (Operations Director)

The point of significance is the departing gesture by the Operations Director. Essentially, because an employee nominated one of his own family members for the position, then this implied a degree of responsibility for the apprentice's performance. Furthermore, such practices were not confined to a single case; for example, of the employees interviewed, three had been recruited directly because they had been nominated by a friend or family member, and in total eight had nominated other people.

In contrast, labour market pressures for technical and specialist workers led to a very different set of problems, with labour shortages for higher specialist positions. According to the Operations Director, such employees had to be educated to a required standard and have relevant employment experience. What is significant here is that the few difficulties that did occur were not due to a lack of qualified applicants, but due to the fact that when interviewed for employment, prospective chemists had to demonstrate a capacity to add commercial value to the organisation. One supervisor explained:

> Recruitment is really down to line managers these days, and that's right across the company. We say what we need, [Operations Director] gives the go ahead or not, and then I'd say it's very much hit and miss. If you're lucky, you get one out of three that might be very good. One might be mediocre, one might be very bad. The decision to employ someone is not based on technical ability, there's plenty of them, but it is based on, do they fit? Will they actually give something that we don't currently have. If they don't then we don't want them. You're recruiting somebody who is capable of at least two jobs higher, that's the name of the game now. Whether they do that 'two jobs higher job' or whether we have the opportunity for them to do that is another issue, but they have to have the potential or the ability.
>
> (Departmental supervisor)

In summary, for Chem Co. the product market was competitive, although this was because many customers were also competitors engaged in similar activity. It is this type of competition which was a key source of influence, rather than the barriers and/or ease of entry for other organisations. For the labour market, those employees who are central to the future development of products (specialist chemists) are more difficult to recruit, although this is due to selection criteria of Chem Co. itself, rather than any apparent shortage of applicants, and once recruited there is a high retention rate. Against these factors is a combination of internal dynamic processes concerning labour market pressures; in particular, where existing employees nominate potential recruits for less skilled positions, this generated a form of peer group pressure to conform to certain behaviours.

Management style and the psychological exchange

In using established schemes to map management style (e.g. McLoughlin and Gourlay 1994; Bacon and Storey 1993; Purcell 1987), Chem Co. could be seen to display a higher individual than collective dimension of style, with a minimalist degree of strategic integration. For example, Chem Co.

had a non-union works council, individual appraisals and pay reviews, and a variety of communication channels between employees and management. However, as in the previous chapter, the objective here is to go beyond descriptive policies as a potential indicator of style, and seek to assess the impact of managerial *intent* and *action* as an influence. At Chem Co., while a series of policies existed that pointed towards a form of union substitution, the discourse and articulation of management intentions lend themselves to a more subtle form of suppression peppered with a touch of benevolence. The complexity here is that management's preference for a non-union relationship ultimately remained ideological, though often couched in a language of business pragmatism. For example:

> A lot depends upon the nature of the influence from outside the business from certain unions and we're lucky I suppose in that respect, we don't have them worries. You've got national executive committees who are awfully interfering into what's going on within a company ... The T&G used to be terrible because something had been decided somewhere, and then everywhere, up and down the country, it was going to happen in all their members' companies ... Now some local organisations, local trade unions that were capable of saying hang on, that's crap and won't work in their company, and that would be fair representation to me; you don't get that. What you do get is awful interference by people who don't know what's going on in the real business world.
>
> (Operations Director)

At one level, the above sentiments demonstrate a preference for a non-union relationship because of a *perception* of union interference in company affairs. Yet at the same time management evidently understood that remaining non-unionised came at a cost. To quote:

> I mean, for me anyway, I would say it's a personal slagging-off if people came to me and said I want a trade union. The first question in my head would be, Why? ... I'd also be thinking, OK, if I really am that bad, then that's the time for me to go, you don't need a trade union just get rid of me ... If you just want people to come to work to sweat, then yes, the Tories have made it a lot easier and I'm sure there's a lot of sweat shops about, we're not one of them though ... To keep the confidence of people, that it's me they can rely on without a trade union, you've got a lot more work to put in because you've got to sell it to everybody. Once trade unions were the best thing to have in the world, because it was a piece of cake to be a manager. All you'd do is deal with one or two people, you'd end up doing your deal with an area organiser or your shop steward or chapel rep, whatever they are these days, and it's his job then to go and sell it.
>
> (Operations Director)

This draws attention to some of the more explicit behavioural *intentions* concerning management style at Chem Co. In particular, the overall company strategy towards people management and possible unionisation is derived exclusively from the personal experiences of one senior manager, the Operations Director, and this is worth a brief explanation. Several years previous to his current position he was employed as a union official in the printing industry. He was also a highly flamboyant character who took an active (even experimental) role in trying to shape the behaviour of people. In addition to his union background, he had a PhD in social psychology from the Open University which, in his own words, allowed him to understand where workers were coming from. For example he organised a variety of employee discussion and educational forums to create an atmosphere of participatory management. These included such things as outward-bound team building exercises, basic literacy classes (maths and English), leadership skills for supervisors, and even classes in industrial democracy. He was highly supportive of the views articulated by Maslow and Hertzberg, and would use these motivational theories in many of the educational and discussion forums with employees. Significantly, these approaches legitimised a subjective discourse about how people were to be managed. To quote:

> You need to know where I'm from ... I used to be in SLADE, that's one of the older print unions, and we used to say what goes in them days, not the management ... I'm also a divorced catholic married to a jewess, so that tells you a lot about me – you can't have divorced catholics and catholics don't marry jewesses. I was taught by Jesuits and the way Jesuits teach is to make you think and not to accept everything. I'm a socialist, but not like the socialists who think like Blair or Brown, give me Tony Benn over these 'new' labourites any day ... I'm in the business of making things happen that shouldn't happen – a socialist managing director and a catholic married to a jewess ... If people want a trade union they can have one, but I'm going to make sure they persuade me first that it will add something, which isn't going to be easy. I'm not going to encourage anyone to be a trade unionist and at the same time I'm not going to stop anyone.
>
> (Operations Director)

Employees often spoke of the Operations Director as a highly dynamic and likeable character, although a few responses were critical. In a humorous way some people thought he was a bit mad, while many suggested he passionately cared about people and the company. One employee commented:

> [*The Operations Director*] is what you could call a hands-on type of manager ... he's out and about all day, he's here one minute and then when you're looking for him, find he's driving up to Leeds.
>
> (Technical chemist)

Other examples were less complimentary, but nonetheless illustrate powerful images in tracing the sources of management style. One respondent suggested that managers with a like-minded approach to that of the Operations Director would fit in at Chem Co. For example:

> The managers here stick together ... it doesn't matter if one makes a big cock-up, they're always sorted and it's us who end up getting it in the neck one way or another ... there was a spillage this morning which could have been fairly lethal with bromide solutions. Big, big panic stations for a few minutes because one of the barrels split open ... Don't get me wrong, the *Operations Director* was straight on the scene, protective gear and all that, helping out like ... But he knew it was [*name, supervisor*] who screwed-up. When its one of their own, you know, it's all forgotten.
>
> (Process operative)

Another employee commented that the site manager for Leeds had been *moulded in* [Operations Director's] *minds eye*. Indeed, the Operations Director referred to the site manager at Leeds as:

> a local lad [*from Merseyside*] that I've put a lot of patience into bringing along. He knows what's what now, which means I can leave Leeds to him.
>
> (Operations Director)

At Leeds, another employee summed-up similar views articulated by different respondents, that the Operations Director has an extremely strong influence on the way other managers manage:

> We're all managed by a lot of shouting and brawling and then more shouting. The *Leeds manager* gets that from the (*Operations Director*), you see that when they're here together.
>
> (Clerical officer: Leeds)

The patterns of management style at Chem Co. are considerably more dynamic than those evident in Water Co.; although, as reported in the previous chapter, the influence of one senior manager has the potential to significantly shape managerial intent and action. It is tempting to explain such similarity in terms of organisational size, given that both organisations are SMEs. However, the data also indicates that SMEs are far from homogenous, and a combination of other internal as well as external factors would appear to be more important than size per se. At Chem Co. management style portrays a very different set of dynamics. There is a clear and strong rhetoric of caring for workers, although this is caring according to management subjectivity and meanings. There may well be a philanthropic edge to management, but this varies by occupational category as well as location. Arguably, while these intentions indicate a degree of benevolence, the benevolence is firmly controlled (and even restrained) in order to maintain a preferred non-unionised relationship.

Employee voice and the psychological exchange

For a small firm, there existed a broad range of policies connected with employee voice at Chem Co., and as noted above, many of these were a result of the active participatory approach of the Operations Director. These included the employee educational and discussion forums previously noted, team briefings, a non-union works council, individual staff briefings, health and safety meetings, individual appraisals, and daily cell meetings at shop floor level. Given the small social setting at Chem Co., informal dialogue also underpinned voice channels, with line managers and the Operations Director frequently walking the floor and actively speaking to individuals.

It was evident that different forms of communication occurred on a regular basis, in particular the daily cell meetings. However, in terms of the depth and scope for employees to have a say, these mechanisms were extremely limited. For instance, the non-union works council had not met for over a year prior to our research. In addition, when it did meet, this was outside working hours and employee reps were required to attend in their own time. Significantly, the issues it discussed were trivial and shallow. Moreover this appeared to be part of the managerial *intent*:

> The works committee has died here and doesn't exist in Leeds ... The main reason was in that works committee meeting you'd be discussing things like the number of toilets on the site, or whether something was safe or unsafe; very, very rare anything to do with pay ... With pay reviews, I make an announcement now to every site and to individuals, what the pay rise is going to be, so if there's any comeback on that I deal with it. When I introduced things like the safety meeting most of those concerns which came under the works committee disappeared.
>
> (Operations Director)

In terms of the more direct mechanisms for employee voice, workers commented that such practices tended to be haphazard and infrequent. For most employees, monthly team briefings did not occur or, when they did, were ad hoc. While the cell meetings for each production process existed on a daily basis, these were confined to immediate production issues. The main purpose was to reinforce output schedules and targets expected of employees. There was little, if any, scope for upward feedback from workers through these cell meetings.

The argument that these voice mechanisms were shallow in both coverage and depth also emerges from the employee survey. For example, Table 6.1

Table 6.1 Employee voice at Chem Co. (percentage of respondents)

Question/statement	Agree	Not sure	Disagree
In your job do you often inform supervisors that you can do your job well	28	26	46
In your job do you often suggest to supervisors improvements in the way your job is done	74	18	8
I speak to management often about my wages and conditions	15	14	71
Employees are very much involved with management in making decisions in this company	15	3	82
When decisions are taken which affect my pay or work, employee views are taken into account by management	10	14	76
Management communicate changes about work often	27	12	61

Note
N = 67.

shows that 82 per cent of employees disagree that they are involved in making decisions with management, and only 15 per cent confirm they speak to management about their wages or conditions, despite the existence of appraisals and individual meetings for this purpose. Moreover, only 10 per cent of respondents suggested that management actually take account of their views when decisions are made, even though team and cell meetings were cited as one of the main channels to tap into employee ideas.

Taken together, the data suggest that employees were highly dissatisfied with the utility of their voice opportunities, and that in contrast with Water Co., where there were fewer voice mechanisms, but a higher degree of perceived utility, there was an inverse relationship between voice mechanism and its utility. This could mean that employees are aware of managerial intentions to by-pass any collectivised employment relations structures. In addition, at Water Co. informal practices often buffered employees from the harsh realities of an antagonistic and exploitative managerial prerogative, which suggests that a small social setting can be a key factor in modifying the employment relationship. However, in terms of deeper analysis, explanations of management's ability or inability to deliver the deal point to the idea that the perceived lack of voice utility could have represented a source of violation of the psychological contract.

Shop floor relations and employee well-being

It has already been acknowledged that the nature of work and shop floor dynamics are important influences that can mediate and modify work relations. However, as noted in Chapter 3, there is a lack of data with regard to these shop floor dynamics in the absence of a collective intermediary. At Chem Co., observation of these shop floor relations serves to illustrate how labour can act as an agent of change, even in the absence of a trade union.

On entering the shop floor at Chem Co. one cannot help but notice the highly structured and bureaucratised organisation of work, as noted earlier in this chapter. At one level this can be explained by the technical and specialist nature of chemical manufacturing, with detailed health and safety procedures and production-like processes across both plants. At another level, however, certain quality management practices appeared to over-bureaucratise the nature of work, and this led to a number of tensions and reactions from different employees. For example, Chem Co. had adopted various British and international quality procedures several years earlier, and one consequence of this was a significant increase in paperwork as part of the quality assurance programme. Interestingly, for the professional employees in laboratories this emerged as a particular bone of contention. Ultimately, these various quality processes were regarded as managerial interference in employees' professional judgement. Similar expressions of concern were also noted from skilled maintenance engineers, with concerted attempts among employees to circumvent such additional job requirements.

According to the employer, the structured nature of work at Chem Co. was also at the root of some of the more recent employee relations issues. One policy was to integrate people across different parts of the organisation, in the hope that this engendered greater commitment through job rotation and job enlargement. Indeed, as noted earlier, the site manager at Leeds was selected by the Operations Director from those suitable for promotion who were based on Merseyside. Similarly, other employees had been moved across sites and placed on different shifts. Of twelve employees interviewed, five had been moved either between sites or onto different production lines and one employee commented:

> My job is maintenance engineer and I worked at Leeds for six years ... I'm now based here [*Merseyside*], and that decision was taken about three months ago.
>
> (Maintenance engineer: Merseyside)

This objective of workforce integration, no matter how admirable the intention, appeared to be at the root of on-going shop floor tensions and served to undermine any notion of a favourable psychological exchange, and the same employee commented:

> there was no asking for volunteers. I've been married eight months, a new baby on the way. I'm not too pleased I have to travel from Leeds to Merseyside now, every day, getting home sometimes at 7 or 8 o'clock at night.
>
> (Maintenance engineer: Merseyside)

These shop floor issues may be minor, or even appear trivial, yet for employees they were seen to affect management's ability (or inability) to deliver the deal. What is crucial here is not so much the detail of managerial imposed regulation, (important as it is for this study) but also the context in which these issues are socially constructed and negotiated, and how they impact on employees' perceptions. For example, the same maintenance engineer quoted above explained that he had become increasingly dissatisfied with managerial *inaction* with respect to his particular circumstances. This employee explained that even though he was recently married and his wife was expecting a new baby, such concerns were handled with a degree of dismissiveness by management. To quote:

> [*The Leeds manager's*] response was he has to do it, he's married with kids, and gets on with it, and that's the only answer I got between getting told I had to move, and actually coming down here.
>
> (Maintenance engineer: Merseyside)

The same employee later commented about raising the matter at a more senior level:

> I've had two meetings with [*Operations Director*] over this move, and to be fair, he's always been very nice and sympathetic ... he's spoke to Joan [*employee's wife*] over the phone about it because she's pregnant and worried ... and I've been told I will go back to Leeds, but exactly when we're not sure, a lot depends on some restructuring that's taking place.
>
> (Maintenance engineer: Merseyside)

Other respondents explained that when employee relations matters were raised at supervisory level, there seemed to be an unofficial policy of inaction in terms of providing an answer. Examples included requests for odd days off at short notice, with no definitive answer until it was often too late. One employee commented:

> you would get more of a response from guards at Colditz! That's no joke that. I've been here eight years now, at 51 I'm coasting downhill, I can say I'm off next Wednesday morning – you have to tell them what for like, but that's it, nothing more. I don't wait to get the nod to stay off. Some of the lads though, they can be their own worst enemies, they keep asking is it OK, is it OK.
>
> (Process operative, paints line)

Some of the psychological indicators of employee well-being were also captured at Chem Co. through an employee survey, the results of which are shown in Table 6.2.

Table 6.2 Psychological indicators of employee well-being at Chem Co. (percentage of respondents)

Question/statement	Agree	No opinion	Disagree
The values of this company are similar to my own personal beliefs	40	48	12
There are good career and promotion prospects in this company	35	33	32
I am willing to stay with this company if offered another job on similar terms and conditions	58	15	27
I am loyal to my employer	33	32	33
There is a great deal of tension at my workplace between management and employees	80	12	8
I am willing to put in a great deal of effort for the success of this company	77	14	10
I am satisfied with my pay and conditions	3	19	78

Note
N = 67.

As with Water Co., the results are somewhat complicated. Given some of the qualitative data reported above, it can be noted that 80 per cent of all employees report that there is a great deal of tension in their workplace. At the same time however, almost the same number (77 per cent) agree that they are willing to put in a great deal of effort to help the company be more successful. Nevertheless there appears to be a strong indication that employees at Chem Co. lack a sense of well-being and an appropriate psychological exchange. For example, while 40 per cent of employees say that they share the same values as the company, just over one-third (35 per cent) commented they have good career and promotion prospects and one-third feel they are loyal to their employer. Nevertheless, 27 per cent of those surveyed said they would be willing to leave Chem Co. if offered another job on the same pay and 78 per cent report dissatisfaction with pay and conditions, both of which are indicative of a low sense of well-being on the part of employees.

Worker attitudes to trade unions

As with each of these non-union case study organisations, the attitude of workers towards trade unions was explored in a number of ways. Of all four case studies, workers at Chem Co. ranked highest with regard to their support for the general principles of trade unionism. However, as can be seen from Table 6.3, and as was also found at Water Co., there was an important difference between ideological and instrumental attitudes towards trade unions.

Table 6.3 (Non-union) employee attitudes to unions at Chem Co. (percentage of respondents)

Question/statement	Agree	No opinion	Disagree
Trade unions provide necessary protection for employees generally[a]	68	21	11
Trade unions can be beneficial to employees[a]	58	31	11
Trade unions are generally a good thing for workers[a]	90	9	1
There are benefits in having the views of all employees represented to management[a]	96	4	0
Trade unions are, on the whole, sensible[a]	91	9	0
A trade union would make my job more secure in my company[b]	66	28	6
My pay/conditions would be improved if a trade union represented my interests in this company[b]	81	13	6

Notes
N = 67.
Factor analysis revealed two factors, a = ideological union factor; b = instrumental union factor.

For the most part those employees who were older and had longer employment tenure (in particular, those with over four years' service) tended to be more positive on both the ideological and instrumental scales. Workers with either a graduate or post-graduate qualification were also more supportive towards unions than workers with no qualifications.

Of the employees interviewed, only one was a current union member and two had prior experience of a unionised relationship with a former employer. The respondent who was currently a union member belonged to the Amalgamated Engineering and Electrical Union (AEEU) and this appeared to be linked to a sense of craft identity. That is, he had remained a union member regardless of where he worked since completing an engineering apprenticeship twenty years before. As he explained:

> I'm in the AEEU now. We all moved in with the electricians' union and … [*membership*] is part and parcel of my life. Part of my lifestyle as a tradesman.
>
> (Maintenance engineer)

When asked to comment on management's reaction to possible unionisation, he suggested:

> Oh, that'd cause some worrying for them [*management*], wonderful for me *but* they won't entertain one, that's been said many times has that.
>
> (Maintenance engineer)

Other employees were in general agreement that there is an implicit understanding that management will resist unionisation, possibly resulting in reprisals for employees. As one employee commented:

> it all comes down to whether you fear for your job, and that's been a thing for people here over the years.
>
> (Process operator)

The same employee later couched these views within a clear them and us divide between workers and management:

> [*unionisation*] would depend a lot on the quality of the managers, and they are part of their own set-up, they look after one another, but there's no one to look after us in that way. I think we have people in positions of authority who abuse their position and get away with that abuse ... their word is always going to be stronger than someone else's off the line ... another view is like a check against any abuse.
>
> (Process operator)

Thus the experiences of workers and the particular style of management articulated by the Operations Director sent clear and unambiguous signals to workers about what trade unionism could mean. Discussions with managerial respondents could easily lead to the view that Chem Co. is perhaps a lucky non-union company; lucky in that unionisation had never emerged as an issue in the company. However, at least one employee told a different story, which broadly fits the pattern of union avoidance using a range of semi-collectivist voice arrangements. For example:

> Someone in the past tried to start a union and they [*management*] violently opposed it. We had the works committee instead, and that was about 6 or 7 years ago as far as I understand.
>
> (Chemist)

In comparison to Water Co., employees at Chem Co. were more supportive of unions, both ideologically and instrumentally, and one explanation is that the structural features of the relationship resembled a rudimentary form of collective participation, albeit on management's terms. Indeed, management were unequivocally anti-union, and they also sought to substitute as well as suppress potential triggers to unionisation as an influence on possible employee mobilisation. Thus the most striking similarity between Water Co. and Chem Co. and its effects on employee attitudes to unions is the role of management as a barrier. Significantly, one of the more interesting issues to emerge thus far is that union substitution and/or suppression are not bipolar opposites. Both were present in different degrees in both companies.

Summary and conclusions

Chem Co. has been categorised as benevolently autocratic, which is due to the effects of a number of key sources that mediate and moderate employment relations. Management had a tendency to impose its own rules and procedures, although at the same time they sought to socially construct the image of a participatory type of strategy towards employees. This equated with a surprisingly wide range of voice mechanisms, although deeper analysis shows these to be rather superficial in terms of their breadth and coverage. In effect, an increase in the number of mechanisms does not equate to workers having a greater say on matters that affect them. Indeed, it can give rise to significant symbolic tensions and violations of the psychological contract. In particular, formalised and bureaucratised structures sat uncomfortably with the informal relations of a relatively small social setting at each of the two sites.

In addition, and as was also reported for Water Co., a distinctive them and us climate could ultimately be traced to the people management preferences of a key senior actor. However, in the case of Chem Co., the flamboyant (if not entertaining) character of this person resulted in a very different dynamic to the relationship than was the situation in Water Co. At Chem Co. there is little doubt that management believed they cared for workers, even though at times they had difficulty in convincing workers of this. In many ways this suggests that strategies for people management can be interpreted and transmitted in very disjointed ways, particularly at shop floor level. These tensions were evident across different occupational groups, which included process operators, as well as professional and technical employees. While Chem Co. has been labelled benevolently autocratic, at times the benevolence was also guarded and restrained. Thus stylised employment relationships can be more complicated, uneven and contradictory than static images would have us believe. For this reason, at Chem Co. there was little point separating substitution from suppression. In the minds of workers, the two went hand in hand.

7 Merchant Co.

A case of manipulative regulation

Introduction

This chapter describes the third case study firm. This is Merchant Co., a national organisation supplying materials to the building trade, which has just under 150 outlets across the UK. The company has a long history in the builders' merchant market, having started trading in 1936 as a Glasgow-based family enterprise. Its growth occurred mainly in the 1970s, with a strategy of acquisition of smaller building suppliers, and in the 1980s started to venture into home DIY products through its established branch outlets. As a whole the organisation employs 2,800 people; a reduction from a peak figure of over 4,400, which occurred from a reorganisation and a redundancy programme that took place in the mid 1990s. The focus of our study at Merchant Co. is based on the company's head office site in North Yorkshire, which employs 120 people covering distribution, warehouse staff, contract fitters, clerical and retail employees, as well as the company's personnel and management functions. Thus, unlike the two previous case studies, Merchant Co. is a very different organisation in terms of its size, structure, centralised management activity and occupational categories. As with the previous case studies, the key features of the employment relationship at Merchant Co. are set out within the conceptual framework given in Chapter 2. This is then followed by an assessment of the factors influencing the relationship in terms of the nature of work, management style and employee voice.

The employment relationship: key characteristics

In this organisation, the employment relationship is classified as manipulative because:

- Regulation of employment is managerially controlled, often using the sanction of employment insecurity, although as we shall see, there is considerable variation across the organisation.
- Overall, non-unionism is a downstream consideration in the company's strategy. This state of affairs is a matter of *intent* on the part of management, and is associated with the disposability of and dependency on

different groups of workers, which was regarded as an important factor in organisational survival.

- Employee voice arrangements are mostly direct, but with a very low level of voice utility expressed by workers.
- A general climate of employment insecurity pervades the relationship, with a poor psychological exchange and minimal feelings of employee well-being.

Influences on the employment relationship organisational context

Structure and the nature of work

Merchant Co. first began trading in 1936, by supplying materials to the building trade. The company witnessed considerable expansion during the late 1970s through a strategy of acquisition, and by the early 1980s Merchant Co. had established a national network of outlets for both building supplies and DIY retail outlets. The 1980s also witnessed a restructuring in both operations and human resource policy. In 1983 the company's head office, incorporating the northern distribution and warehouse centre, was located on one site with a centralised personnel function. During this time Merchant Co. adopted a non-union strategy according to circumstances and market conditions, in which union de-recognition occurred in a small, but nonetheless strategic way. That is, a number of different unions (TGWU, GMB, AEU) were de-recognised when Merchant Co. acquired smaller suppliers, which, prior to a merger or take-over, had been unionised.

The *Builders Merchant Journal* described the company as the fourth largest supplier to the construction trade, with a particularly strong presence in Scotland and the south-west, relative to the company's size. The core business activities include supplying materials to trade customers; plumbers, heating engineers, house-builders, housing associations, local authorities and a constellation of sub-contracting organisations. There is a light and heavy trade classification to the company's business activities, where the former denotes plumbing materials (ceramic tiles, copper tubing, taps, bathroom products, radiators etc.) and heavy business is synonymous with materials for house building, for instance, bricks, plaster, cement, aggregates and ironmongery. At the time of this study, Merchant Co. had a 5 per cent share of a £7 billion builders' supplier market. It is of particular interest that in a predominantly fragmented industry with around 600 builders' merchants, Merchant Co. stood out as one of the largest single companies.

The mid 1990s however, witnessed an economic slump in the construction and building trades and as a result, a redundancy programme reduced the numbers employed by the organisation from 4,440 to 2,800. In 1995 the company was floated on the stock exchange to raise capital to meet a borrowing deficit, and by 1998 the organisation registered an annual turnover of £374 million (13.5 million pre-tax profit). Interestingly, in floating the company on the stock exchange, Merchant Co. publicly articulated non-unionism as a virtue to prospective share buyers, emphasising that *only a very small number of employees are members of trade unions.*[1]

The organisational structure is shown in Figure 7.1. The largest single site is the company's head office, which also incorporates a warehouse, distribution centre and showroom. It is at this head office, employing 120 staff, that the research took place.

There are a number of qualifications in relation to how the above structure translates into the organisation of work. Within some of the separate functions there exists a mix of occupational and skill groups. For instance, within the distribution depot there are groups of skilled employees, such as warehouse personnel and delivery drivers, but also skilled fitters and builders. The latter group tend to work on contract for other organisations, for example, on local authority housing projects and as noted by Rubery *et al.* (2001), the boundaries of the employment relationship for these workers can be somewhat blurred. While in strict legal terms these employees have a contract of employment with Merchant Co., they are continuously based at, and often directly answerable to the managers of other organisations. Moreover, this varies according to contract type, location and duration. These employees could be fitting kitchens in local council homes and managed for the most part by local authority managers, after which they might work on other large-scale projects elsewhere in the region, the most significant of which was for the prison service.

There is an almost equal split between the numbers of men and women employed at the head office, although for retail outlets in other parts of the country the majority of staff are women. In total there are 148 branches, and although these vary in terms of actual size, from over 100 employees to others employing as few as five, the typical branch employed about 20 staff. It is also common for most branches to have a showroom to display products

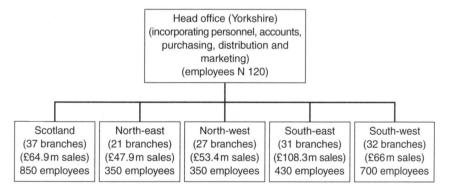

Figure 7.1 Organisational structure of Merchant Co.

and to employ different occupations; for example, clerical employees, drivers and contract fitters.

However, the male–female divide is not equal across all occupations. At the head office site, all warehouse employees, contract fitters and delivery drivers are men, while all clerical and retail assistants are female. Of the latter, 6 per cent of the 120 employees work part time (all women), while the remainder are full-time employees. As a whole the organisation is characterised by a relatively young workforce, and this is also reflected at the head office site. Around 45 per cent of all employees are under 30 years of age, with another 30 per cent aged between 30 and 40. The reason for this is that a recent severance package was more attractive to older employees with longer service. Consequently, the vast majority of employees (74 per cent) have been employed with the company for less than seven years, and 30 per cent of these for less than three years.

The nature of work varies considerably for employees at the head office site. Warehouse employees receive orders from clerical assistants, and load and unload vehicles, and several warehouse employees are licensed fork-lift truck operators. The bulk of the younger warehouse employees are known as pickers, who basically retrieve smaller items from stock for customers who collect orders at the depot. There is also a physical divide between clerical and warehouse workers, with the former located in an office on the next storey of the building. Delivery drivers tend to be located with warehouse workers, and regard themselves as one cohesive group, while employees based upstairs are considered as a separate group; even viewed as a distant part of the company. This may be because those located upstairs include senior managers and Directors of the company. Here there are several managerial functions: accounts, marketing, buyers, contract managers and the centralised personnel function. Within personnel there is a senior personnel manger and several personnel officers (for example, specialists for health and safety). However, the senior personnel manager does not have a seat on the company's board.

For a non-union organisation there appeared to be a surprising degree of regulation and job demarcation between occupations. Overall, each occupational group remained a separate unit with very little, if any, flexibility between jobs and this seems to be a matter of conscious management choice. For example, warehouse pickers, drivers or contract fitters were discouraged from entering the showroom because this is the place for customers. Similarly, very rarely was it observed that clerical employees would enter the warehouse. Instead, paper orders were dispatched and sent to the loading bay, where the warehouse supervisor would lodge the order on the computer system, then leave it on an in-tray for warehouse staff to sort and retrieve items from stock. It was also observed on several occasions, that when large deliveries of warehouse stock arrived shortly before lunch or shortly before clocking off time, these would be left until after lunch and on some occasions drivers asked to return the next day for unloading. Where areas of flexibility did appear to exist, this related to opportunities to work overtime. This occurred for example, on warehouse stocktaking, which would occur on a Sunday or a Saturday afternoon, or when large orders were required for some of the main contracts to fit kitchens and bathrooms for housing and prison service projects.

Product and labour markets

The products and services supplied by Merchant Co. were classified into three types. Light side business, which referred to goods such as plumbing materials, bathrooms, kitchen units and tiles for both corporate (e.g. builders) and individual customers (e.g. DIY enthusiasts). Heavy side business related to those materials such as bricks, cement and building aggregates sold mainly in bulk to corporate customers. Finally, contract services, where Merchant Co. supplied both the goods and labour to construct and/or refurbish large-scale projects for certain clients, such as local authority housing projects or various prisons around the country. The latter accounted for about 30 per cent of all business and the only area of market growth for Merchant Co. Extensive training and investment had been directed at regional and in some cases branch managers, as these were regarded as key managers in direct contact with external project clients. The heavy and light side areas accounted for about 20 per cent and 50 per cent of business respectively, with the greatest loss occurring in heavy side supplies.

As with Water Co., to a large extent market pressures were often beyond the immediate control of company management and a range of exogenous factors were responsible for this state of affairs. For example, the weather (which affected construction patterns), the demand for new houses and/or government changes to interest rates, which affected mortgage rates, all had an influence on the demand for Merchant Co.'s products. It was these external factors that were frequently cited by managerial and employee respondents as a source of competitive pressure that resulted in the redundancy programme mentioned earlier, which was particularly focused on heavy building supplies. In this respect it is important to note that Merchant Co. had experienced the harsh realities of economic conditions to a greater extent than any other organisation studied. This resulted in a shift in market strategy towards contract support services, rather than the previous emphasis on supplying building materials, and this had a number of implications for employment relations. Moreover, it indicates the extent to which management regarded certain occupations as commercially crucial, while others were seen as disposable, with greater dependency on those employees who work for the most part at a distance from the company and based alongside employees of other organisations. Given their direct links with contract clients, another implication was that Merchant Co. targeted regional and store managers for training and development purposes. For example:

a good branch manager can be what we call a good trader, they know what the market place is like, they know what they can get for the business, and the fact they can go out and get contracts has been a bedrock for us when the market [*for building materials*] is at rock bottom.

(Manager, internal auditing department)

However, not all employees were regarded in the same way. In some areas of the company growth provided new opportunities for workers, while in other parts of the company insecurity and instability were much more common. The personnel manager explained that because of market conditions in the south of the country, coupled to some extent with the preferences of the regional management team, promotion and career opportunities were more favourable for employees than elsewhere in the company:

Take the south east, which seems to have a lot of opportunities for promotion, and that Regional Director is a believer in going for a younger team, so it gives people within that region hope if they're on the younger side.

(Personnel manager)

In contrast, other parts of the country experienced the opposite, with the spin-off effects of the redundancy programme leaving a lasting mark of insecurity on those who remained with the company. As one employee commented:

we've been lucky in DC [*distribution centre*] with the stuff for branches ... supplying them for their own contract jobs has actually kept us going but it's always in your mind whether we're next.

(Warehouse employee)

Another employee, whose job was to visit branches on a regular basis, recalled:

I've been in some offices and girls (sic) are in tears because it's getting closed ... it's not nice auditing them and they're all losing their jobs ... it definitely brings it home to you.

(Clerical employee, internal audit department)

The people management implications of this were much broader and related to areas of recruitment and labour retention against a climate of adversity. For example, since the redundancy exercise, labour turnover had been slowly increasing from what had been below 4 per cent for several years, to around 10 per cent shortly after the redundancy situation. The personnel manager explained the reaction thus:

We did start to have some exit interviews and I know people who were offered jobs elsewhere took them, first, I think, for the money [*and secondly*], things were very very uncertain after we'd lost some on the severance.

(Personnel manager)

One employee reflected the same sentiments:

Some have left because they felt they were next to go anyway ... [*the redundancy has*] made everyone scared and ... we all keep an eye open for something else, just in case.

(Clerical employee, marketing department)

This also affected the retention of key employees such as contract fitters and those regional managers who were capable of negotiating and maintaining contract services, whose positions were not in jeopardy because of their centrality to areas of market growth. For example, skilled fitters and joiners represented a more transient labour pool than other employees based at warehouses or in showroom outlets, particularly when contracts meant they had to work away from home for lengthy periods of time. Similarly, quite a few of the branch managers cited earlier as good traders because they could negotiate new client contracts, were at times in high demand by other companies, and several were poached from Merchant Co.:

Branch managers who are on the ball with the requisitions, they know what's what when it comes to costings. They've been doing this for years, they can really work for whoever and we have lost a few good managers that way.

(Manager, internal auditing department)

In summary, the market environment for Merchant Co. represented several contradictions, but on balance had a high degree of influence in shaping the employment relationship, particularly through economic threats of insecurity. While many of these market difficulties were at times beyond the control of management, little attempt was made to try and ameliorate the sense of insecurity or perceived loss of any psychological exchange, even for those workers who remained with the organisation after the redundancy programme. As a result, many workers actively sought alternative employment.

Management style and the psychological exchange

In terms of the general proxies for management style, Merchant Co. could be characterised as having a traditional HRM approach. There is a highly centralised approach to policy formation through the personnel function at the head office, although many local managers exercise a considerable degree of freedom in terms of policy implementation, including the selection for redundancy and in areas such as recruitment, discipline and dismissal. There also exists a range of individualised HR policies suggesting a high degree of strategic integration, such as the centralised personnel function, devolved managerial decision making and formalised policies published extensively in a company-wide personnel handbook.

In addition to these proxies, an attempt was made to analyse managerial *intent* and style at a deeper level of discourse and practice. This managerial *intent* is most evident when probing respondents about the motives and rationale for non-unionism as a preferred managerial approach. As noted earlier, union de-recognition had occurred when Merchant Co. purchased small companies during a period of acquisition, and this reinforces a very strong anti-union flavour to how management prefer to manage. For example:

> This company will not go into dealing with a union, not ever I'd say. About two years ago was the last one when we took over [*a firm*] that had a trade union and we ... de-recognise[*d*] them ... Staff were told they'd be better off under [*Merchant Co.*] which is a non-union based company ... and [*the law*] makes it less argumentative to do that now than it would have been 10 years ago.
>
> (Personnel manager)

Further critical scrutiny of the methodological indicators of strategic integration and what it can mean in practice can also paint a very different picture to that of a traditional HRM type employer. Despite the range of formal HR policies, several of these fell short of those recommended in ACAS codes of practice. For example, discipline was stated in the personnel handbook to be a tool to modify employee behaviour, indicating a punitive rather than corrective approach. In addition, equal opportunities and health and safety regulations all fell short of ACAS recommendations, and in some health and safety areas, such as job risk assessments, these were completely absent. Perhaps more significantly, line managers simply by-passed and blocked policies, which in turn appeared to shape the notion of (mis)trust as a central component of any psychological exchange. As the personnel manager commented:

> Tribunals galore here. Tribunals galore. We have two personnel officers dealing with them on a full time basis these days. A lot is to do with unfair dismissal or unfair selection ... It could be where management have done things that did not follow the proper procedure or go through proper channels ... managers think its simple: 'well, I don't believe him, I'm gonna dismiss him'. They don't take into account how long he's been with you, the reasons, there may be personal reasons. The

problem is getting them to go through this department [*personnel*] ...
some managers don't even wanna deal with us and think we're a waste
of time and space. Some managers out there are a bit, 'I know what I'm
doing' sort of attitude.

(Personnel manager)

What is significantly different here from either the Water Co. or Chem
Co. case studies is the interdependency between the centre and other outlets
across the country; and indeed, between the different functions at the head
office site. Essentially, the approaches to managing people varied considerably by department, and as one manager explained:

there's really a very wide spectrum. Some managers have staff meetings,
some are keen on wall charts showing the graphs on how well they are
doing and some tell employees about health and safety issues or get
manufacturers in to give training on products that we stock. What
makes it very difficult is you've got those who just don't seem able to
confront a situation and they never adopt the direct managerial
approach.

(Manager, accounts department)

These differences indicate the complex and variable nature of management style and its impact on employment relations. For some workers we
interviewed, underpinning the centralised structures there existed a more
informal exchange at departmental level. At the head office, clerical
employees were more favourably disposed towards management than were
warehouse staff, even though both occupational groups were employed in
the same (notional) team. This suggests (as was also the case at Water Co.)
that an attachment to a work unit or immediate supervisory structure is an
important dynamic of the relationship. However, for many employees, management style was often couched in a language of mistrust and them and us
divisions, as the following employees comment:

I think they put a lot of trust in us as staff in the department that I'm
in, but that wouldn't necessarily be the case downstairs [*i.e. warehouse*].

(Clerical employee, marketing department)

[*employees*] probably trust their own branch manager, but they certainly
don't trust head office management is the feeling I get very much.

(Joiner/contract fitter (working on housing client project))

I know there's some [*managers*] who can take a general dislike to staff
and then find any excuse to discipline them and at the end of it sack
them ... and others are much nicer in how they speak and that.

(Clerical employee, accounts department)

In contrast to the previous two case studies, a range of hierarchical managerial philosophies, rather than any measurable indicator of strategic integration, appeared to influence management style. This implies that while management style can be shaped by board level strategies, the ideologies of certain managers are important sources of modification that cannot be easily disregarded. One employee summed-up the variability of line management style (and arguably, their power) thus:

> If your gob doesn't fit then you know not to apply for posts that might come up ... it'll be sorted anyway.
>
> (Clerical employee, typing services)

Employee voice and the psychological exchange

Merchant Co. had several employee voice mechanisms. These ranged from team briefings, individual communications, appraisals, a company newsletter, noticeboards, and e-mail communications for clerical employees. It was also suggested to us that informal communication is preferred, which was underpinned by a belief that employees always have the opportunity to speak to management direct. However, there was reliance on e-mails for office staff but not for drivers, warehouse employees or fitters working on client contracts. For the latter, internal memos and company notice boards were used extensively to disseminate information. Merchant Co. also had a staff newsletter, entitled *Good News–Bad News*, which reported areas of commercial success as well as areas of weakness. Significantly, none of these voice mechanisms sought to consult employees and they therefore represented little more than a series of top-down information channels. The personnel manager commented:

> reliance [*is*] on supervisory views ... We don't give people much choice ... it's implemented in here through the board, personnel or line manager teams ... the message [*is*] that the rules are important and should be used.
>
> (Personnel manager)

It was also evident that there had been no recent initiatives in the area of employee involvement, and the voice channels that did exist had remained the same for some time. More importantly, many of the mechanisms had lapsed or appeared to be bolted-on to existing structures. Some managers carried out team briefings infrequently, while others conducted staff meetings on a more regular basis. In short, the use of these voice mechanisms correlated almost perfectly with the preferences and choices of different managers across the organisation.

Given the limited range of consultative techniques, it is thus important to explore employee perceptions of how well they can articulate their voice with management, and summary frequencies from the employee survey are provided in Table 7.1. If voice utility is related to how well employees perceive that management deliver the deal, then the psychological contract is certainly found wanting at Merchant Co. For example, there was no respondent who said they had the opportunity to speak to management about wages. While a small majority (45 per cent) said that management communicated about change often, only 7 per cent felt involved and only a very small number (6 per cent) believed management took their views into account.

Shop floor relations and employee well-being

As with previous case studies, the day-to-day relations at workplace level can capture a great deal about the salience of employment issues and extent of employee well-being and associated psychological exchanges. On several occasions workers at Merchant Co. appeared suspicious of management, which indicates a pattern of low trust for certain occupations. Both the personnel manager and several employees commented about the high level of petty grievances across the company. All respondents interviewed were aware of the discipline and grievance procedure, and three of the twelve employees who were interviewed had direct experience of raising a formal complaint with management. Examples were given of alleged unfair treatment for overtime (warehouse employees) and an appeal against a supervisor's disciplinary warning (clerical employee for lateness). Interestingly, all respondents rated the role of the personnel function extremely positively,

Table 7.1 Employee voice at Merchant Co. (percentage of respondents)

Question/statement	Agree	Not sure	Disagree
In your job do you often inform supervisors that you can do your job well	3	33	64
In your job do you often suggest to supervisors improvements in the way your job is done	25	33	42
I speak to management often about my wages and conditions	0	18	82
Employees are very much involved with management in making decisions in this company	7	13	80
When decisions are taken which affect my pay or work, employee views are taken into account by management	6	15	79
Management often communicate changes about work	45	21	34

Note
N = 39.

and their concerns were directed specifically at line and departmental managers. For example:

> I've been given two warnings with the lates ... I'd ring-in and explained that ... [*the*] childminder was sick and [*I*] had to travel to my parents ... [*the personnel manager*] was very understanding and had more time to listen than my manager ... that helped me a lot with the worrying and all.
>
> (Clerical employee, marketing department)

One of the more recent shop floor issues, which occurred shortly after the redundancy exercise, concerned the introduction of teams. The objectives were explained as twofold: to create a more fluid communication flow from the head office down to the branch networks, and second to engender a greater sense of identity and commitment to the idea of the team as a unit among staff. At the distribution centre this included an attempt to merge previously demarcated job roles of warehouse personnel (pickers and fork-lift truck operators) and clerical support staff (buyers and purchase order clerks). However, the impact of this was problematic. As noted earlier, a physical and psychological demarcation existed between clerical employees and warehouse staff, who were located in different parts of the distribution centre. This militated against the philosophy of a team spirit and the very idea of a team was notional, because employees continued work in different locations, with only occasional interactions.

The implications of this were further complicated when a new Just-in-Time (JIT) system was introduced alongside the team based structures. What this meant is that warehouse employees were no longer required to perform regular stock-takes of goods held in the warehouse, and in effect, the JIT ordering system made the task of manual stock-taking redundant. The net effect of this was to streamline clerical tasks and stock orders, while simultaneously eliminating overtime earnings for warehouse employees; a practice that had long been regarded as part of their implicit contract. One employee summed-up the situation as:

> there's hardly any overtime since we're on to Just-in-Time. We used to get every second Sunday [*overtime*] ... that's all done upstairs [*clerical employee*] through what they call the ledger system ... print-outs tell them what's needed every day.
>
> (Warehouse employee)

The single issue of JIT illustrates the dynamic and contested nature of shop floor relations at the distribution centre. Management introduced the JIT system, evidently with efficiency savings in mind, though this clearly had other implications that shaped behaviour and was bound up with the introduction of a new team based structure. Critically, there had been no consultation with affected employees and the outcome represented a division between warehouse employees on the one hand, who preferred the older manual system with subsequent overtime, and clerical employees who recognised the benefits for their own work tasks.

However it would be misleading to assume there existed distinct sub-cultures or inter-departmental divisions among employees across the organisation as a whole. Prior to the new team-based structures there were close-knit groups of workers who appeared to share a common identity (as was also found at Water Co.). This was particularly evident among drivers and contract fitters, who frequently spoke about the crack with their work mates. Significantly, those included in this definition of work mates were employees directly employed by a client organisation with whom they worked each day, for instance, local council trades people and builders. In addition, clerical employees commented on social evenings after work with colleagues, which pointed to a sense of occupational solidarity and/or departmental identity.

As with our other organisations, research at shop floor level provides the opportunity to assess some of the psychological indicators about employee well-being in the context of social exchange. Of all the organisations in our study, employees at Merchant Co. were the least satisfied on a range of indicators. For instance, as can be seen from Table 7.2, only one-third of all workers agreed that the values of the company are similar to their own beliefs, and given the redundancy programme, it is not surprising that only 20 per cent believed the company provide good career and promotions prospects. Of course, these results may be obscured by a climate of insecurity, which might also explain why less than half the sample (44 per cent) were willing to stay with the company if offered another job elsewhere. Also, given that only just over half of all workers surveyed felt loyalty to their employer, the notion of a favourable psychological exchange is certainly found wanting at Merchant Co.

In terms of modifying the relationship, these results point to a need to recognise the role of group cohesion, based on occupational identity. Significantly, despite the large size of Merchant Co., there existed a strong undercurrent of informal, close and friendly relations within separate work units, rather than any obvious identification with the organisation per se. Indeed, for fitters employed by Merchant Co. but working away on client sites, to all intents and purposes the employment relationship was *permeable*, and the boundaries that delineate colleagues and co-workers of other organisations with Merchant Co. as the employer, were increasingly blurred.

Worker attitudes to trade unions

Given that a series of manipulative aspects to people management are evident at Merchant Co., it is not surprising to find that workers remain

Table 7.2 Psychological indicators of employee well-being at Merchant Co. (percentage of respondents)

Question/statement	Agree	No opinion	Disagree
The values of this company are similar to my own personal beliefs	33	15	52
There are good career and promotion prospects in this company	21	8	71
I am willing to stay with this company if offered another job on similar terms and conditions	44	19	37
I am loyal to my employer	55	14	31
There is a great deal of tension at my workplace between management and employees	35	36	29
I am willing to put in a great deal of effort for the success of this company	67	11	22
I am satisfied with my pay and conditions	42	19	39

Note
N = 39.

unorganised, particularly when it is considered that there were managerial threats of an economic stick, should unionisation be considered.

As can be seen from Table 7.3, workers gave a mixed bag of responses when asked about their attitudes towards trade unions. While views about unionism are generally positive, employees at Merchant Co. are second only to those at Delivery Co. in terms of their level of support for trade unions (see Chapter 8). Perhaps more importantly, a distinction between ideological and instrumental union attitudes similar to that already noted in both prior case studies was found to exist. At Merchant Co. workers generally thought trade unions to be a good thing, though there was less agreement about whether a union could improve employment security (40 per cent), or pay and terms and conditions (48 per cent).

As with other companies in our study, these attitudes cannot be extrapolated from the specific environment experienced by workers themselves. As noted earlier in the chapter, an important contextual factor is the message that Merchant Co. sent to prospective investors that the company is proud is of its non-union status. Indeed, this was even portrayed as a commercial advantage, and similar views were articulated by the personnel manager:

We're a non-union based company and we will not go into a union environment ever, that's important here and for the board very much I'd say.

(Personnel manager)

Table 7.3 (Non-union) employee attitudes to unions at Merchant Co. (percentage of respondents)

Question/statement	Agree	No opinion	Disagree
Trade unions provide necessary protection for employees generally[a]	71	16	13
Trade unions can be beneficial to employees[a]	36	50	14
Trade unions are generally a good thing for workers[a]	65	22	13
Are there benefits in having the views of all employees represented to management[a]	83	14	3
Trade unions are, on the whole, sensible[a]	54	28	18
A trade union would make my job more secure in my company[b]	40	33	27
My pay/conditions would be improved if a trade union represented my interests in this company[b]	48	32	20

Notes
N = 39.
Factor analysis revealed two factors, a = ideological union factor; b = instrumental union factor.

Interestingly, at Chem Co. the cost of avoiding triggers to unionisation emerged through a labyrinth of non-union voice arrangements, together with the proactive style of the Operations Director. However, this was not an area of concern for Merchant Co. Departmental and regional managers often promoted the stick of redundancy, market turbulence and insecurity rather than the carrot of substituting union demands. In short, given the market situation, managerial power and prerogative was legitimised and the sanctions employees could subsequently experience were significant and real. As one departmental manager (surprisingly) commented:

> By virtue of the fact that there is no trade union representation here and management don't have to accept one, means the employees really do suffer under the management at the end of the day ... they don't have the wherewithal to mount any alternative case.
>
> (Departmental manager: head office)

These experiences of employees provided some explanation of the differences in ideological and instrumental attitudes towards unions, with the main barrier to unionisation being a combination of managerial action and the prevailing socio-political climate engineered from previous government (anti-union) laws. For example:

> the position is that unions haven't the clout they used to have ... this lot [*management*] know they don't have to listen to unions, so they won't.
>
> (Warehouse employee)

> I think for staff a union would probably be good, but I don't think the
> management would allow it because some of the changes that they keep
> making I'm sure would not stand up to trade union pressures at all.
>   (Clerical employee, internal auditing department)

As with other case studies, it is evident that management prefer a non-
union relationship and behave in such a way as to maintain a union-free
organisation. Similarly, employees appear to be largely supportive of the
general principles of trade unionism, although less so when the role of
unions is contextualised within their immediate work environment. What is
perhaps more complicated is that compared to the two previous case studies,
there is a degree of dissonance in the reactions of departmental managers. At
least one departmental manager (along with employees) thought trade
unionism had a constructive contribution to make in terms of modifying
the relationship, though this is certainly the exception. The variance of
managerial approaches indicates that a simple dichotomy between union
suppression and/or substitution is more complicated. Moreover, Merchant
Co. appear to avoid unions by manipulation and tactical use of the prevailing market environment, and this can help in understanding why employees
feel lacking in terms of their psychological needs and wants.

Summary and conclusions

Merchant Co. represents an interesting non-union case study for several
reasons. In contrast to both Water Co. and Chem Co., it is a considerably
larger and nationally dispersed organisation. At the surface level at least, the
company displayed some of the hallmarks of what has been referred to as a
traditional HRM model, although on closer examination this was shown to
be somewhat misleading. It had also been non-unionised for over 50 years,
and there was some evidence of union de-recognition. Moreover, Merchant
Co. illustrates the close linkages between market circumstances and employment relations outcomes under harsher economic circumstances. Overall,
Merchant Co. is categorised as a manipulative type of organisation. As
Wood and Kelly (1988) have noted, management does not revolve around
the issue of workforce control per se, because it has circumstances that
compete for its attention. For Merchant Co., unionism and non-unionism
were for the most part *de facto* downstream considerations and the ways in
which the employment relationship was modified, and how wider business
decisions were made ultimately served to consolidate the non-union status of
the organisation. In turn these decisions legitimised managerial power over
employees, although it is unlikely this was to any great extent the main strategic objective or primary concern confronting the organisation during a
period of economic uncertainty.

8   Delivery Co.

A case of sophisticated human relations?

Introduction

Delivery Co. is the final case study organisation reported in this book. It is an interesting and valuable non-union case study for a number of reasons. The organisation differs considerably from those considered in previous cases. It is part of a large foreign-owned multinational, with a wide geographical spread across the UK. Delivery Co. also employs a number of very different occupational groups, has its own separate human resource (HR) function and is engaged in a competitive service sector market. Importantly, it is characteristic of those large non-union employers that pay above average market rates of remuneration, to give what many would describe as an attractive employment package with good terms and conditions. In addition it has a favourable psychological contract and utilises a range of individualised HRM policies and practices that might substitute for the demands for unionisation. In short, Delivery Co. is reminiscent of the larger and more sophisticated household name non-union employers. As with the previous case study chapters, the key features of the employment relationship at Delivery Co. are identified and this is followed by an assessment of factors that appear to shape and modify the relationship.

The employment relationship: key characteristics

In relation to some of the key characteristics of non-union employment relations, as depicted in Chapter 2, Delivery Co. could be located towards the sophisticated human relations end of the continuum (see Figure 2.2). For a variety of reasons however, there are questions about the extent of such sophistication. Its key characteristics are:

- There is a high degree of involvement, information-sharing and systems of employee voice used across the organisation.
- People are regarded as strategic assets and accordingly, a competitive and individualised employment package is offered to core employees, although often at the expense of peripheral workers.

- A culture of informality is used to create a friendly and trusting work-place environment, against which unionisation is said (by its management) to be unnecessary. Nevertheless, employees support the principles of collective representation.
- According to employees there is a favourable psychological exchange. However, this also appears to cultivate a dependency on the organisation.
- A more pleasant work environment does not remove the tensions and ambiguities associated with a them and us division in the employment relationship.

Influences on the employment relationship organisational context

Structure and the nature of work

Delivery Co. commenced trading in 1969 in America as an air and freight transport service. By 1974, the company was established on a global footing, and is regarded as the market leader for door-to-door parcel deliveries. It has a presence exceeding those of American Express or Coca-Cola and company assets and profits are significant by any measure. Delivery Co. employs 53,000 people worldwide, with 3,500 employed in the UK, where this case study took place. It has over 2,000 separate sites in 227 countries, owns over 12,000 vehicles and 200 aircraft, and it continues to grow.

While employees and customers generally regard Delivery Co. as an American-owned company, the actual source of ownership is complex. It includes literally hundreds of other holding companies based in different parts of the world, for example different American, French, Dutch, German and Japanese holdings are listed as significant shareholders. While all commercial branding, technical infrastructure and to a large extent general HR policies are identical across the globe, legally, Delivery Co. in each country is registered as a separate business, with profits retained by a holding company in the West Indies. In practical terms, Delivery Co. World-wide is divided into two principal divisions: Delivery Co. Airways, serving all US locations; and Delivery Co. International, serving all locations outside the USA. Operational decisions for all non-US business are taken at its head-quarters in Brussels. Human resource policies are modelled on a Delivery Co. World-wide handbook, although a variety of practices can be independently determined in each host country to reflect market conditions and legal requirements.

In the UK, where this study took place, all business activity is focused around two international hubs (East Midlands and Heathrow). These hubs are linked to regional distribution centres (known as Gateways), which then feed a network of individual stations that collect and despatch parcels throughout the country. For Delivery Co. (UK) there is an HR function located at the London hub, where there is an HR director, although he does not have a seat on the company's (UK) board of directors. Employee relations matters are directed from both the Brussels and UK head offices. However, station managers have some degree of autonomy in relation to modifying the relationship to reflect local market factors; for example about pay, benefits and approaches to recruiting staff. There is a European Works Council, to which employees elect one of their peers as the UK representative. Each station mirrors three core business functions, which are shown in Figure 8.1. These are: customer services, clerical support and operations.

In commercial terms, Delivery Co. (UK) has experienced consistent and impressive growth, with the most recent turnover exceeding £230 million with a net annual profit of £26.6 million. The company also believes that sophisticated human resource management (HRM) policies and practices are linked to company performance, at the core of which is said to be a culture that espouses the virtues of openness, innovation, creativity and employee involvement. Highly publicised examples that praise individual employees in company literature include: the delivery of a pair of socks for the All Blacks rugby team, a curry delivered from a London restaurant to Moscow, Prince Charles's cap and gown for a University ball and a new set of drums delivered to a U2 concert. Employees are strongly encouraged to put forward their own suggestions that will promote Delivery Co. as a dynamic and vibrant organisation to the outside world.

Given the size and variety of occupations at Delivery Co., the nature and organisation of work is highly variable. Occupations include delivery drivers (known as couriers), administrative and clerical staff, call centre operators (known as agents), supervisors, team leaders, and employees who sort parcels

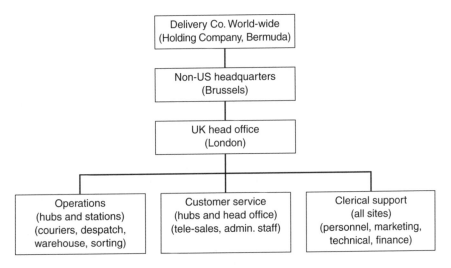

Figure 8.1 Organisational structure of Delivery Co.

(known as operations staff). For each of these jobs, the nature and organisation of work is fundamentally different, as might be anticipated in such a large multi-divisional company.

Couriers are regarded as key customer contact staff. They collect and deliver parcels direct to clients, and are required to conform to high standards of customer service and appearance. They are also responsible for different stages of a parcel's delivery for clients that they might never meet on a face-to-face basis; for instance, responsibility for the transit of items between sorting offices, international hubs or another delivery station. Thus their jobs are much more than the simple delivery of parcels. They have to record, code and track parcels that can be delivered anywhere in the world. One of the most significant aspects of this work is the use of tracking and surveillance technology in vehicles, so that a driver's location can be pinpointed at any time. For instance, messages are conveyed between a centralised despatch function and the driver, and in this way, changes to delivery details or new notification about parcels for collection are conveyed direct to the driver on the road. Equally important, some of the more important clients are provided with Internet technology designed and patented by Delivery Co. so that they can track their parcel anywhere in the world; on a plane, in a warehouse or in the back of a van.

For couriers this means that technology has important control implications. For example, in order to meet deadlines set by customers and the centralised despatch function, most couriers spoke of breaking legal speed limits as a normal part of their work. Furthermore, the role of courier as delivery driver was much more complicated because of the technology used to record and send messages while out on the road, and as one of them commented:

> When we are actually collecting a shipment you are sorting the paperwork out there, you have to do it then because there's that much pressure on you. I'm quite fast because I've been doing it for five years. I know a lot off by heart. It's not hard, but when you are in a rush it can be easy to make a mistake ... everything is worked to a time-scale. You have to be in one place at a certain time and then you have to get to the next place.
>
> (Courier)

In contrast, the organisation of work for call centre agents was very different. The East Midlands hub is also the location for the company's call centre operation, employing 1,000 people (mostly women). Employees work in teams of approximately twenty, and each team is divided into smaller units of five. Each team has a set geographical area from which calls are fed automatically. There is an electronic message board (as was also evident at the call centre in Water Co.) informing employees of their team performance (calls answered, calls waiting etc.). All employees have to follow a carefully worded telephone salutation, and team leaders and supervisors periodically monitor employee calls. Each agent has to answer 70 calls per day, which does not take account of the nature of the customer query or problem to be dealt with. Exceptionally, lengthy queries (known as traces) can be used to trade-off below target results, which are often left to the discretion of team leaders. One agent explained the nature of her work thus:

> It's a very heavy workload. You have obviously a lot of targets you have to meet, like your calls, you're monitoring how many calls you take, also you have traces to deal with. You have got [*to receive*] 70 calls ... and also get your 5 out of 5 bookings to reach your target to get the bonus ... Every month they check randomly five bookings, so you have got to have them 5 right each month to get your bonus ... which is Next vouchers or the like.
>
> (Call centre agent)

Unlike the situation at Water Co., employees were not physically separated from their co-workers by partitions. Another difference at Delivery Co. was a flatter managerial structure and in practice, lead agents and team leaders were engaged in the same work as other call centre employees. Indeed, there was a great deal of emphasis placed on team working and employee involvement at Delivery Co.'s call centre, whereas many of the associated people management practices such as team meetings, email communications and newsletters were all absent at Water Co.

The nature of work for other groups of employees was also different. Clerical staff at stations would manage specific client contracts; that is, clients who have regular shipments on a daily basis. This work involved arranging collections and monitoring price and tariffs, as well as general administrative duties particular to a station or office. Operations staff sorted parcels to be delivered direct to customers, or to be shipped to other stations or hubs. Many of these employees were temporary and part-time, often recruited from among students. The reason for this is that there was considerable fluctuation in demand for their services, depending on customer shipments, seasonal variations and time of day. Arguably, because the work is expected to be casual and short-term, the nature of relations was very different and more exploitative than for other categories of worker. For instance, at some (but not all) of the stations these peripheral employees usually worked towards the end of the day, when more and more customer parcels would arrive for sorting and onward shipment. Typically, the shifts for casual and temporary employees were 4pm–10pm during the week, and Saturday morning. This meant that temporary employees had very little interaction with other (core) employees. In some stations they were also separated from office, courier or sales staff and worked in a loading/sorting bay. Moreover, hourly rates of pay for temporary and casual staff were between 20–35 per cent below those of comparable permanent grades.

One of the more common features of work across these different occupations was the nature of supervision. While this differed to some extent between couriers and call centre agents, it was evident that management sought to empower staff to a greater extent than was the case with other organisations. In general, employees appeared to have a degree of discretion about how they carried out their work as long as they met set targets, and it was noticeable that supervisors and team leaders refrained from adopting a direct overseeing approach. Of course, this may be because the technologies used by Delivery Co. allowed for a more distant form of supervisory surveillance than was evident at any other organisation. Indeed, management would frequently stress the importance of technology in people management activities. As the HR director commented:

> Customer expectations are changing as they are in every market. They want more, they want more sophisticated interaction with our people, and we're putting more technology in place so our people have to learn to use some quite complex functionality now than they ever had to in the past.
>
> (Human resources director)

Employees were not unaware of the functional control aspects arising from technology. Both couriers and call centre operatives often deployed their own tactics to avoid managerial interference or circumvent the intensity of constant surveillance. For example, couriers would find space and time in their schedules for occasional unofficial breaks and use traffic congestion to their own advantage.

Market factors

The market for parcel delivery was subject to intense competitive pressures, with price cutting one of the main market characteristics. Nonetheless, this case illustrates the choices and options available to management, and how these relate to people management policies and practices. Unlike some of the other case studies, Delivery Co. promoted quality, customer satisfaction and reliability as its main differentiator in a competitive market place. The HR director explained:

> The market is a very vast market, everything's offered as overnight for Europe ... So just around the place people get energised by achieving very tangible results which are more often than not only very short-term results ... in addition to all that, we do play on the humour a lot, make our service a very warm, customer quality friendly service to stay ahead in a vast and fast market.
>
> (Human resources director)

At the level of separate stations, where managers had more direct experience of day-to-day customer interactions, the emphasis on a warm and friendly customer service was less apparent. In particular, there was tension between centralised control and the opportunity for local managers to respond to specific market conditions, particularly on price setting. A manager at one station reflected the issues encountered at other stations:

> We try and stay ahead of the competition basically by trying to counter any moves that they may make ... We do keep our ears and eyes open as to what [competitors] are doing and try to keep one or two steps ahead of them ... I'm not allowed to touch the price. The actual prices are set as per the tariff but I have a certain limit at which I can discount to the main competitor in my area. Above that, discounts go higher up the field to an area director.
>
> (Station manager)

Interestingly, at more senior levels such local issues were well known, as the HR director commented:

> There are guidelines as you'd expect. [*Station managers*] can't paint their vans blue with green logos; salary scales and a grading process have to keep on track with budgets. But within those parameters they can hire, they can fire, they discipline as necessary. To me these are line managers' decisions.
>
> (Human resources director)

The importance of creating a particular commercial image over and above price competition, and with certain local managerial freedoms, cannot be overstated. Staff who had direct customer contract such as couriers, or office sales teams and call centre agents would frequently receive training on how to project Delivery Co.'s market strategy to customers, and a regional manager for the north of England summed up the objectives of such employee training and induction programmes:

> We don't offer overnight deliveries. We can't make that guarantee, our competitors give that guarantee but we know they can't meet it because there's so much that can go wrong. We guarantee delivery and what we can guarantee is it's in the same time as any competitor; better, more efficient and more professional and that's where we've stood out. We do overnights most of the time but it's not to be given in any guarantee and we explain that to customers. You don't get [*Delivery Co.*] vans running on baldy tyres for example, which is what we compete against a lot of the time.
>
> (Regional manager)

Crucially, promoting a more professional and reliable service than competitors (instead of price) was a conscious strategy that had very specific people management implications. Training and induction was one such outcome and another is arguably the extent of employee surveillance mentioned earlier; for example, the courier who explained that breaking legal speed limits was required if customer deadlines were to be met. Nevertheless, the response of finding space in schedules for unofficial breaks was also a relief valve to cope with the intensity of market pressures. In this respect a similarity with Chem Co. can be noted. That is, the way Delivery Co. responded to market pressure is its way of countering the ease of market entry for competitors, which illustrates the idea that management often has a range of choices which can impact on people management practices.

In addition to product market influences, conditions in the labour market also relate to employment relations. Delivery Co. had a very low turnover of staff, which fluctuated between 2 and 5 per cent, depending on the occupation and geographical locality. Staff turnover was higher in the south of England and the call centre than at any other individual station or sorting office. However, two surprising findings were particularly noteworthy. One was the mix of both formal and informal recruitment and selection methods. Delivery Co. used a multitude of selection techniques, including detailed psychometric and attitudinal testing to match employee and organisational values. These tests may or may not be used to screen potential trade unionists, although this could not be confirmed from those interviewed. On the other hand, and running alongside these sophisticated selection techniques, there existed an informal network of contacts through employees, which were similar to those found at Chem Co. For example, workers would receive gifts and small cash incentives when they nominated family or friends who were later successfully recruited after they had been screened and selected. One courier explained how he came to work for Delivery Co.:

> My brother-in-law put in a word for us!
>
> (Courier)

Similarly, in the larger East Midlands call centre employing over 1,000 people, another employee remarked:

> My sister actually worked here and she phoned and said do you want to come for an interview, because a new cohort had been set up and some people had not turned up. I came and had an interview and was offered the job. I actually started the following Tuesday.
>
> (Call centre agent)

While such practices are not in themselves bad or suspect – indeed, labour turnover at both Delivery Co. and Chem Co., who also used informal methods of recruitment were relatively low – one potential implication is that employees are recruited and replaced on a like-for-like basis. This may have equal opportunities implications (males recruit males etc.) but it also implies an informal screening process. If existing employees have very little or no experience of unionisation, then there is a probability that this may also apply to family members. While this is of course speculative, the descriptive data from the employee survey shows that 70 per cent of those sampled had no prior union experience.

In summary, while the actual market for parcel delivery is characterised by ease of entry for competitors, especially for local and national deliveries, the promotion of a professional customer service over and above price cutting shows that a range of employer choices remain available. Some of these choices required very specific people management policies, such as customer service training and organisational induction and socialisation, and to some extent, these were strongly integrated with recruitment and selection techniques in response to labour market conditions. In addition, there is the core-periphery divide, which was noted in the previous section. It could be the case that a sophisticated link between people management strategies and market factors was used to consolidate the non-union status of Delivery Co.

Management style and the psychological exchange

In accordance with the indicators for mapping management style considered in Chapter 3, Delivery Co. could be categorised as having a *Strategic HRM style*. Of all the organisations studied, it ranks highest in terms of its strategic integration and has an extensive range of individualised approaches to the employment relationship. In general terms, the company is regarded as a good employer that provides an attractive employment package, shows empathy and concern for individual employees and has an open and inclusive approach. Some of its integrated policies include: individual pay reviews together with performance related pay, individual appraisals, incentive bonuses, suggestion schemes and the use of a variety of employee voice techniques. However, for the purposes of explanation, the objective here is to go beyond these indicators of policy and seek to assess the importance of style in terms of actual practices and managerial *intent*. At Delivery Co. management style contributed to a favourable psychological exchange, although the way in which this was interpreted and experienced across the organisation varied.

At a surface level there appeared to be a close alignment between corporate aims and people management activities. In many smaller organisations informality and friendly relations are often spontaneous and organic, but at Delivery Co. there was a recognition that the large size of the organisation could counter notions of friendly relations, and so a concerted attempt was made to engineer an informal approach to people management. The HR director explained the overarching style thus:

> We do play on the humour a lot … a very light heartedness [style].
> We're a fairly big organisation and we're getting bigger. We want to
> keep the small identity … [*Station managers*] are responsible for morale
> in their station. Most stations will have days out every six months and
> they'll go to Alton Towers. Whole stations will come out on a Sunday
> and there's quite a lot of spirit within stations which I think helps lots
> of small bits work well, on the whole it tends to gel quite well together.
> You don't feel part of a big name which can be faceless.
>
> (Human resources director)

While the head of HR carried the title of director, he did not have a seat
on the company's (UK) board of directors. Nevertheless the HR function
appeared to be highly proactive in helping to engineer this friendly sense of
identity. For example, employee performance targets (i.e. at the call centre
and courier delivery schedules) were established at head office and filtered
down, thus eliminating supervisory manipulation. Training for the organisation as a whole was also designed at the HR function level, and the HR
director and other senior HR managers took part in road shows travelling
the country to visit different stations. To some extent the language and discourse involved was important. The company used the term human
resources instead of personnel, employee empowerment would be used
instead of involvement or participation, and culture was often interchange-
able with the style of people management. Both HR and station managers
frequently talked of managing staff in the context of market influences and
worldwide corporate values. For example:

> We very much see our culture [*e.g. team spirit, openness, innovation, creativ-
> ity, humour*] as a commercial differentiator … We put a lot of effort into
> the op's supervisors and the station managers to communicate various
> issues. Sometimes that breaks down and you know that you don't get
> some messages right through, [*supervisors*] just get lost … There's
> almost a scan proof system which incorporates the HR advice, confiden-
> tial focus groups and it helps, not always, it helps them stop getting
> too lost.
>
> (Human resources director)

Examples of placing workers at the centre of the corporate approach were
also evident in company documentation. For instance, the first two items
listed in the corporate mission placed the role of managing staff at the heart
of company performance. Moreover, expressions such as employees are a core
corporate competence and success comes through people, feature prominently in company literature. Similarly, there existed a detailed staff handbook which not only outlined employee responsibilities, terms and
conditions, it also emphasised a desire for people to achieve their ambitions
through innovation and creativity. While much of the literature could be

little more than company propaganda, it appeared to send a strong and clear message to employees about how the organisation values people.

However, a content analysis of this documentation revealed that in terms of being a guideline for managerial action, it fell short in several ways. For example, while the discipline code emphasised a corrective rather than punitive approach, its was barely consistent with ACAS recommendations. That is, although there was an appeals process, there was no explanation of the precise stages, time-scales or managerial levels of decision making. Similarly, health and safety policies referred to employer and employee responsibilities under the 1974 Health and Safety at Work Act, but there was no reference to European Directives incorporated into British law over the last decade. Finally, while there was an equal opportunities policy, contravention of which was listed as an offence in the discipline code, this was little more than a statement about eliminating outdated attitudes, with no explanation of what constituted an offence, or how managers should deal with such incidents. Thus on balance, a great deal was left to line management interpretation in carrying out policy objectives.

The impact of management style and *intent* on relationship outcomes is always difficult to evaluate. At Delivery Co. style appeared to consolidate and even legitimise the non-union status of the company. At a senior level, the official line was that the company is not anti-union, but rather pro-individual and the relatively attractive employment package with higher rates of pay compared to competitors, good terms and conditions and fringe benefits were cited as rendering the triggers to unionisation irrelevant. For instance:

> [We] couldn't see what a union could add. We've got extremely good employee relations, we benchmark our employees with normal groups and with other companies across the UK and we come out best. What more could a union add to that, we seem to be fair, our turnover's well below the industry average … If there are issues around health and safety and around things like discipline then [*Delivery Co.'s*] got processes and policies to tackle them as well.
>
> (Human resources director)

However, managerial intent can also be inferred from other actions. Even though union representation had never been an issue for Delivery Co., management felt obliged to consider the implication of statutory provisions for union recognition in the Employment Relations Act (1999). As the HR director explained:

> I'd be surprised if there was a ground-swell of interest from staff for these [*union recognition laws*] … We're not too sure how to tackle them yet. We understand a bit more, we'd put some effort in to handle it our way because we think it's the right thing to do … I can see that where you haven't got a particularly progressive employer, wages rates are

below the market, you've got health and safety issues and a lot of incon-
sistencies and inequities. In our environment you've only got better
working conditions, better pay conditions.

(Human resources director)

What is significant here is that statutory support for union recognition
evidently influenced the underlying approach to people management. This
seems to accord with Gall's (2003a) hypothesis that where there are legally
enforceable rights for workers, latent employer opposition to trade unionism
is likely to transform itself into more subtle forms of tangible union substitution. Thus management at Delivery Co. actively sought to understand what
union recognition *could* mean, should the issue become a reality at some point
in the future. In this way, the discourse associated with management style
was ultimately anti-union, albeit in a more subtle and covert form.

Against these broader indicators of managerial intent, variations in style
were also evident at local level. In particular, the meanings and interpretations ascribed by different respondent groups demonstrates a more complicated and uneven picture at workplace level. For instance, in some of the
smaller stations, different managerial approaches resulted in significant
sources of tension and disagreement. Employees spoke of a lack of clarity
between what may be viewed as the overall corporate approach on the one
hand, and the styles adopted by local (station) managers on the other. For
example:

The style of management is very them and us, between the couriers and
the top management team ... It's not we don't want to get on with the
management, but they say one thing then do another – e.g. a national
conference on a Sunday. Everyone that goes will be paid double time.
What actually happened was lots of people give up their day off only to
be told on the Tuesday after that no overtime will be paid. Say one
thing, but then the station manager [does] the other.

(Courier)

While the latter indicates a distinction between senior and local managers, other employees regarded the specific personalities of local managers
as important, which suggests that line managers are important agents in
shaping and influencing managerial intent. For example, although the call
centre has an employment environment that could be identified as problematic (Fernie and Metcalf 1997; Bain and Taylor 2000), many employees
appeared to support the managerial approach, and the use of team meetings,
a friendly style and social interactions outside the office were particularly
favoured. In contrast, at a number of other stations employees were less complimentary about specific managerial styles, because more aggressive managerial tactics appeared to dominate. As one clerical employee explained the
situation in her office:

Showing people up I think is the worst thing about managing people in this place. [*Supervisor A*] is really nice. If he's got something to say to me he will tell me quietly and so he's not showing me up, but [*Supervisor B*], he will just come out with it and show you up in front of everybody. He's the main problem in here. [*Supervisor B*] says you're too fat to wear those trousers. That's what he's like ... then he will say I'm sorry for saying that, but I can't forgive him. When [*the regional manager*] is here it's different, everybody just gets on and more work's done because she's so much nicer in how she speaks to people.

(Sales employee (station))

In summary, there was dissonance about how management style was articulated and experienced at Delivery Co. At a broader, more conceptual level, managerial intent appeared to contribute towards a favourable psychological exchange. At the same time however, as might be expected for such a large organisation, local managerial freedoms can and do distort the application of a given style or approach towards people management. Thus it is difficult to trace the effects of management style in any particular organisation. At times the underlying approach was carefully engineered, shaped by market concerns as much as a latent anti-union prerogative. At other times personal traits and localised conditions show a less sophisticated and harsher managerial style. Moreover, style is not a static preference of how to manage employees, but a highly disjointed, uneven and contradictory phenomenon, even in an organisation that may be described as one of the more pleasant non-union settings.

Employee voice and the psychological exchange

As might be expected for a company characterised as a sophisticated non-union employer, a wide range of both formal and informal employee voice mechanisms existed. These can be categorised as top-down communication channels, together with upward problem-solving techniques. With the exception of a European Works Council (EWC), the methods for employees to receive information and comment on matters affecting them at work all tended to be direct and individualised. The range of mechanisms included staff newsletters, magazines, individual appraisals, senior managerial road shows and extensive use of email communications. The range of techniques classified as upward problem-solving included team briefings, quality circles, staff focus groups, attitude surveys and staff suggestion schemes. The EWC was a more recent initiative for Delivery Co. (UK). While other operations across Europe were similarly non-unionised, employees in France and Germany had requested an EWC several years previous to this study. In response, the headquarters in Brussels decided that all European operations would come under the remit of the EWC, in part so that the system could be managed without competing requests, and also because management recognised a number of benefits from their own experiences of works councils in other EU countries.

In practice, the methods for team briefings and quality circles appeared to be utilised across all the sites visited, although with some variation in terms of the depth and scope of information disseminated to employees. At the East Midlands site, for example, employees approved of team briefings and regular email communications, but also commented that on occasion work pressures and the demands from customers often meant that regular voice mechanisms did not always occur. In addition, at some of the smaller stations, informal day-to-day communications with the station manager/supervisor were viewed as more important than the formal structures such as team meetings. In general, a linkage between management communications and some notion of a psychological exchange was evident among many of the employees interviewed. For example:

> I think it's all quite good here ... They send you emails and thank you for jobs well done and for all working hard, or if we've had an enormous amount of telephone calls in the day, they will say, well done ... They are only little things I know, but I've never had anything like that before.
>
> (Call centre agent)

However, receiving information can be very different from the opportunity to have a say, and it was evident that the frequency of some of the more consultative-type of voice channels was neglected. In the larger call centre, for instance, customer demand and work pressures often meant that team meetings did not occur, while in the smaller stations employees approved of the more informal day-to-day conversations with supervisors and managers as a voice channel.

In assessing the utility of employee voice, as well as the incidence and range of techniques used, the employee survey sought to capture worker perceptions about the value of such mechanisms in practice and this is shown in Table 8.1. Interestingly, despite the existence of various techniques, the survey data further reinforces the conclusion that the opportunities for the employees to have a say on matters that affect them at work remained rather limited in the scope and depth of issues covered.

Table 8.1 also shows a mixed picture in terms of the perceived utility of employee voice at Delivery Co. For example, over 70 per cent of the sample disagree that management often communicate information about changes to work, with 50 per cent of the respondents saying they do not feel involved with management when decisions are taken about their work. Only a minority (23 per cent) reported having the opportunity to speak to management about their wages or conditions. Significantly, despite the range of employee voice techniques, workers at Delivery Co. were less satisfied on some of these scales than employees at Water Co., where it was reported in Chapter 5 that there was an absence of voice mechanisms.

Table 8.1 Employee voice at Delivery Co. (percentage of respondents)

Question/statement	Agree	Not sure	Disagree
In your job do you often inform supervisors that you can do your job well	43	20	37
In your job do you often suggest to supervisors improvements in the way your job is done	66	26	8
I speak to management often about my wages and conditions	23	30	47
Employees are very much involved with management in making decisions in this company	33	17	50
When decisions are taken which affect my pay or work, employee views are taken into account by management	38	22	40
Management often communicate changes about work	20	9	71

Note
N = 109.

Shop floor relations and employee well-being

Given the overall size of Delivery Co., analysis of day-to-day shop floor relations was often complicated and uneven. At the head office or call centre, for example, employment issues were fundamentally different from events reported at the smaller stations. To some extent this might well be anticipated in an organisation as large and fragmented as Delivery Co. At the same time, however, the range of day-to-day relations also illustrates the diversity of people management, and the salience of some of these key issues is explained.

One particular issue was the attempt to socially engineer a distinctive corporate culture that permeated shop floor relations, of which some of the main features have already been noted in relation to management style and employee voice. As noted, in the smaller stations employee voice was more a matter of general day-to-day conversation, whereas in the larger hubs and call centre, different teams were encouraged to come up with their own social activities at work, such as inter-team games and charity fund-raising events. The HR director approved of this as a way to promote humour and a fun side to work. Of course, while these activities can be a form of social control (Grugulis *et al.* 2000) they also acted as a release-valve for employees from the pressure and stress of call centre work.

A second area associated with shop floor relations that resonates well with notions of employee well-being and psychological exchange was much more apparent at the smaller stations, rather than the larger call centre or international hubs. In particular, there was considerable disagreement among employees as to the ability and/or willingness of management to handle issues of concern to workers. While the specifics of certain issues varied across sites and occupations, areas of concern tended to focus on the intensification of work and/or changes introduced by local managers. For example, at one station the requirement to attend new Delivery Co. training courses at the behest of station management led to considerable tensions among part-time employees. Several of them commented that management had a lack of understanding of the particular concerns of part-time workers, many of whom were women with family commitments. Interestingly, the issues were resolved not by management, but through a sense of solidarity among co-workers at the station. For instance, full-time employees would offer to take the next training course when it was too difficult for part-time employees to do so. One part-time worker explained:

> I haven't gone yet and Angela [*another employee*] volunteered for my place cos she knows how difficult it's going to be and how upset I've been over all this ... I just can't seem to get it through to [*supervisor A*].
> (Operations employee (station))

At another station, employees reacted to a particular issue about safety shoes, which demonstrates that areas of tension and ambiguity existed in other parts of the company. Briefly, couriers we interviewed explained that they had raised a complaint about the corporate uniform code. The issue was that the code did not include safety shoes for couriers, although it did for operational employees, and that both occupational groups handled the same packages. The grievance had been unresolved for some months and couriers eventually took their own form of resistance by refusing to drive fork-lift trucks while working at the station:

> You're not supposed to wear training shoes; you have to wear the company issued ones ... safety shoes are now a big bone of contention. If you're picking up heavy parcels you should have them, all the people who drive the stacker truck or op's on the processing bench have them, so a lot of the couriers have decided we won't use the fork lift truck for that reason ... It's just like an agreement between the couriers ... We've asked for them and it's always getting looked into. The thing is sometimes they can't and other times they just won't sort it. Any uniform that's purchased comes off the station budget so they try to keep the budget to a minimum ... if it's always getting looked into it's never gonna come out of the budget, is it!
> (Courier)

In addition to the diversity of shop floor relations, and how these appeared to feed into notions of employee well-being, the employee survey also provides evidence of broader patterns from across the organisation as a whole. In terms of favourability of employee attitudes, Delivery Co. ranked the highest of all the companies in our study. As can be seen from Table 8.2,

Table 8.2 Psychological indicators of employee well-being at Delivery Co. (percentage of respondents)

Question/statement	Agree	No opinion	Disagree
The values of this company are similar to my own personal beliefs	70	14	16
There are good career and promotion prospects in this company	76	5	19
I am willing to stay with this company if offered another job on similar terms and conditions	65	11	24
I am loyal to my employer	82	8	10
There is a great deal of tension at my workplace between management and employees	52	12	36
I am willing to put in a great deal of effort for the success of this company	86	8	6
I am satisfied with my pay and conditions	64	14	22

Note
N = 109.

a significant number of employees (70 per cent) report that the values of the organisation are similar to their own beliefs, perhaps suggesting a linkage between the various selection practices noted earlier and the human resource policies of the organisation. In terms of management delivering a psychological contract, it is noteworthy that 76 per cent of workers believe there are good career and promotion prospects, with 82 per cent saying they are loyal to the company and 64 per cent feel satisfied with their pay and conditions.

In summary, the picture at Delivery Co. is one where employees appear to be more positively disposed towards the company than in the other case studies. What is significant here is that a level of approval towards the company seemed to exist amidst areas of disagreement and tension between employer and employee, reflecting the uneven and dynamic nature of relations across a large multi-divisional organisation. It is perhaps appropriate at this point to ask how these issues related to employee attitudes towards trade unions.

Worker attitudes to trade unions

As with the previous case studies, questions about trade unions gave rise to mixed responses. Importantly, workers at Delivery Co. were the least supportive of trade unions in all the case studies. While this can perhaps be expected in the light of the general literature about so-called sophisticated non-union employers, it does not mean that attitudes were negative. Indeed, as can be seen from Table 8.3 many workers displayed a very positive orientation towards trade unions. For example, 58 per cent thought trade unions

Table 8.3 (Non-union) employee attitudes to unions at Delivery Co. (percentage of respondents)

Question/statement	Agree	No opinion	Disagree
Trade unions 'provide necessary protection' for employees generally[a]	58	30	12
Trade unions 'can be beneficial to employees'[a]	38	40	22
Trade unions are generally a good thing for workers[a]	60	31	9
Are there benefits in having the views of all employees represented to management[a]	78	17	5
Trade unions 'are, on the whole, sensible'[a]	54	31	15
A trade union would make my job more secure in my company[b]	33	31	36
My pay/conditions would be improved if a trade union represented my interests in this company[b]	44	30	26

Notes
N = 109.
Factor analysis revealed two factors, a = ideological union factor; b = instrumental union factor.

provide necessary protection, are generally a good thing for workers (60 per cent), and 78 per cent believe there are benefits in having the views of all employees represented to management.

What is also important is that there was a difference between instrumental and ideological support, as was found in other companies in our case studies. For instance, one-third of respondents believed a trade union would make their job more secure, while 44 per cent commented that a trade union could improve pay. However, these figures are much lower than those found at any other case study and the only response with statistical significance was for employees with longer employment tenure (over four years' service), who were marginally more supportive in general terms. Graduate employees expressed a more positive instrumental attitude towards unions than non-graduates.

As with the other case studies, the environment in which these attitudes are formed and shaped can be an important explanatory factor. As noted earlier, the HR director stressed that Delivery Co. is not an anti-union employer per se, but argued the case that a trade union was irrelevant because a range of individualised HR policies and practices promoted fairness and consistency. To some extent employees appeared to support the notion that a favourable psychological exchange existed, although a number of tensions and ambiguities were found at different locations.

Most of the workers interviewed tended to contextualise their attitudes about trade unions in relation to their experiences at Delivery Co., which suggests that management are an important source of influence. For example, many employees re-iterated the importance of the market environment when asked about trade unionism. In contrast to Merchant Co., where an economic stick was evident in relation to possible unionisation, at Delivery Co. the softer messages communicated by management were much more subtle and seemed to have percolated down the organisation. For example:

> Basically, in the industry that we're in, I don't think we can afford to go into that sort of union thing. We have got to be flexible and flexible enough to suit our customers' needs … And if that can't be done due to union regulations then we would go backwards rather than forwards.
>
> (Operations employee (station))

> The fact is we are governed by our customers and we tend to recruit and do things on what the client wants. It's not a bad working environment, it's not like a factory where it's dirty or filthy, we get free coffee, we have a laugh, there's a good environment. If people have problems they say so, they can be re-trained if they need it. If we need help we can have help, so at the end of the day I don't think unions are necessary or help with the client needs for the direction of our industry.
>
> (Call centre agent)

In addition to this impact of market pressures on trade union values, other employees sought to rationalise the benefits of non-union voice channels as a substitute for unionisation. These feelings can be summed-up by the remarks of one employee thus:

> I don't think we need a union, you can always go to somebody. If you are not happy with your manager's decision then you go to the big boss, and they don't mind you doing that.
>
> (Call centre agent)

Of those employees interviewed, no respondent was a current union member, though several had experience of a unionised relationship with a former employer, and this prior experience seemed to shape their perceptions about the relevance of union organisation. A few suggested that a trade union presence could actually counterbalance managerial control, while others made reference to the idea that a union could help articulate employee views without any one individual being singled out. Most recognised that management would be resistant to the idea of unionisation.

> I don't think [*management*] would be too happy with unions. Any qualms or anything they could just turn round and say to us, no it's like

this. If a union is involved then they have obviously got to sit and listen to what they have to say, which can make you feel a bit better knowing someone will do that for you

(Clerical employee (station))

[*Delivery Co.*] don't believe in unions, they think they can handle their own employees. I think it would be a good thing personally because they are there to look after you and nobody else, where the management basically want more packages being sent and more money making.

(Operations employee (station))

The majority of couriers would appreciate a union. It would save them standing and arguing with supervisors over certain aspects, their routes and jobs and that.

(Courier)

A final issue that emerged from employee interviews is the inter-relationship between union attitudes and management style. To some extent this suggests that the boundaries between union suppression and substitution are not separate, but in fact interact and vary according to circumstance and management preferences. Above all, how employees perceive potential managerial action, in response to the idea of unionisation, illustrates the power of management intent over employee behaviour and attitudes. Several employees commented that the very idea of unionisation would be frowned upon by company management. Other employees suggested that trade union membership would, in all probability, be an unwise career move while further responses elaborated on incidents that had apparently happened in the past, which left employees under no illusion as to possible managerial reprisals. For example:

There was a lady who worked here. She made sure every employee was treated fairly ... She was quite happy for a union to be here ... She doesn't work here anymore – she was too much that way and not enough the management way. She did leave on her own accord, but I think it was because she was made uncomfortable.

(Call centre agent)

The following short and simple message, conveyed by another call centre employee, illustrates the significance of possible managerial reprisals:

At my last place they had a union ... I mentioned it when I first came here and I said to someone, 'Have you got a union?' And they said, 'Don't mention unions here or you will be out on your ears.' So I've never brought it up again.

(Call centre agent)

Summary and conclusions

Delivery Co. provides data on employment relations from an organisation characterised as a so-called sophisticated non-union employer. Overall, the evidence suggests that claims of sophistication can be questionable. It depends on who you ask and when you ask them. On one hand employees seemed to approve of the psychological exchange that was evident at Delivery Co., partly because of the more attractive employment package on offer. On the other hand, however, the evidence also points towards a dependency relationship for employees that included tensions, conflicts and contradictions in the legitimisation of managerial control. Employees certainly spoke favourably about involvement (but not participation), were encouraged to be creative (but not allowed freedom), and perceived their employer to be fair (but not always equitable). It is these tensions and ambiguities that suggest that the level of sophistication can be interpreted in different ways.

What is also important is that the data collected at Delivery Co. coincided with a shift in public policy and a legal environment more sympathetic to trade union rights with statutory union recognition procedures. The fact that management sought to respond to such potential recognition claims in the future (should they arise) is highly significant. Above all, this shows the importance of managerial *intent* towards the idea of unionisation, with a corresponding impact on employee attitudes and behaviours that consolidate the non-union position of the organisation.

9   Towards an explanation of non-union employment relations

Introduction

The purpose of this chapter is to integrate and evaluate the evidence from our four case study organisations. Our principal objective in conducting this study was to assess how the employment relationship is made and modified in the absence of a trade union. We also sought to capture a range of possible influences that could shape such relationships; for instance, employer actions to avoid unions, and the capacity of workers to influence the relationship and/or mobilise collectively.

In Chapter 2, we reviewed a number of theoretical approaches that could be used to help explain some of the issues we were likely to encounter. While it was pointed out that each of these has a number of inherent advantages and limitations, our underlying rationale recognised that employment relations are more eclectic than a straightforward wage–effort bargain. In particular, organisational activity involves the combined interaction of social, legal, psychological and political and economic dimensions. With these in mind, Figure 2.2 in Chapter 2 helped conceptualise some of the key characteristics of the employment relationship for the purposes of empirical inquiry. Effectively this meant that we categorised relationships along a continuum, with bipolar opposites. This allowed us to suggest amendments to existing theory and towards the end of this, the final chapter in the book, we present an output framework for the analysis of managerial action and intent, in which we ground the findings reported in Chapters 5 to 8.

Non-union employment relationships and typologies

Since the Donovan Commission of the late 1960s, an increasing degree of attention has been focused on the management of the employment relationship in different settings. Some of this work advocates a more strategic approach to people management, through various methods of enhancing employee commitment, workforce productivity and organisational effectiveness. Historically these approaches focused on systems of trade union involvement and joint regulation. However, managerial motives for non-union employment relations have received very little attention, and the data from our case studies offers additional insights into some of these issues. In all our case studies managerial ideologies had a huge influence, and management expressed a strong ideological aversion to the idea of collective forms of employee representation. In many respects this is indicative of a neo-unitarist approach to people management and for the most part, managers viewed trade unions as an unnecessary interference in management's right to manage. However, ideological opposition is not quite the same thing as ideological hostility. It is certainly the case that some of the key senior managers (and owners) in our case study firms were extremely hostile to the idea of unionisation, particularly at Water Co., Chem Co. and Merchant Co. Nevertheless, other managers in these firms were more ambivalent. At Merchant Co. one regional manger was even in favour of trade unionism, while at both Water Co. and Delivery Co., the views of supervisors were mixed, ranging from opposition to indifference. Thus it is important to recognise that the ideological motivation to remain union-free is not a universal phenomenon, but is often tempered by different managerial styles of action (see below).

These ideological sentiments were also mixed with other motives for remaining non-union, although it is possible that the so-called imperatives of market flexibility, or recruiting the right type of people served as euphemisms to obscure the real extent of ideological opposition. At Delivery Co., the articulation of pragmatic business reasons featured quite prominently among managers and (some) employees. This often took the form of an expressed need for market responsiveness, or good customer relations, which were matters that respondents felt would be hindered with a trade union presence. At Merchant Co. the motivation to remain union-free was based on the need for managerial freedom of action, particularly in the areas of labour supply and cost savings through redundancy. Moreover, at both Delivery Co. and Chem Co., other objectives to remain non-union included control over the labour process, which, according to management, included the need to select employees who fitted-in with company values.

While the motives for non-union status are one thing, the form of non-union relations can be quite a different matter, and each of the four case study organisations displayed very different non-union relationship characteristics. Because of its virtually unilateral regulatory approach, Water Co. was categorised as exploitatively autocratic. What stood out at this company are the extremes to which management would go in treating workers as a highly disposable factor of production. Potential unionisation was not only unwelcome, it was vigorously discouraged by the firm's owners and senior management team, and in doing so they often circumvented statutory employment protection rights. In contrast, Merchant Co. was classified as engaging in manipulative regulation. As such it displayed some indications of management acting as the leader in making and modifying the relationship, more by manipulation than anything else. This organisation had embarked on a strategy of union de-recognition during a period of acquisition and takeover, which sent a clear symbolic message to workers about employer attitudes and the potential reprisals that could arise from any attempts to unionise. In particular, management frequently promoted a climate of insecurity by using the implied economic threat of job losses.

Whereas Water Co. lies at one extreme of the continuum shown in Figure 2.2 and Merchant Co. is located at the middle position, Chem Co. and Delivery Co. are positioned towards the opposite end of the relationship continuum. As such these two organisations had some similarities, but also important differences. Both companies displayed a mixture of joint and unilateral regulatory approaches and in each one management sought employee commitment and identification with corporate goals, by promoting a meritocratic relationship. Both utilised a range of what is often referred to as union substitution techniques, such as extensive voice mechanisms. However, at times these techniques were artificial and shallow. For example, Chem Co. management expected employees to participate in the works committee outside of company time.

Delivery Co. was purposely selected as an organisation that used a range of so-called sophisticated human relations practices, in which the underlying managerial objective was to discourage unionisation by seeking to win employees' hearts and minds. There was a much stronger identification with a corporate culture than was found among workers in the other case studies, and many employees appeared to approve of the attractive employment package. This included above-average remuneration, employee involvement and an articulation of the idea that the workplace can also be a place of fun. However, it also illustrates the difficulties and complexities of managing a non-union relationship through above-average remuneration, extensive employee involvement techniques and the promotion of a strong cultural identity. This is what Flood and Toner (1997) suggest is the catch-22 face of non-unionism. At Delivery Co., employees were increasingly dependent on the organisation and, despite the more attractive environment in which they worked, a number of tensions were evident.

This short comparison draws attention to the idea that there are both advantages and disadvantages associated with using an idealised classification scheme for categorising relationships. On the one hand there is a clear utility in making these distinctions between organisations, because it allows a mass of data to be managed and subsequently assessed by the researcher. In addition, typification gives a degree of internal consistency to the particular phenomenon under investigation, and this gives it empirical utility (Yin 1993; Kitay and Marchington 1996). Typologies can also act as a springboard to pinpointing key explanatory variables, such as those used to categorise management style (Purcell 1987; Purcell and Ahlstrand 1993; McLoughlin and Gourlay 1994); or Guest and Hoque's (1994) four faces of non-unionism (the good, bad, luck and ugly). Subsequent analysis can then lead to refinement of these concepts, together with informed corrections and amendments to existing theories.

On the other hand, however, our evidence would suggest there are some important limitations to the use of typologies. In particular, it can be very difficult to generalise from them. Of the four case studies in this book, it would be possible to label each of them in accordance with Guest and Hoque's (1994) four faces of non-unionism. Water Co. would be an ugly non-union employer; Chem Co. probably lucky; Merchant Co. might be bad; while Delivery Co. would be the so-called good non-union organisation. In addition, McLoughlin and Gourlay's (1994) styles of management could be applied to the case study results and more will be said on this below. However, and as we comment in each of the case study chapters, one shortcoming of such typification is the comparative neglect of factors internal to each organisation. Thus while Water Co. could be classified as a bad, ugly or exploitative employer, at the same time there was a friendly element to the social relations among co-workers (and some supervisors) that helped explain a positive aspect of the psychological exchange particular to this organisation. Workers at Water Co. were also important change agents, who shaped the environment in which they worked, which can be noted by their capacity to question (and at times resist) some of the unilateral and exploitative conditions imposed by management. The same is also true in each of the other case studies. For instance, the level and extent of participation that was said to exist at Chem Co. was highly questionable, as is a broad brush picture of so-called good non-union employers being good in every respect. The problem is that typification using idealised classifications can actually prompt a neglect and polarisation of practices that are remarkably diverse, complex and contradictory. For this reason, we have purposely made an attempt to capture a spectrum of factors that help to explain more fully how and why these relationships are made, modified and amplified. Later in this chapter we will introduce an output framework that can help capture a range of managerial actions. Before then however, it is more appropriate to review some of these separate relationship influences that we uncovered in the research.

Influences on the employment relationship

In Chapter 3 (Figure 3.1) and following a review of the literature, a set of possible influences that could be used to explain the processes of relationship modification was presented. We also stressed the interconnections between these possible influences and recognition of the variability between organisational contexts. The purpose of this section is to compare the range of influences from our case studies with the extant literature, and comment on which of them were the most significant.

Management style and attitudes to trade union recognition

There is a considerable literature on management style. In industrial relations and HRM the expression is used to reflect an employer's overall approach to people management activities and in particular, the way that management exercises control and authority in the relationship. Chapter 3 identifies a range of internal and external constraints on management influence and style. In reviewing the literature on management style, McLoughlin and Gourlay (1994) make important amendments that are more applicable to the non-union setting and these, together with Marchington and Parker's (1990) call to recognise managerial *intent*, informed the basis for our research and data analysis.

In each of our four case studies management style was an important source of influence and, as noted elsewhere (Roy 1980; Knox and McKinlay 2003), style remains an enduring (if not *the* most enduring) influence on labour–management relations. However, while different categorisation schemes can be useful, they also tend to obscure the dynamic processes within these relationships and this is for several reasons. First, as noted earlier in this chapter, typification can be a problematic matter, particularly where the information to categorise style is solely obtained from the completion of questionnaires by managerial respondents, which can lead to a *cul-de-sac* positioning (Purcell 1999). In other words, it is never explained whether these respondents really know why, or to what extent, their personnel policies are strategically integrated. Second, these schematic frameworks rarely take account of the meanings and interpretations of the principal recipients of management style: employees. Finally, collectivism versus individualism (a principal measure in some categorisations of style) are not necessarily mutually exclusive dimensions; they have been found to coexist simultaneously within an organisation (Bacon and Storey 1993). Thus while style categories are useful, they can also obscure some of the deeper influences and meanings of management action and strategy. As Gall (2003b) notes, there is no Chinese wall separating dichotomous approaches (nor the attendant techniques). It may be that the classification of union suppression and/or substitution can be self-defeating, as there are many other permutations that can be used to assess managerial intent.

The evidence from our case studies suggests that management style is primarily an expression of power and coercion that also reflects (employee) consent. In each of the case study chapters, we stressed the importance of deeper meanings and interpretations associated with managerial intent. This would not have been possible if we relied solely on the reports of managerial respondents, or attempted to assess style by evaluating policies that appear (or not) to be strategically integrated. Given the exploitative practices shown towards employees at Water Co., the idea that management style is *ad hoc* or opportunistic can be misleading. That is, the dominant role of the Chief Executive at Water Co. was consistently calculated and pre-determined, despite the absence of formalised policies. The most significant issue here was a management style that reflected an *intent* to view labour as a disposable factor of production, which was coupled with strong personalised and ideological sentiments that gave rise to a propensity to suppress unionisation through unilateral imposition. In this case, employee reactions to the way they were managed formed a barrier which counterbalanced any possible triggers to unionisation for fear of managerial reprisals. To a lesser extent, this barrier was evident at Chem Co. and Merchant Co., although for different reasons. As a very small company it was evident that Water Co. could simply not afford the required sophisticated techniques that could be used to substitute for unions, as were found at Delivery Co.

It is also important to note that both Water Co. and Chem Co. were SMEs, and this may have some bearing on management style in these organisations. At Chem Co. the boundaries between benevolence and paternalistic approaches were crucial in maintaining workplace discipline and order. The charismatic figure of the Operations Director engendered a duality of roles and control measures. In Friedman's (1977) terms, professional and technical employees were granted areas of responsible autonomy, while many other workers were subject to direct supervision and control. Such an approach to managing people created what have been termed *father-like* roles for management, with employees placed in subordinated *child-like* roles (Newbury 1975; Wray 1996). The implication is that workers are dependent on the employer for more than wages; they are part and parcel of deeper social and psychological exchange processes, which helped maintain order according to managerial objectives. For instance at Chem Co. employees were expected (required) to attend workshops run by the Operations Director, and worker representatives on the non-union works council were also expected (required) to participate outside of company time, even though management knew the system was effectively defunct. It is these combined influences that provide a more insightful picture about managerial style and its attendant influences on how these relationships are made and modified.

Merchant Co. provides further evidence about these issues. Arguably, a case could be made that Fox's (1974) Standard Modern category, with its deeper unitarist overtones, is relevant in such a non-union setting. In particular, there was a dissonance between the centralised personnel function and fragmented retail outlets spread across the country and this pointed to a range of competing pressures on management style. Similarly, centralised people management policies as opposed to local managerial styles were also evident at Delivery Co. However the organisational contexts were very different. At Merchant Co. the legacy of policies emanating from a (former) hostile government provided some legitimisation to union de-recognition. These, coupled with a more difficult product market, meant that managerial approaches were conditioned to a great extent by market pressures.

In contrast, at Delivery Co. there were different explanatory factors. There was a strong link between Delivery Co. (UK) and a corporate headquarters that sought to mirror a commercial and people management image with the outside world. In this organisation, management style fits more closely to the Marchington and Parker (1990) description of an *investment-orientation* towards employees. However, despite this, workers were not ignorant of their position as a controllable cost, and several ambiguities and contradictions were evident. It is also important to note that these were not isolated events. Tensions and social processes were not unique to any single site or office, but evident across different parts of the country. Examples included the call centre employee who innocently asked about unionisation, to which her peers commented that such matters should not be raised. Other examples included couriers in dispute with station management over health and safety. In short, beneath the sophistication of human relations, the coexistence of other managerial practices was found which would not have been as evident if we had relied on measuring a range of individual–collective or strategic integration proxies.

Product and labour markets

As discussed in Chapter 3, there is a wealth of literature on the influence of product and labour markets on employment relations. In this study it was certainly evident that the experiences of product and labour markets shaped the employment policy choices made by managers. In some organisations, such as Merchant Co. and Water Co., these tended to be straightforward, in the sense that they conformed to a large extent to Marchington and Parker's (1990) twin components of *competitive* (monopoly power) and *customer* (monopsony power) pressures, and often simultaneously. However, Chem Co. and Delivery Co. presented a slightly different picture. At Chem Co. the small size of the organisation and its market niche meant that the company was well known to its customers and competitors, and a rudimentary set of oligopoly conditions was evident. For instance, other smaller chemical companies concentrated on slightly different market segments, and given the intermediary nature of the chemicals it manufactured, it was also common for customers to be competitors. This afforded management a degree of market stability that helped reinforce its authority through long production cycles. Consequently, management style was very personalised and ideologically driven, rather than directly influenced by the prevailing market environment.

Delivery Co. was rather different. The company was already a market leader, with a wealth of global resources at its disposal. This provided greater scope for managerial choice, and some of the employment practices reinforced product quality policies, rather than price cutting, even though the organisation operated in a cut-throat market. In many ways this reinforces the notion that the choice between union suppression and substitution is one that can be very dependent on available resources. In other words, for the other three case study organisations, sophisticated union avoidance strategies were simply not a viable option.

In many respects Merchant Co. was even more unique, which provides fresh insights on the debate about market pressure. This was the only company in our sample to experience a serious decline in market share, with subsequent redundancies. In part this was explained by knock-on effects in other markets on which Merchant Co. was dependent, for instance, house construction and large-scale contract projects. At the same time however, branch managers had a significant degree of influence on the maintenance of client contracts, with some occupational groups (e.g. branch managers and skilled fitters) effectively occupying a more strategic bargaining position within the organisational structure.

A more recent observation, evident across all case studies with the exception of Chem Co., is the centrality of the customer in day-to-day worker interactions. At one extreme, in Delivery Co., couriers were not only subject to surveillance by management at the central dispatch function, but also under the watchful eye of clients through integrated technologies to track parcels anywhere in the world. This translated into corporate codes of employee behaviour and standards of dress when dealing directly with customers. Similarly, call centre staff at both Water Co. and Delivery Co., were subject to an array of customer satisfaction measures and supervisory monitoring that fed into and shaped the nature of work in these companies. At the other extreme, contract staff at Merchant Co. were not employed on company premises, but at various client sites and had to deal with a more complex accountability structure. Some customers, for example local authority housing trusts, also represented a managerial chain of authority that complicated organisational boundaries and the employment relationship. In contrast, customer interaction for staff in the retail outlets was more obvious and consistent with the sector as a whole. What these observations suggest is a fusion between market pressures and organisational initiatives that place the role of the customer/client as central in employment relations decisions. As Beynon *et al.* (2002) note, the growth of customer service work has either allowed management to intensify work through longer hours, or widen job tasks and responsibilities.

Non-union employee voice

An interest in employees having a say about matters that affect them has received increasing attention in the employment relations literature, both from those seeking higher levels of organisational performance, and from those desiring better systems of employee representation (Freeman and Medoff 1984; Marchington *et al.* 2001). As discussed in Chapter 3, our main interest was in assessing both the extent of non-union voice arrangements, and also employee perceptions of the utility of such mechanisms.

In all case studies some form of briefing system by management was evident, although the extent of these mechanisms varied considerably. At Water Co., staff briefings were the only formal voice mechanism available and they tended to be extremely limited in scope. That is, employees and managers commented that such interventions often indicated that there is something important or major to report to the workforce. In the main therefore, informal communications (mainly via the grapevine) were more important at Water Co. In contrast, Chem Co. employed a surprisingly wide range of techniques for such a small organisation, although how these different mechanisms translated into actual practice varied. Here, many of the voice arrangements were designed by the Operations Director, who favoured a hands-on approach in trying to create a participatory culture through employee educational and discussion forums. It was also evident that such schemes were selective in terms of the employee groups involved. For most production operatives, monthly team briefings did not occur and other techniques, such as daily production meetings tended to reinforce output targets, rather than tap into the ideas of employees.

While Water Co. had virtually no formal voice arrangements, Merchant Co. was quite different. Several mechanisms were reported and these had been present for many years. Nevertheless, it was apparent that some schemes had fallen into disuse, while for others, management assumed that because they circulated information, employees had received and understood the message. Moreover, management relied on a series of top-down communications and took these to mean that they consulted and informed employees, which was not the case in practice.

Delivery Co. employed an extensive range of voice mechanisms, and this is consistent with the picture of a non-union firm that seeks to introduce substitutes for some of the features of unionised representation. It was also evident that many employees approved of these schemes, because they were perceived to be taken seriously by management. At the call centre, work pressures occasionally meant that some briefings schemes were lacking. At different stations there was often a reliance on informal day-to-day conversation to strengthen the relationship among workers and station managers, and this was often perceived to be more important than formal mechanisms.

Overall, however, there tended to be an inverse relationship between a set of voice mechanisms on the one hand, and employee perceptions of the utility of these schemes on the other. For example, at Water Co. there was no formal voice arrangement, yet employees reported a high degree of satisfaction with their opportunities to speak to management. At Chem Co., which had a range of both information and consultative techniques, significant numbers of employees reported they were dissatisfied with the voice arrangements, and only a small number suggested they had the opportunity to contribute to organisational issues or work decisions. A similar pattern was also evident in this respect at Delivery Co., where, despite an extensive range of mechanisms, there were noticeable areas of dissatisfaction according to workers. Thus if voice utility is related to how well employees perceive that management deliver the deal, then the psychological contract was found wanting at these organisations, albeit with differences in degree and kind.

With the exception of Delivery Co., and to a lesser extent Chem Co., it was difficult to ascertain the impact of non-union voice channels on the relationship. These schemes were all designed and controlled by management, and where employees could contribute, it is important to recognise that these contributions were on matters deemed appropriate by management. Perhaps the most striking feature is that on the more substantive issues, such as wages or conditions, only a small number of employees in all these case studies were satisfied with the arrangements to speak to their employer. Indeed, at Merchant Co., no employee in our survey said they had the opportunity to speak to management about wages.

Employment relations climate

The final group of influencing factors set out in Figure 3.1 included the prevailing climate in each organisation. Given some of the limitations of questionnaire data, which is often completed by a single managerial respondent, we sought to capture this at a number of levels: through day-to-day shop floor relations among the parties, from worker attitudes to trade unions and by gauging the extent to which management handles and/or responds to the concerns expressed by employees. When taken together, these aspects of climate can influence behaviour and perceptions of whether management delivers on the deal. From our evidence, it would appear that climate represents an intervening variable that shapes employment relations. That is, the prevailing climate in an organisation can influence a number of psychological components such as trust or feelings of employee well-being in indirect ways. At times this intervening influence mirrored changes in public policy, such as at Delivery Co. and Merchant Co. in relation to government policies towards unionisation. In other situations the climate constituted a series of symbolic meanings articulated by the preferences of senior managers, particularly at Water Co. and Chem Co., and these sent clear messages to employees about managerial intent and possible action.

From our evidence, the prevailing climate would also appear to constitute a central element in Kelly's (1998) argument about the capacity for unorganised workers to mobilise. That is, the climate experienced by employees shaped their attitudes towards group identity (collective mobilisation), attribution (blaming management) and a perceived instrumental efficacy for a trade union to correct an injustice. At Water Co. employees obtained some psychological satisfaction from group membership: a group that stood up to managerial threats. Similarly, workers at Delivery Co. displayed solidarity in challenging management's lack of issue handling, and this served as cement, to bond key occupational groups together. In contrast, at Chem Co. management attempted to institutionalise an orientation to a group identity focused around the organisation, rather than a unionised collectivity. In many respects, employees viewed this as enforced compliance, although distinctive patterns of inter-group identity prevailed, often along occupational lines.

This is consistent with other research data (Freeman and Rogers 1999) which shows how feelings such as these can be translated into worker attitudes towards unions. These remained remarkably consistent across very different organisational settings, and while there were some differences in degree, workers were generally positive towards trade unions, although they displayed a higher ideological than instrumental orientation.

A final observation in relation to climate is the importance of social relations at shop floor level. For instance, at Water Co. the use of a distinctive banter coupled with informal relations between employees and supervisors helped to fill a psychological void and, in so doing, ameliorated some of the harsher exploitative conditions found there. Similarly at Merchant Co. small groups of employees (in the warehouse and offices) ascribed certain roles to themselves and others. For example, the actions of workers in the warehouse meant that rather than enforce company rules, it was easier for management to allow these employees to determine their own work routines. In contrast, at Delivery Co. personalised relations were much more visible through a friendly culture of involvement, particularly at the call centre. Arguably, a coalescence of personal and employment relations served to protect group members against management interference.

Re-mapping non-union relations: an output framework

The above descriptions and explanations make it clear that making and modifying the employment relationship is a process which is subject to a host of competing pressures. These pressures vary between different companies, and they can also vary in different parts of the same organisation. To account for these broader patterns of influence, and to accommodate the interrelationships between factors that are noted in Chapter 3, we introduce an analytical framework adapted from Peetz (2002), which is shown in Figure 9.1.

We introduce this now for a number of reasons. First, the employment relationship is not a set of static variables but is made up of interacting multi-level and multi-dimensional components. That is, rather than producing some easily identifiable outcome on its own, each component can influence others.

The second reason is that, given the data from our case studies, some of the prescriptive models outlined in earlier chapters cannot fully account for the complexity, diversity and contradictory nature of employment relations found in these firms. For instance, individualism and collectivism, or union suppression and substitution, may well represent polar opposites but that does not mean they are dichotomous. In other words, apparently contradictory processes can coexist over the same space and time, and the objective here is to understand how similar conditions (e.g. non-unionism) produce very different relationship outcomes.

Finally, as Edwards (2003: 348) suggests, there is a need to subject existing models to critical scrutiny, in order to advance the level of analysis and

	Exclusivist	Dual exclusivist/inclusivist	Inclusivist
Employment practices	• Redundancy • Casualisation • Climate of insecurity • Threats to employment • Reassigned work tasks • Discrimination and dismissal	• Dual (internal) labour markets • Job freedoms/task discretion • Non-union premiums • Performance inducements (e.g. pay, appraisals) • Recruitment and selection	• Standardisation of conditions • Friendly/informal climate • Uniformity of regulation
Relational	• Union de-recognition • Delay or refuse to negotiate with union • Latent employer opposition to unions • Legal action	• Supervisors as change agents • Social relations between employees and supervisors • Group meetings (captive audience)	• Non-union employee voice arrangements • Apparent employee participation schemes • Social events
Informational	• Control of inward information flows • Threats of economic sanction from market conditions (e.g. closure) • Anti-union messages (unions are unnecessary or will harm company performance)	• Corporate language and symbols • Direct, simple, bureaucratic and/or cultural control • Peer surveillance • Combined formal and informal regulation	• Induction and training programmes • Corporate mission statements

Real dimension (vertical axis)

Symbolic dimension (horizontal axis)

Figure 9.1 An output framework of managerial action and intent.

Source: adapted from Peetz (2002).

understanding. The following is but one small attempt to explain some of the contradictory patterns and influences reported throughout this book.

At the core of the framework outlined in Figure 9.1 is the idea that employer action and intent has both a *real* and a *symbolic* output. Our starting point is that managerial intent and action are shaped by a combination of influences, as previously depicted in Figure 3.1 in Chapter 3, and reported in each of the case study chapters of this book. The *real* and *symbolic* outputs of employer action and intent are shown respectively on the vertical and horizontal axes of Figure 9.1. The *real* output from managerial style (the physical expression of action) can manifest itself in a number of ways, which are covered in the three rows of the matrix. That is, as an employment practice, as something that is relational and part of the day-to-day relations between the parties to an employment relationship, or as something that is concerned with information flows between the parties, and often relates to the conditions under which work is performed. The *symbolic* outputs are concerned with the meanings and interpretations that employees ascribe to managerial action and intent. These can be grouped into three categories: *exclusivist, inclusivist*, or a combination of both. *Inclusivist* messages usually seek to incorporate employees into the organisational culture, and promote uniform behaviours and norms within the relationship. In contrast the *exclusivist* dimension sends messages to employees that certain behaviours are not welcome, for example, a diversion from managerial objectives, or the idea of unionisation (Peetz 2002). Note that this analytical framework is relatively unconnected with matters such as individualism, collectivism or the strategic integration of policy objectives, as in the McLoughlin and Gourlay (1994) scheme. Rather its focus is on whether the employer makes attempts to engineer a monoculture that embraces individuals with different sets of skills, but who have a single, common set of values that exclude unionism (Peetz 2002: 255). In what follows, the different cells in the matrix are related to the four case study organisations.

A set of *exclusivist employment practices* can be identified in each of the case studies. A pronounced climate of insecurity was prevalent at Merchant Co. and Water Co., and this often took the form of redundancy, or threats to employment security. Other practices that would fall within this part of Peetz's model include the practice of using casualised labour at Delivery Co. – e.g. the use of temporary and agency employees. It would also include some of the harder discriminatory practices relevant to potential unionisation evident at Water Co., where it can be recalled that many employees did not even receive written particulars of their contracts of employment, and they would often be dismissed (but re-employed a few weeks later) as a tactic to avoid statutory employment protection.

Inclusivist employment practices in Figure 9.1 might include a spectrum of techniques, such as the attractive employment package at Delivery Co.; the prevalence of informal relations on the shop floor at Water Co.; or a uniformity in the regulation of employment conditions at Merchant Co. However, the most significant real indicator of intent is the attempts that were made at Chem Co. to standardise practices across the organisation in order to reinforce a sense of identity with the company, rather than to an external third party, such as a trade union. Nevertheless, in the same organisation there was also a *duality of inclusivist and exclusivist* dimensions. For instance, at Chem Co. professional and technical employees enjoyed a greater degree of job freedom than process operatives, and at Merchant Co. warehouse and clerical grades were treated less favourably than contract fitters because of prevailing labour market conditions. Moreover, the existence of a dual labour market at Delivery Co., which had core and peripheral groups of employees, provided the basis for standardisation, but was also the basis for differences in the wage–effort reward. While this may seem paradoxical, it actually legitimises the coexistence of variable practices. For example, temporary employees who worked the more unsocial shift patterns often comprised those employees such as students, who had few alternative employment opportunities. This dual inclusive and exclusive nature of employment practices is also evident in the variety of recruitment and selection practices used at each firm. These ranged from the use of sophisticated testing and screening methods, to the use of an informal network of contracts (often simultaneously), as evident at Delivery Co. and Chem Co.

Exclusivist relational measures, as shown in Figure 9.1, are also evident across our case study firms. At Merchant Co., when management effectively de-recognised unions during the process of acquisition, this effectively removed (without consultation) the opportunity for employee representation. Delivery Co. provides a more subtle and possibly more strategic use of tactics than this. In response to the introduction of statutory legislative provisions for union recognition, Delivery Co. sought to respond to the possibility of unionisation; even though company management was convinced employees did not want or desire such representation.

Some of these managerial actions also have *relational inclusivist* messages. For instance, the range of non-union voice mechanisms found across our sample of organisations often sent a signal that management regarded unions as unnecessary. At Delivery Co., and to a lesser extent Chem Co. and Water Co., *relational inclusivist measures* also extended beyond the workplace, to include social events at the company's expense, as well as activities such as sponsored company soccer teams. The role of supervisory management also helps to explain how these actions and intentions have *dual inclusivist and exclusivist* meanings. At Merchant Co. there was a significant gap between the expression of corporate slogans and the practices employed by local managers. This was also evident at Delivery Co. and Water Co., where local managers circumvented policies from head office. At Water Co. this led to a more coordinated form of worker resistance when shift supervisors appeared to condone the (late) attendance of employees in response to the Chief Executive's decision to remove the perk of using company vehicles. At Chem Co. some of these actions resulted in a different output. That is, the use of employee educational programmes, which provided a captive audience to articulate company messages, or the use of team meetings in other companies would be a further example of this duality.

Inclusivist informational methods relate to the messages, other than those communicated through day-to-day relationship interactions, which are taken by employees to be a symbolic indication of managerial action and intent. As evident at Delivery Co. and Chem Co., employee induction, training and socialisation programmes are particularly important in this respect. Similarly, a corporate mission statement that located the role of employees within the overall corporate strategy, such as that evident at Delivery Co., is also embraced by this inclusive dimension.

In contrast, *exclusivist informational messages* can include a broader range of actions, such as threats of dismissal or economic sanctions that are communicated by managers as being beyond their control. This was certainly the view of employees at both Merchant Co. and Delivery Co., although for very different reasons. The attendant output is not so much managerial action itself, but rather the perceptions and behaviours of employees. Thus when one of the supervisors at Water Co. explained that no one is ever sacked, but a lot are told to leave, this conveys a clear and unambiguous message to employees about managerial intent and likely actions. Similarly at Merchant Co., when the company articulated the virtues of non-unionism during the share floatation, this was taken by employees as a sign that henceforth, trade unions would be unwelcome. In addition, as Peetz (2002) comments, exclusivist measures can relate to excluding part of a message, in an attempt to control inward information flows so that certain thoughts are prevented from flourishing. At Water Co., management removed all questions that related to trade unions from data collection instruments (without our consent). The explanation was that the owner did not want to raise the idea of unionisation in the minds of employees.

Dual inclusivist and exclusivist informational methods, the final component of Figure 9.1, relates to the use of language, discourse and the interpretation of meanings that are then ascribed to certain situations by different stakeholders. This duality can help correct some of the deficiencies associated with the mapping of management style considered in Chapter 3, and discussed earlier in this chapter. It allows us to chart the range of managerial actions from direct, informal and simple methods to more structured, bureaucratic and even subjective controls through corporate culture. For example, recruitment and selection methods at both Delivery Co. and Chem Co. were formal and informal, structured and unstructured. The use of informal peer control via family and friends can reshape attitudes and orientations towards the company, as well as allowing an element of screening of prospective employees in less intrusive ways. This is perhaps one of the more contradictory aspects inherent in managerial action and style that is often missed in other models and frameworks. Non-union employers frequently stress a unitarist culture by emphasising employee trust, yet, given the range of manipulative and deceptive tactics used to try to secure commitment and loyalty, at the same time management evidently mistrusts employees.

Concluding comments

In Great Britain the majority of workers now have their terms and conditions determined in ways that exclude trade unions. In this chapter we have sought to make a number of connections between the debates considered in Chapters 2 and 3, and the evidence reported in Chapters 5 to 8. It comes as no surprise that the various means of making and modifying these non-union relationships are virtually the sole prerogative of management. Neither is it surprising that the way employees seek to assert their influence and pursue their own interests in the employment relationship appear to be significantly inferior to those available to workers who have access to systems of effective and independent trade union representation. Notwithstanding differences in context and location, what stands out above all else is the influence and complexity of management action in shaping the experience of employment for workers in these firms. From this we have a number of general observations to make.

The first is that the reality of employment is often very different from the images espoused in corporate documentation or policy objectives. In all our case studies there were pronounced differences between the meanings that employees attributed to managerial action, and management's policy prescriptions. Although management style (intent and action) could have been categorised very differently, as we have argued earlier, this would have missed some of the deeper and arguably much richer experiences associated with these employment conditions. Furthermore, to assume that employees have a say in matters that affect them simply because management ticks a box on a questionnaire which asks whether team working or briefing groups are used in the organisation gives a misleading and unsatisfactory picture of employee voice opportunities. This suggests that despite the valuable insights obtained from large surveys, there remains a need for more detailed, exploratory research at enterprise level in order to evaluate the extent and meanings of these practices.

The second observation concerns the ontological assumptions underpinning this and other related areas of research. In Chapter 2 we considered a number of debates about the limitations of orthodox industrial relations, the legal contract, HRM and the suitability of these for the study of non-union firms. The main shortcomings here relate not so much to the labels used – industrial, employee, employment or even HRM – but rather the analytical frameworks and tools deployed. In the past, the difficulty has been that much industrial relations analysis has tended to study the parties and outcomes of collective bargaining, although as Edwards (2003: 338) recently comments, industrial relations as it should be understood studies: rules, conflict, and negotiation ... process[es] through which the terms of the exchange of wages for effort are altered or re-asserted. For this reason, and perhaps because of our criticisms of mainstream industrial relations, the perspective we adopted was more eclectic, in that we purposely took a social exchange perspective when examining the management of the employment relationship. Moreover, we adopted this view as a field of study, rather than as a perspective within a particular field (see also Ackers and Wilkinson 2003; Edwards 2003). This led to a number of adaptations from social theory, social mobilisation and psychological exchange.

The use of social exchange theory led fairly naturally to the use of the concept of a psychological contract, and this gave a convenient way of operationalising the range of processes by which employment relations can be conceptualised, both economically and socially. From our evidence this would certainly appear to be a useful analytical framework for future research and theorising, because both industrial relations and social exchange assume an inherent conflict of interest, together with the coexistence of antagonism and commitment. Therefore, in conceptualising social and psychological exchange as the principal lens through which to view the processes of employment relations, we have been able to illustrate the complexities of managing the employment relationship, as experienced by employees. A key attraction in using this perspective was a realisation that the broader social context can reveal a range of inherent ambiguities, and this shows just how indeterminate the relationship is in reality. In this way issues such as fairness, social justice, dignity or trust can be more fully integrated, or their absences exposed. So far as we can determine, there is no reason to assume that this perspective could not be applied to organisations where collective representation exists.

There are, of course, limitations. If the psychological contract is the principle instrument for evaluation, then there is an implicit assumption that employers have an obligation to meet a set of unspecified obligations. This may not be the case in reality, and from our case studies, particularly at Water Co. and Merchant Co., the idea of a psychological contract was in many respects an alien concept for managers.

Future implications

Our final concluding comments are concerned with the future implications for trade unions and employers as a result of the evidence in this book. If the 1980s was a nightmare decade for trade unions (Bradley 1994), the new millennium is a realisation of their loss of influence and general decline. A central debate in this matter is the ability of unions to widen membership among previously unorganised groups; what Kelly and Heery (1989) describe as *distant expansion*. While unions are reinventing themselves through a range of new and innovative organising methods, the focus of such activity appears to be limited to those areas where membership already exists (Heery *et al.* 2000). Arguably, to recapture lost membership would require organising efforts in non-union firms that are not too dissimilar to the case studies examined in this book. Our evidence tends to confirm that the main barrier to such expansion is managerial hostility, rather than a lack of interest among workers. It is not so much that some employers are *non-union* and others are *anti-union*, it is that managers who manage without unions prefer to keep matters that way. At Water Co. and Delivery Co., for instance, the context of work and managerial systems were very different. At Delivery Co., the use of more sophisticated techniques tended to obscure the commodity status of employees, while at Water Co. management was unashamedly exploitative. Merchant Co. and Chem Co. fell between these two extremes. The implication for trade unions is that strategies which seek distant expansion would need to define more precisely the target constituencies and range of issues that they need to combat (for example, managerial hostility and employee concerns) and this would need to be done for very diverse organisational contexts.

For employers the implications are many. Employment relations in these organisations were neither straight-forward, harmonious nor conflict-free. One implication is that remaining union-free comes at a price. At Delivery Co. this was evident through a more attractive employment package and use of non-union voice arrangements. At Water Co. and Merchant Co., the price of enforced managerial prerogative equated to a lack of trust and poor psychological exchange. In many respects, managers appear to still have difficulty recognising that employees can, and do, have different interests to those of the employing organisation. Indeed, despite the vocabulary of so-called new industrial relations or strategic HRM, deep-rooted tensions remain the cornerstone of employee–employer relations. The existence of such tensions harks back to a well-respected (although often forgotten) adage that management seems to have found it difficult to accept, that it can only regain control by first learning how to share it (Flanders 1970). The implication here is that the structures and processes to mediate and moderate such tensions were for the most part absent in the firms we studied.

Another implication for management arises from the shift in public policy. The environment is now more favourable towards trade unions and supported by new legal regulations. Given the statutory recognition procedures, non-union employers might either wind up courting trade unions, or they may decide to continue to work without trade unions by incorporating employees through more extensive non-union voice channels, such as the provisions in the European Directive on Employee Information and Consultation. This was most evident at Delivery Co. and Chem Co. These future directions suggest that employers have a number of choices, although the precise configuration of policy options depends to a large extent on the ideology of managers, the prevailing market context and also the capacity and agency of workers inside these organisations. Although it occurred in different ways and to a different extent, management in each of our case studies underestimated the role of workers in shaping the relationship, because of their own perceptions of identity and interest formation.

Finally, given that workers in these firms were generally sympathetic to trade unionism, and in particular, had a recognition that unions can counterbalance the downside of unilateral regulation and arbitrary rule, we would argue that trade unions can act as a conduit for management as much as workers. There are distinct benefits that can accrue from more efficient employee voice arrangements, a climate that is more democratic, and which involves more equitable managerial systems and actions.

Notes

2 The employment relationship re-visited

1 In contrast, self-employment would be legally defined as a 'contract for services'.
2 Examples here include pension arrangements for part-time workers and the implications for indirect sex discrimination, or peripheral employees who fall on the fringe of 'self-employment' and outside statutory employment protection such as unfair dismissal.
3 Such multi-disciplinary approaches tend to incorporate history, the law, economics, organisational politics and power, business strategy, psychology and sociology.

7 Merchant Co.: a case of manipulative regulation

1 Natwest Securities Ltd document, sponsors for Merchant Co.'s sale of shares.

Bibliography

Ackers, P. and Wilkinson, A. (2003) 'Introduction: the British industrial relations tradition – formation, breakdown and salvage', in P. Ackers and A. Wilkinson (eds), *Understanding Work and Employment: Industrial Relations in Transition*, Oxford: Oxford University Press.

Ackers, P., Smith, C. and Smith, P. (1996) 'Against all odds? British trade unions in the new workplace', in P. Ackers, C. Smith and P. Smith (eds), *The New Workplace and Trade Unionism: Critical Perspectives on Work and Organisation*, London: Routledge.

Adam, R. (1995) *Industrial Relations Under Liberal Democracy*, Columbia: University of Carolina Press.

Ajzen, I. (1988) *Attitudes Personality and Behaviour*, Milton Keynes: Open University Press.

Alderfer, C.P. and Smith, K.J. (1982) 'Studying intergroup relations embedded in organisations', *Administrative Science Quarterly* 27(1): 35–64.

Allport, G.W. (1954) 'Attitudes in the history of social psychology', in G. Lindzey and A. Aronson (eds), *Handbook of Social Psychology* vol. 1, Reading, Mass: Addison-Wesley.

Ansoff, I.H. (1965) *Corporate Strategy*, Harmondsworth: Penguin.

Argyris, C. (1960) *Understanding Organisational Behaviour*, Homewood, Ill: Dorsey.

Armstrong, E.A.G. (1969) 'The role of the State', in B. Barrett, E. Rhodes and J. Beishon (eds), *Industrial Relations and the Wider Society*, London: Macmillan.

Ashness, D. and Lashley, C. (1995) 'Empowering workers at Harvester Restaurants', *Personnel Review* 24(8): 17–32.

Ashtorth, B.E. and Mael, F. (1989) 'Social identity theory and organisation', *Academy of Management Review* 14(1): 20–39.

Bacon, N. (1999) 'Union derecognition and the new human relations: a steel industry case study', *Work, Employment and Society* 13(1): 1–17.

Bacon, N. and Storey, J. (1993) 'Individualization of the employment relationship and the implications for trade unions, *Employee Relations* 15(1): 5–18.

Bacon, N., Ackers, P., Storey, J. and Coates, D. (1996) 'It's a small world: managing human resources in small businesses', *International Journal of Human Resource Management* 7(1): 82–100.

Bain, G.S. and Clegg, H. (1974) 'A strategy for industrial relations research in Great Britain', *British Journal of Industrial Relations* 12(2): 91–113.

Bain, G.S. and Price, R. (1983) 'Union growth: dimensions, determinants and density', in G.S. Bain (ed.), *Industrial Relations in Britain*, Oxford: Blackwell.

Bain, P. and Taylor, P. (2000) 'Entrapment by the electronic panopticon? Worker resistance in call centres', *New Technology, Work and Employment* 15(1): 2–18.

Barnett, A. (1999) 'US union-busters get busy in the UK', *The Observer*, 24 January.

Barrett, B., Rhodes, E. and Beishon, J. (1975) *Industrial Relations and the Wider Society*, London: Macmillan.

Bassett, P. (1988) 'Non-unionism's growing ranks', *Personnel Management*, March: 44–47.

Bassett, P. (1986) *Strike Free*, London: Macmillan.

Beardwell, I. (1994) 'Managerial issues and the non-union firm', paper presented to the Centre for Economic Performance Workshop, London, April.

Beaumont, P.B. (1995) 'HRM and the non-union sector', in P. Beaumont (ed.), *The Future of Employment Relations*, London: Sage.

Beaumont, P.B. and Cairns, L. (1987) 'New towns – a centre of non-unionism?', *Employee Relations* 9(4): 14–15.

Beaumont, P.B. and Harris, R.I.D. (1988) 'High technology industries and non-union establishments in Britain', *Relations Industrielles* 43(4): 829–46.

Beaumont, P.B. and Harris, R.I.D. (1989) 'Non-union establishments in Britain: the spatial pattern', *Employee Relations* 10(4): 13–16.

Beaumont, P.B. and Rennie, I. (1986) 'Organisational culture and non-union status of small businesses', *Industrial Relations Journal* 17(3): 214–24.

Beynon, H., Grimshaw, D., Rubery, J. and Ward, K. (2002) *Managing Employment Change: The New Realities of Work*, Oxford: Oxford University Press.

Biasatti, L.L. and Martin, J.E. (1979) 'A measure of the quality of union management relationships', *Journal of Applied Psychology* 64(4): 387–90.

Billot, H. (1993) 'Fast Moving Cultural Change Programs at Co-Steel Sheerness: Improving Attitudes and the Work Ethic of Employees', paper presented to the ISS 21st Century Steelmaker Conference – The Human Technology Symposium, Williamsburg, USA, 31 October.

Billot, H. (1996) 'Business alloys', *People Management* October: 34–41.

Bird, D., Beatson, M. and Butcher, S. (1993) 'Membership of trade unions', *Employment Gazette* 101: 174–89.

Blau, P. (1964) *Exchange and Power in Social Life*, New York: Wiley.

Blauner, R. (1964) *Alienation and Freedom: The Factory Worker and Industry*, Chicago: University of Chicago Press.

Blyton, P. and Turnbull, P. (1998) *The Dynamics of Employee Relations* (2nd edn), Basingstoke: Macmillan.

Bolton, J.E. (Chair) (1971) *Report on the Commission of Enquiry on Small Firms*, Cmnd 4811, London: HMSO.

Boxall, P. and Purcell, J. (2002) *Strategy and Human Resource Management*, London: Macmillan.

Bradley, H. (1994) 'Divided we fall: unions and their members', *Employee Relations* 16(2): 41–52.

Braverman, H. (1974) *Labor and Monopoly Capital: The Degradation of Work in the Twentieth Century*, New York: Monthly Press Review.

Broad, G. (1994) 'Japan in Britain: the dynamics of joint consultation', *Industrial Relations Journal* 25(1): 26–38.

Broadbent, J. and Laughlin, R. (1997) 'Developing empirical research in accounting: an example informed by a Habermasian approach', *Accounting, Auditing and Accountability Journal* 10(3): 622–48.

Brown, W. (1972) 'A consideration of custom and practice', *British Journal of Industrial Relations* 26(1): 68–82.

Brown, W. and Rea, D. (1995) 'The changing nature of the employment contract', *Scottish Journal of Political Economy* 42(3): 363–77.

Brown, W. and Wright, M. (1994) 'The empirical tradition in workplace bargaining research', *British Journal of Industrial Relations* 32: 153–64.

Buroway, M. (1979) *Manufacturing Consent*, Chicago: University of Chicago Press.

Buroway, M. (1985) *The Politics of Production*, London: Verso.

Callinicos, A. (1996) *New Labour or Socialism?*, London: Bookmark Publications.

Cappelli, P., Bassi, L., Katz, H., Knoke, D., Osterman, P. and Useem, M. (1997) *Change at Work*, Oxford: Oxford University Press.

Chalmers, A. (1982) *What is this thing called Science?* (2nd edn), Buckingham: Open University Press.

Child, J. (1972) 'Organisational structure, environment and performance', *Sociology* 6(1): 1–22.

Clark, I. (1994) 'The employment relationship and contractual regulation', in I. Beardwell and L. Holden (eds), *Human Resource Management: A Contemporary Perspective*, London: Pitman.

Claydon, T. (1989) 'Union derecognition in Britain during the 1980s', *British Journal of Industrial Relations* 27(2): 214–23.

Claydon, T. (1996) 'Union derecognition: a re-examination', in I. Beardwell (ed.), *Contemporary Industrial Relations: A Critical Analysis*, Oxford: Oxford University Press.

Claydon, T. and Doyle, M. (1996) 'Trusting me trusting you? The ethics of employee empowerment', *Personnel Review* 25(6): 13–25.

Clegg, H. (1979) *The Changing System of Industrial Relations in Britain*, Oxford: Blackwell.

Cohen, A. (1992) 'Attitudinal militancy and propensity to strike among unionised technicians', *Human Relations* 45(12): 1333–66.

Cohen, G. (1988) *History, Labour and Freedom*, Oxford: Clarendon Press.

Collins, D. (1999) 'Born to fail? Empowerment, ambiguity and set overlap', *Personnel Review* 28(3): 208–21.

Cook, S. and Selltiz, C. (1964) 'A multiple indicator approach to attitude measurement', *Psychological Bulletin* 62: 36–55.

Cressey, P. (1985) 'Recasting collectivism: industrial relations in two non-union plants', in G. Spyropoulos (ed.), *Trade Unions Today and Tomorrow* vol. II, Maastricht: Presses Interuniversitaires Europeennes.

Cressey, P., Eldridge, J. and MacInnes, J. (1985) *Just Managing: Authority and Democracy in Industry*, Milton Keynes: Open University Press.

Cully, M. and Woodland, S. (1996) 'Trade union membership and recognition: an analysis of data from the Labour Force Survey', *Labour Market Trends* May: 212–25.

Cully, M., O'Reilly, A., Millward, N., Forth, J., Woodland, S., Dix, G. and Bryson, A. (1998) *The 1998 Workplace Employee Relations Survey: First Findings*, London: Department of Trade and Industry/HMSO.

Cully, M., O'Reilly, A., Woodland, S. and Dix, G. (1999) *Britain at Work: As Depicted by the 1998 Workplace Employee Relations Survey*, London: Routledge.

Cunningham, I. and Hyman, J. (1999) 'The poverty of empowerment? A critical case study', *Personnel Review* 28(3): 192–207.

Cunningham, I., Hyman, J. and Baldry, C. (1996) 'Empowerment: the power to do what?', *Industrial Relations Journal* 27(2): 143–54.

Curran, J. (1990) 'Rethinking economic structure: exploring the role of the small firm and self-employment in the British economy', *Work, Employment and Society* 4(2): 125–46.

D'Art, D. and Turner, D. (1997) 'An attitudinal revolution in Irish industrial relations: the end of Them and Us?', paper presented to the annual conference of the British Universities Industrial Relations Association, Bath, July.

Daniel, W. and Millward, N. (1984) *Workplace Industrial Relations: The DE/ESRC/ PSI/ACAS Surveys*, Aldershot: Gower.

Darlington, R. (1994) *The Dynamics of Workplace Unionism: Shop Stewards' Organization in Three Merseyside Plants*, London: Mansell.

Darlington, R. (2000) 'Shop stewards' leadership, left-wing activism and collective workplace union organisation', paper presented to British Universities Industrial Relations Association study group, Manchester Metropolitan University, 11 February.

Davies, P. and Freedland, M. (eds) (1983) *Kahn-Freund's Labour and the Law*, London: Stevens.

Delbridge, R. (1998) *Working on the Line*, Oxford: Oxford University Press.

Denison, D. (1996) 'What is the difference between organisational culture and organisational climate? A native's point of view on a decade of paradigm wars', *Academy of Management Review* 21(3): 619–45.

Denzin, N. (1970) *The Research Act*, Chicago: Aldine.

Department of Employment (1981) *Trade Union Immunities*, London: HMSO.

Department of Employment (1991) *Industrial Relations in the 1990s*, London: HMSO.

Dickson, T., McLachlan, M., Prior, P. and Swales, K. (1988) 'Big blue and the unions: IBM, individualism and trade union strategy', *Work, Employment and Society* 2(4): 44–56.

Donovan, Lord (Chair) (1968) *Royal Commission on Trade Unions and Employers Associations Report*, Cmnd 3623, London: HMSO.

DTI (2001) *Small and Medium Sized Enterprise Statistics for the UK (1997)*, London: Department of Trade and Industry (www.sbs.gov.uk/statistics/smedefs.asp).

Dubin, R. (1973) 'Attachment to work and union militancy', *Industrial Relations* 12(1): 51–64.

Dundon, T. (2002) 'Employer opposition and union avoidance in the UK', *Industrial Relations Journal* 33(3): 234–45.

Dundon, T. and Wilkinson, A. (2003) 'Employment relations in SMEs', in B. Towers (ed.), *A Handbook of Employment Relations Law and Practice* (4th edn), London: Kogan Page.

Dundon, T., Grugulis, I. and Wilkinson, A. (1999) 'Looking out of the black hole: non-union relations in an SME', *Employee Relations* 21(3): 251–66.

Dundon, T., Grugulis, I. and Wilkinson, A. (2001) 'New management techniques in small and medium sized enterprises', in T. Redmond and A. Wilkinson (eds), *Contemporary Human Resource Management: Text and Cases*, London: Pearson.

Dunlop, J. (1958) *Industrial Relations Systems*, New York: Holt Press.

Dunn, S. (1993) 'From Donovan to wherever', *British Journal of Industrial Relations* 31(2): 169–87.

Dunn, S. and Metcalf, D. (1996) 'Trade union law since 1979', in I. Beardwell (ed.), *Contemporary Industrial Relations: A Critical Analysis*, Oxford: Oxford University Press.

Durkhiem, E. (1933) *The Division of Labor in Society*, New York: Free Press.

Edwards, P.K. (ed.) (1995) *Industrial Relations: Theory and Practice in Britain*, Oxford: Blackwell.

Edwards, P.K. (2003) 'The Future of industrial relations', in P. Ackers and A. Wilkinson (eds), *Understanding Work and Employment: Industrial Relations in Transition*, Oxford: Oxford University Press.

Edwards, P.K. and Scullion, H. (1982) *The Social Organisation of Industrial Conflict*, Oxford: Blackwell.

Edwards, P.K. and Whitston, C. (1993) 'FinCo: the regulation of white-collar work', in P.K. Edwards and C. Whitston (eds), *Attending to Work: The Management of Attendance and Shopfloor Order*, Oxford: Blackwell.

Edwards, R. (1979) *Contested Terrain: The Transformation of the Workplace in the Twentieth Century*, London: Heinemann.

Eisenhardt, K. (1989) 'Building theories from case study research', *Academy of Management Review* 16(3): 613–19.

ERA (1999) Employment Relations Act, London: HMSO.

Evans, S. (1987) 'The use of injunctions in industrial disputes', *British Journal of Industrial Relations* 25(3): 419–35.

Fazio, R.H. and Zanna, M.P. (1978) 'On the predictive validity of attitudes', *Journal of Personality* 46(2): 228–43.

Felstead, A. and Jewson, N. (1999) *Global Trends in Labour Flexibility*, Basingstoke: Macmillan.

Fernie, S. and Metcalf, D. (1997) '(Not) hanging on the telephone: payment systems in the new sweatshops', Centre for Economic Performance, London School of Economics.

Fernie, S., Metcalf, D. and Woodland, S. (1994) 'Lost your voice?', *New Economy* 1(4): 231–7.

Finlay, P. (1993) 'Union recognition and non-unionism: shifting fortunes in the electronics industry in Scotland', *Industrial Relations Journal* 24(1): 28–43.

Flanders, A. (1965) *Industrial Relations: What is Wrong with the System?*, London: Faber.

Flanders, A. (1970) *Management and Unions: The Theory and Reform of Industrial Relations*, London: Faber.

Flood, P. and Toner, B. (1997) 'Large non-union companies: how do they avoid a Catch 22?', *British Journal of Industrial Relations* 35(2): 257–77.

Flood, P.C., Gannon, M.J. and Paauwe, J. (1994) 'Managing without unions: a pyrrhic victory', in P.C. Flood, M.J. Gannon and J. Paauwe (eds), *Managing Without Traditional Methods: International Innovations in Human Resource Management*, Wokingham: Addison-Wesley.

Formbrun, C., Tichy, N.M. and Devanna, M.A. (1984) *Strategic Human Resource Management*, New York: Wiley.

Foulkes, F. (1980) *Personnel Policies in Large Non-union Companies*, New York: Prentice Hall.

Fox, A. (1966) 'Industrial sociology and industrial relations', *Donovan Commission Research Report No. 3*, London: HMSO.

Fox, A. (1974) *Beyond Contract: Work, Power and Trust Relations*, London: Faber and Faber.

Fox, A. (1985) *Man Mis-management* (2nd edn), London: Hutchinson.

Freeman, B. and Medoff, J. (1979) 'The two faces of unionism', *The Public Interest* 25: 69–93.

Freeman, B. and Medoff, J. (1984) *What Do Unions Do?*, New York: Basic Books.

Freeman, R. and Rogers, J. (1999) *What Workers Want*, Ithaca: Cornell University Press.

Friedman, A. (1977) *Industry and Labour: Class Struggles at Work and Monopoly Capitalism*, London: Macmillan.

Gall, G. (2001) 'Management control approaches and union recognition in Britain', paper presented to the Work, Employment and Society Conference, Nottingham, September.

Gall, G. (2003a) 'Union recognition legislation as a stimulant to employer anti-unionism in three Anglo Saxon countries', paper delivered at Symposium on Union Busting and Union Organising: Comparative Reflections and International Trajectories, International Human Resource Management Conference, University of Limerick, 3–6 June.

Gall, G. (2003b) 'Employer opposition to union recognition', in G. Gall (ed.), *Union Organizing*, London: Routledge.

Gall, G. and McKay, S. (1994) 'Trade union derecognition in Britain, 1988–1994', *British Journal of Industrial Relations* 32(3): 433–48.

Gall, G. and McKay, S. (2001) 'Facing fairness at work: union perceptions of employer opposition and response to union recognition', *Industrial Relations Journal* 32(2): 94–113.

Gallie, D. and White, M. (1998) *Restructuring the Employment Relationship*, Oxford: Clarendon.

Garrahan, P. and Stewart, P. (1992) *The Nissan Enigma: Flexibility at Work in a Local Economy*, London: Macmillan.

Glaser, B. and Strauss, A. (1967) *The Discovery of Grounded Theory: Strategies for Qualitative Research*, Chicago: Aldine.

Godard, J. (1997) 'Whither strategic choice: do managerial ideologies matter?', *Industrial Relations* 36(2): 206–28.

Gollan, P. (2002) 'So what's the news? Management strategies towards non-union representation at News International', *Industrial Relations Journal* 33(4): 316–31.

Goodrich, C. (1975) *The Frontiers of Control*, London: Pluto Press.

Goss, D. (1988) 'Social harmony and the small firm: a reappraisal', *Sociological Review* 36(1): 114–32.

Goss, D. (1991) *Small Business and Society*, London: Routledge.

Gouldner, A. (1955) *Wildcat Strike*, London: Routledge & Kegan Paul.

Gratton, L., Hope-Hailey, V., Stiles, P. and Truss, C. (1999) *Strategic Human Resource Management*, Oxford: Oxford University Press.

Grey, C. and Garsten, C. (2001) 'Trust, control and post-bureaucracy', *Organisation Studies* 22(2): 229–50.

Grugulis, I., Dundon, T. and Wilkinson, I. (2000) 'Cultural control and the culture manager: employment practices in a consultancy', *Work, Employment and Society* 14(1): 97–116.

Guest, D. (1987) 'Human resource management and industrial relations', *Journal of Management Studies* 24(5): 503–21.

Guest, D. (1995) 'Human Resource management, industrial relations and trade unions', in J. Storey (ed.), *Human Resource Management: A Critical Text*, London: Routledge.

Guest, D. and Conway, N. (1997) 'Employee motivation and the psychological contract', *Issues in People Management No. 21*, Wimbledon: Institute of Personnel and Development.

Guest, D. and Conway, N. (1999) 'Peering into the black hole: the downside of the new employment relations in the UK', *British Journal of Industrial Relations* 37(3): 367–89.

Guest, D. and Conway, N. (2002) 'Communicating the psychological contract: an employer perspective', *Human Resource Management Journal* 12(2): 22–38.

Guest, D. and Hoque, K. (1994) 'The good, the bad and the ugly: employment relations in new non-union workplaces', *Human Resource Management Journal* 5(1): 1–14.

Guest, D. and Peccei, R. (1994) 'The nature and causes of effective human resource management', *British Journal of Industrial Relations* 32(2): 219–42.

Guest, D., Conway, N., Briner, N. and Dickman, M. (1996) 'The state of the psychological contract', *Issues in People Management No. 16*, Wimbledon: Institute of Personnel and Development.

Gunnigle, P. (1995) 'Collectivism and the management of industrial relations in greenfield sites', *Human Resource Management Journal* 5(3): 24–40.

Gunnigle, P., MacCurtain, S. and Morley, M. (2001) 'Dismantling pluralism: industrial relations in Irish greenfield sites', *Personnel Review* 30(3): 263–79.

Hakim, C. (1994) *Research Design: Strategies and Choices in the Design of Social Research* (2nd edn), London: Routledge.

Hall, M., Broughton, A., Carley, M. and Sisson, K. (2002) *Works Councils for the UK? Assessing the Impact of the EU Employee Consultation Directive*, London: Eclipse Group.

Hammer, M. (2000) 'Non-union representational forms: an organisational behaviour perspective', in B.E. Kaufman and D.G. Taras (eds), *Nonunion Employee Representation: History, Contemporary Practice and Policy*, New York: M E Sharpe.

Harbison, F. and Coleman, J. (1951) *Goals and Strategy in Collective Bargaining*, New York: Harper.

Hartley, J.F. (1992) 'Trade union membership and union joining', in J.F. Hartley and G.M. Stephenson (eds), *Employment Relations: The Psychology of Influence and the Control of Work*, Oxford: Blackwell.

Hartley, J.F. (1994) 'Case studies in organisational research', in C. Cassell and G. Symon (eds), *Qualitative Methods in Organisational Research*, London: Sage.

Hayek, F. (1980) 'The trade unions and Britain's economic decline', in W.E.J. McCarthy (ed.), *Trade Unions* (2nd edn), Harmondsworth: Penguin.

Hedges, B. (1994/95) 'Work in a changing climate', in R. Jowell, J. Curtice, L. Brook and D. Ahrendt (eds), *British Social Attitudes: 11th Report*, Aldershot: Dartmouth.

Heery, E., Simms, M., Simpson, D., Delbridge, R. and Salmon, J. (2000) 'Organising unionism comes to the UK', *Employee Relations* 22(1): 38–57.

Hendry, C. and Pettigrew, A. (1990) 'Human resource management: an agenda for research', *International Journal of Human Resource Management* 1(1): 17–43.

Holliday, R. (1995) *Investigating Small Firms: Nice Work?*, London: Routledge.

Homans, G.C. (1961) *Social Behaviour*, New York: Harcourt, Brace and World.

Honeyball, S. (1989) 'Employment law and the primacy of contract', *Industrial Law Journal* 18(2): 97–108.

Huse, E.F. and Bowditch, J.L. (1973) *Behaviour in Organisations*, Reading, Mass: Addison-Wesley.

Hyman, R. (1975) *Industrial Relations: A Marxist Introduction*, London: Macmillan.

Hyman, R. (2001) *European Trade Unionism: Between Markets, Class and Society*, London: Sage.

Ingham, G. (1970) *Size of Industrial Organisation and Worker Behaviour*, Cambridge: Cambridge University Press.

IRS (1998) 'Predicting union membership', *Employment Trends No. 669*, Industrial Relations Services, December.

ISR (1995) *Employee Satisfaction: Tracking European Trends*, London: International Survey Research.

James, L.R. and Jones, A.P. (1974) 'Organisational climate: a review of theory and research', *Psychological Bulletin* 83(8): 1096–112.

Jick, T. (1979) 'Mixing qualitative and quantitative methods: triangulation in action', *Administrative Science Quarterly* 24(2): 602–11.

Johnson, G. and Scholes, K. (1999) *Exploring Corporate Strategy: Text and Cases* (5th edn), Hemel Hempstead: Prentice Hall.

Jones, A.P. and James, L.R. (1979) 'Psychological climate dimensions and relationships of individual and aggregated work environment perceptions', *Organisational Behaviour and Human Performance* 23(2): 201–50.

Jowell, R., Curtice, J., Brook, L. and Ahrendt, D. (eds) (1984–96) *British Social Attitudes (annual reports)*, Aldershot: Dartmouth.

Kahn-Freund, O. (1967) 'A note on status and contract in British labour law', *Modern Law Review* 30: 635–44.

Kahn-Freund, O. (1977) *Labour and the Law*, London: Stevens.

Kaufman, B.E. and Taras, D.G. (eds) (2000) *Non-union Employee Representation: History, Contemporary Practice and Policy*, New York: M E Sharpe.

Keenoy, T. (1997) 'Review article: HRMism and the language of re-presentation', *Journal of Management Studies* 34(5): 825–41.

Kelly, J. (1997a) 'The future of trade unionism: injustice, identity and attribution', *Employee Relations* 19(5): 400–14.

Kelly, J. (1997b) 'Long waves in industrial relations: mobilisation and counter-mobilisation in historical perspective', *Historical Studies in Industrial Relations* 4: 3–35.

Kelly, J. (1998) *Rethinking Industrial Relations: Mobilisation, Collectivism and Long Waves*, London: Routledge.

Kelly, J. and Heery, E. (1989) 'Full-time officers and trade union recruitment', *British Journal of Industrial Relations* 27(2): 196–213.

Kelly, J. and Kelly, C. (1991) 'Them and us: social psychology and the new industrial relations', *British Journal of Industrial Relations* 29(1): 25–48.

Kelly, J. and Nicholson, N. (1980) 'The causation of strikes: a review of theoretical approaches and the potential contribution of social psychology', *Human Relations* 33(12): 853–83.

Kessler, S. and Bayliss, F. (1992) *Contemporary Industrial Relations*, London: Macmillan.

Kitay, J. and Marchington, M. (1996) 'A review and critique of workplace industrial relations typologies', *Human Relations* 49(10): 1263–90.

Knox, B. and McKinlay, A. (2003) 'Organizing the unorganized: union recruitment strategies in American transnationals, c. 1945–1977', in G. Gall (ed.), *Union Organizing*, London: Routledge.

Kochan, T. and Katz, H. (1988) *Collective Bargaining and Industrial Relations*, Homewood, Ill: Urwin.

Kochan, T., Katz, H. and McKersie, R. (1986) *The Transformation of American Industrial Relations*, New York: Basic Books.

Kolb, D.A., Rubin, J.M. and McItyre, J. (1974) *Organisational Psychology: An Experimental Approach* (2nd edn), Englewood Cliffs: Prentice Hall.

Koys, D. and DeCotiis, T. (1991) 'Inductive measures of psychological climate', *Human Relations* 44(3): 265–85.

Laughlin, R. (1995) 'Empirical research in accounting: alternative approaches and a case for "middle-range" thinking', *Accounting, Auditing and Accountability Journal* 8(1): 63–87.

Leahy, M. (1996) 'Tempered steel', *People Management* November: 27–30.

Legge, L. (1995) *Human Resource Management: Rhetorics and Realities*, Basingstoke: Macmillan.

Lewin, K. (1951) *Field Theory in Social Science*, New York: Harper and Row.

Lloyd, C. (2001) 'What do employee councils do? The impact of non-union forms of representation on trade union organisation', *Industrial Relations Journal* 32(4): 313–27.

Logan, J. (2001) 'Is statutory recognition bad news for British unions? Evidence from the history of North American industrial relations', *Historical Studies in Industrial Relations* 11(Spring): 63–108.

Marchington, M. and Parker, P. (1990) *Changing Patterns of Employee Relations*, Hemel Hempstead: Harvester Wheatsheaf.

Marchington, M. and Wilkinson, A. (2000) 'Direct participation', in S. Bach and K. Sisson (eds), *Personnel Management: A Comprehensive Guide to Theory and Practice* (3rd edn), Oxford: Blackwell.

Marchington, M., Wilkinson, A., Ackers, P. and Dundon, A. (2001) *Management Choice and Employee Voice*, London: Chartered Institute of Personnel and Development.

Marchington, M., Wilkinson, A., Ackers, P. and Goodman, J. (1994) 'Understanding the meaning of participation: views from the workplace', *Human Relations* 47(8): 867–94.

Marsh, A. and McCarthy, W. (1968) 'Disputes procedures in Britain', *Donovan Commission Research Report No. 2*, London: HMSO.

Martin, R., Sunley, P. and Wills, J. (1996) *Union Retreat and the Regions*, London: Jessica Kingsley.

McAdam, D. (1988) 'Micromobilisation contexts and recruitment activism', *International Social Movement Research* 1: 125–54.

McCaulay, I. and Wood, R. (1992) 'Hotel and catering industry employees' attitudes towards trade unions', *Employee Relations* 14(3): 20–8.

McFarlane, S. and Tetrick, L. (1994) 'The psychological contract as an explanatory framework in the employment relationship', in C. Cooper and D. Rousseau (eds), *Trends in Organisational Behaviour* 1, Chichester: Wiley.

McIlroy, J. (1995) *Trade Unions in Britain Today*, Manchester: Manchester University Press.

McKinlay, A. and Taylor, P. (1996) 'Power, surveillance and resistance: inside the factory of the future', in P. Ackers, C. Smith and P. Smith (eds), *The New Workplace and Trade Unionism: Critical Perspectives on Work and Organisation*, London: Routledge.

McLoughlin, I. (1996) 'Inside the non-union firm', in P. Ackers, C. Smith and P. Smith (eds), *The New Workplace and Trade Unionism: Critical Perspectives on Work and Organisation*, London: Routledge.

McLoughlin, I. and Clark, J. (1994) *Technological Change at Work* (2nd edn), Buckingham: Open University Press.

McLoughlin, I. and Gourlay, S. (1992) 'Transformed industrial relations? Employee attitudes in non-union firms', *Human Resource Management Journal* 2(2): 8–28.

McLoughlin, I. and Gourlay, S. (1994) *Enterprise Without Unions: Industrial Relations in the Non-union Firm*, Buckingham: Open University Press.

Miller, P. (1991) 'Strategic human resource management: an assessment of progress', *Human Resource Management Journal* 1(4): 23–39.

Millward, N. (1994) *The New Industrial Relations?*, London: Policy Studies Institute.

Millward, N. and Stevens, S. (1986) *British Workplace Industrial Relations 1980–84: The DE/ESRC/PSI/ACAS Surveys*, Oxford: Heinemann.

Millward, N., Bryson, A. and Forth, J. (2000) *All Change at Work? British Employment Relations 1980–1998, as portrayed by the Workplace Industrial Relations Series*, London: Routledge.

Millward, N., Stevens, M., Smart, D. and Hawes, W.R. (1992) *Workplace Industrial Relations in Transition: The ED/ESRC/PSI/ACAS Surveys*, Aldershot: Dartmouth.

Minford, P. (1982) 'Trade unions destroy a million jobs', in W.E.J. McCarthy (ed.), *Trade Unions* (2nd edn), Harmondsworth: Penguin.

Mintzberg, H. (1973) *The Nature of Managerial Work*, New York: Harper and Row.

Mowday, R., Porter, L. and Steers, R. (1982) *Employee-Organisation Linkages: The Psychology of Commitment, Absenteeism and Turnover*, San Diego: Academy Press.

Mumford, E. (1995) 'Contracts, complexity and contradictions: the changing employment relationship', *Personnel Review* 24(8): 54–70.

Newbury, H. (1975) 'The deferential dialect', *Comparative Studies in Labour and History* 13: 246–59.

Nicholson, N. (1979) 'Industrial relations climate: a case study approach', *Personnel Review* 8(3): 20–5.

Noon, M. and Blyton, P. (1997) *The Realities of Work*, London: Macmillan.

Oliver, N. and Wilkinson, B. (1992) *The Japanization of British Industry: New Developments in the 1990s*, Oxford: Blackwell.

Parry, D., Waddington, D. and Critcher, C. (1997) 'Industrial relations in the privatised mining industry', *British Journal of Industrial Relations* 35(2): 173–96.

Peach, L.H. (1983) 'Employee relations in IBM', *Employee Relations* 5(3): 17–20.

Peetz, D. (2002) 'Decollectivist strategies in Oceania', *Industrielle Relations* 57(2): 252–78.

Pendleton, A. and Winterton, J. (eds) (1993) *Public Enterprise in Transition: Industrial Relations in State and Privatized Corporations*, Routledge: London.

Phelps-Brown, E. (1959) *The Growth of British Industrial Relations*, London: Macmillan.

Pollert, A. (1988) 'The flexible firm: fixation or fact?', *Work, Employment and Society* 2(3): 281–316.

Poole, M. and Mansfield, R. (1993) 'Patterns of continuity and change in managerial attitudes and behaviour in industrial relations', *British Journal of Industrial Relations* 31(1): 11–35.

Purcell, J. (1979) 'Lessons of the Commission on Industrial Relations: attempts to reform workplace industrial relations', *Industrial Relations Journal* 10(2): 4–22.

Purcell, J. (1987) 'Mapping management style in employee relations', *Journal of Management Studies* 24(5): 533–48.

Purcell, J. (1999) 'The search for best practice and best fit in human resource management: chimera or cul-de-sac?', *Human Resource Management Journal* 9(3): 26–41.

Purcell, J. and Ahlstrand, B. (1994) *Strategy and Style in Employee Relations*, Oxford: Oxford University Press.

Purcell, J. and Sisson, K. (1983) 'Strategies and practices in the management of industrial relations', in G.S. Bain (ed.), *Industrial Relations in Britain*, Oxford: Blackwell.

Rainnie, A. (1985) 'Small firms, big problems: the political economy of small business', *Capital and Class* 25(Spring): 140–68.

Rainnie, A. (1989) *Industrial Relations in Small Firms: Small Isn't Beautiful*, London: Routledge.

Ram, M. (1991) 'Control and autonomy in small firms: the case of the West Midlands clothing industry', *Work, Employment and Society* 5(4): 601–19.

Ram, M. (1994) *Managing to Survive: Working Lives in Small Firms*, Oxford: Blackwell.

Ram, M., Edwards, P., Gillman, M. and Arrowsmith, J. (2001) 'The dynamics of informality: employment relations in small firms and the effects of regulatory change', *Work, Employment and Society* 15(4): 845–61.

Ray, C. (1986) 'Corporate culture: the last frontier of control', *Journal of Management Studies* 23(3): 287–97.

Reddish, H. (1975) 'Memorandum of written evidence to the Royal Commission on Trade Unions and Employers Associations', in B. Barrett, E. Rhodes and J. Beishon (eds), *Industrial Relations and the Wider Society*, London: Macmillan.

Regan, D.T. and Fazio, R. (1977) 'On the consistency between attitudes and behaviour: look to the method of attitude formation', *Journal of Experimental Social Psychology* 13(1): 28–45.

Reitsperger, W.D. (1986) 'Japanese management: coping with British industrial relations', *Journal of Management Studies* 23(1): 72–87.

Rim, Y. and Mannheim, B.F. (1979) 'Factors relate to attitudes of management and union representatives', *Personnel Psychology* 64(4): 387–90.

Roberts, I., Sawbridge, D. and Bamber, G. (1992) 'Employee relations in smaller enterprises', in B. Towers (ed.), *Handbook of Industrial Relations Practice*, London: Kogan Page.

Rollinson, D. (1993) *Understanding Employee Relations: A Behavioural Approach*, Wokingham: Addison-Wesley.

Rollinson, D., with Broadfield, A. (2002) *Organisational Behaviour and Analysis: An Integrated Approach* (2nd edn), Harlow: Financial Times Prentice Hall.

Rollinson, D., Broadfield, A. and Edwards, D. (1998) *Organisational Behaviour and Analysis: An Integrated Approach*, Harlow: Addison-Wesley.

Roloff, M. (1981) *Interpersonal Communications: The Social Exchange Approach*, Beverly Hills: Sage.

Rousseau, D. (1995) *Psychological Contracts in Organisations: Understanding the Written and Unwritten Agreements*, London: Sage.

Rousseau, D. and Parks, J. (1993) 'The contracts of individuals and organisations', in L.L. Cummings and B.M. Staw (eds), *Research in Organisational Behaviour* vol. 15, Greenwich: JAI Press.

Roy, D. (1980) 'Repression and Incorporation. Fear stuff, sweet stuff and evil stuff: management's defenses against unionization in the south', in T. Nichols (ed.), *Capital and Labour: A Marxist Primer*, Glasgow: Fontana.

Rubery, J. (1987) 'Flexibility of labour costs in non-union firms', in R. Tarling (ed.), *Flexibility in Labour Markets*, London: Academic Press.

Rubery, J., Earnshaw, J., Marchington, M., Lee-Cooke, F. and Vincent, S. (2001) 'Changing organisational forms and the employment relationship', *The Future of Work, Working Paper No. 4*, London: ESRC.

Scase, R. (1995) 'Employment relations in small firms', in P.K. Edwards (ed.), *Industrial Relations: Theory and Practice in Britain*, Oxford: Blackwell.

Scase, R. and Goffee, R. (1987) *The Real World of the Small Business Owner* (2nd edn), London: Croom Helm.

Schein, E.H. (1980) *Organisational Psychology* (3rd edn), Englewood Cliffs: Prentice Hall.

Schneider, B., Parkington, J.J. and Buxton, V.M. (1980) 'Employee and customer perceptions of service in banks', *Administrative Science Quarterly* 25(2): 257–67.

Scott, A. (1994) *Willing Slaves? British Workers Under Human Resource Management*, Cambridge: Cambridge University Press.

Scott, M., Roberts, I., Holroyd, G. and Sawbridge, G. (1989) *Management and Industrial Relations in Small Firms*, London: Department of Employment Research Paper No. 70.

Sieff, M. (1990) *Marcus Sieff on Management: The Marks and Spencer Way*, London: Weidenfeld and Nicholson.

Silverman, D. (1970) *The Theory of Organisations*, London: Heinemann.

Sisson, K. (ed.) (1989) *Personnel Management in Britain*, Oxford: Blackwell.

Sisson, K. (1993) 'In search of HRM', *British Journal of Industrial Relations* 32(2): 201–10.

Smith, C. and Elger, T. (1994) *Global Japanization? The Transnational Transformation of the Labour Process*, London: Routledge.

Smith, P. and Morton, G. (1993) 'Union exclusion and decollectivisation of industrial relations in contemporary Britain', *British Journal of Industrial Relations* 31: 97–114.

Sparrow, P. and Pettigrew, A. (1988) 'Strategic human resource management in the computer supply industry', *Journal of Occupational Psychology* 61(1): 25–42.

Stephenson, C. (1996) 'The different experience of trade unionism in two Japanese transplants', in P. Ackers, C. Smith and P. Smith (eds), *The New Workplace and Trade Unionism: Critical Perspectives on Work and Organisation*, London: Routledge.

Storey, D. (1994) *Understanding the Small Business Sector*, London: Routledge.

Storey, J. (1983) *Managerial Prerogative and the Question of Control*, London: Routledge.

Storey, J. (1986) 'The phoney war? New office technology: organisation and control', in D. Knights and H. Willmott (eds), *Managing the Labour Process*, London: Sage.

Storey, J. (1987) 'Development in the management of human resources: an interim report', *Warwick Papers in Industrial Relations*, Warwick: University of Warwick, November.

Storey, J. (ed.) (1995) *Human Resource Management: A Critical Text*, London: Routledge.

Storey, J. and Beardwell, I. (1995) 'Organ grinder or monkey? Personnel management in the non-union firm', paper presented to the annual conference of the British Universities Industrial Relations Association, Durham, July.

Storey, J. and Sisson, K. (1993) *Managing Work and Organisations*, Buckingham: Open University Press.

Sturdy, A. (2001) 'Servicing societies? – colonisation, control, contradiction and contestation', in A. Sturdy, I. Grugulis and H. Willmott (eds), *Customer Service: Empowerment and Entrapment*, London: Routledge.

Terry, M. (1999) 'Systems of collective representation in non-union firms in the UK', *Industrial Relations Journal* 30(1): 16–30.

Thompson, P. and Warhurst, C. (1998) *Workplaces of the Future*, London: Routledge.

Thompson, P. (1983) *The Nature of Work: An Introduction to Debates on the Labour Process*, London: Macmillan.

Thurley, K. and Wood, S. (1983) 'Introduction', in K. Thurley and S. Wood (eds), *Industrial Relations and Management Strategy*, Cambridge: Cambridge University Press.

Tilly, C. (1978) *From Mobilisation to Revolution*, New York: McGraw-Hill.

Torrington, D. and Hall, L. (1998) *Human Resource Management* (4th edn), Hemel Hempstead: Prentice Hall.

Towers, B. (1997) *The Representation Gap: Change and Reform in the British and American Workplace*, Oxford: Oxford University Press.

Trevor, M. (1988) *Toshiba's New British Company*, London: Policy Studies Institute.

Truss, C., Gratton, L., Hope-Hailey, V., McGovern, P. and Stiles, P. (1997) 'Soft and hard models of human resource management: a reappraisal', *Journal of Management Studies* 34(1): 53–73.

Tse, K. (1985) *Marks and Spencer: An Anatomy of Britain's Most Efficiently Managed Company*, London: Pergamon.

TULR(C)A (1992) Trade Union and Labour Relations (Consolidation) Act, London: HMSO.

Turnbull, P. and Wass, V. (1996) 'Marksist management: human relations in a Marks and Spencer's high street store', paper presented to the British Universities Industrial Relations Association annual conference, Bradford, July.

Turnbull, P. and Wass, V. (1998) 'Marksist management: sophisticated human relations in a high street retail store', *Industrial Relations Journal* 29(2): 98–111.

Turner, T. and D'Art, D. (eds) (2002) *Industrial Relations in the New Economy*, Dublin: Blackhall Press.

Tversky, A. and Kahneman, D. (1973) 'Availability: a heuristic for judging frequency and probability', *Cognitive Psychology* 5(2): 207–32.

Tyson, S. (1995) *Human Resource Strategy: Towards a General Theory of Human Resource Management*, London: Pitman.

Tyson, S. (1997) 'Human resource strategy: a process for managing the contribution of HRM to organisational performance', *International Journal of Human Resource Management* 8(3): 277–90.

Von Prondzynski, F. (1985) 'The changing functions of labour law', in P. Fosh and C. Littler (eds), *Industrial Relations and the Law in the 1980s*, Aldershot: Gower.

Waddington, J. (1992) 'Trade union membership in Britain 1980–87: unemployment and restructuring', *British Journal of Industrial Relations* 30(2): 287–324.

Walton, R.E. (1985a) 'Towards a strategy of eliciting employee commitment based on policies of mutuality', in R.E. Walton and P.R. Lawrence (eds), *HRM Trends and Challenges*, Boston: Harvard University Press.

Walton, R.E. (1985b) 'From control to commitment in the workplace', *Harvard Business Review* 63(2): 77–84.

Walton, R.E. and McKersie, R. (1965) *A Behavioural Theory of Labour Negotiation: An Analysis of a Social Interaction System*, New York: McGraw-Hill.

Webb, S. and Webb, B. (1897) *Industrial Democracy*, London: Longman.

Wedderburn, K.W. (Lord) (1986) *The Worker and the Law* (3rd edn), Harmondsworth: Penguin.

Weik, K. (1979) *The Social Psychology of Organising* (2nd edn), Reading, Mass: Addison-Wesley.

Weik, K. (2001) *Making Sense of the Organisation*, Oxford: Blackwell.

Whincup, M. (1991) *Modern Employment Law* (7th edn), Oxford: Butterworth-Heinemann.

Whitaker, A. (1986) 'Managerial strategy and industrial relations: a case study of plant relocation', *Journal of Management Studies* 23(6): 657–78.

White, M. and Trevor, M. (1983) *Under Japanese Management: The Experience of British Workers*, London: Heinemann.

Wickens, P. (1987) *The Road to Nissan*, London: Macmillan.

Wilkinson, A. (1998) 'Empowerment: theory and practice', *Personnel Review* 27(1): 40–56.

Wilkinson, A. (1999) 'Employment relations in SMEs', *Employee Relations* 22(3): 206–17.

Wilkinson, A. and Ackers, P. (1995) 'When two cultures meet: new industrial relations at Japanco', *International Journal of Human Resource Management* 6(4): 849–71.

Willmott, H. (1993) 'Strength is ignorance, slavery is freedom: managing culture in modern organisations', *Journal of Management Studies* 30(4): 515–52.

Winters, J. (1999) 'The final frontier: trade unions and the small business sector', paper presented to the British Universities Industrial Relations Association HRM Study Group, University of Cardiff, January.

Wood, S. and Kelly, J. (1988) 'Taylorism, responsible autonomy and management strategy', in R. Phal (ed.), *On Work*, Oxford: Blackwell.

Wood, S., Moore, S. and Willman, P. (2002) 'Third time lucky for statutory recognition in the UK', *Industrial Relations Journal* 33(3): 215–34.

Wray, D. (1996) 'Paternalism and its discontents', *Work, Employment and Society* 10(4): 701–15.

Yin, R. (1993) *Applications of Case Study Research*, Beverly Hills: Sage.

Index